KRISTALLNACHT

KRISTALLNACHT

THE NAZI NIGHT OF TERROR

ANTHONY READ and DAVID FISHER

RANDOM
HOUSE

Library of Congress Cataloging-in-Publication Data
Read, Anthony
  Kristallnacht : the Nazi night of terror / Anthony Read and David Fisher.
    p.   cm.
  Includes index.
  ISBN 0-8129-1723-5
  1. Germany—History—Kristallnacht, 1938.   I. Fisher, David.
II. Title.
DS135.G33F56   1989
943.086—dc20   89-40184

Title page photograph: The Synagogue in Baden-Baden (*The Wiener Library*)
Book design: J. Vandeventer

This copyright page is continued on page 293.

To those who suffered

Acknowledgments

First, we would like to thank those witnesses and victims of Kristallnacht who wrote to us from all over the world, and in particular to those who replied at length to our never-ending and no doubt tiresome questions. Among those we would like to thank are Mr. J. Abraham, Mrs. E. Abrahams, Mr. Albert Adler, Mrs. Lore Boas, Mrs. Robert Durlacher, Dr. Fritz Engel, Mr. Arnold Erlanger, Mrs. M. Forbes, Mr. R. W. Fraser, Mr. E. Freeman, Mrs. K. Freyhan, Mr. Willie Glaser, Mrs. Vera Gradon, Mrs. T. H. Hurst, Ms. Elizabeth Jennings, Miss Kinstead, Mrs. Lotte Kramer, Mr. R. Layton, Mrs. Ruth Leggett, Mr. Vernon Mosler, Mrs. C. K. Rosenstiel, Mrs. Stella Rotenberg, Mrs. I. Samson, Mrs. Robert Singer, Mrs. Jeannie Strauss-Cypres, Mrs. Ilse Warner, and many, many others.

On forensic and ballistic matters arising from the assassination of Ernst vom Rath, we are grateful for the professional advice and encouragement of Professor James Cameron of London Hospital, Mr. Clarke of Manor Firearms, and David Pryor of the Metropolitan Police Support HQ; on matters of French law, Maître Guy Picarda, barrister and *avocat*, offered invaluable help and advice; as did Michael Alexander on the subject of old films; our thanks, too, to Mr. Aronsfeld of the AJR, Bernt Engelmann, Dr. Ingeborg Fleischauer, Professor M.R.D. Foote, Professor Ian Kershaw, Dr. Bob Moore, and Professor Norman Stone, for their advice and encouragement.

No book of this nature can be written without the help of libraries and archives. We would like to thank therefore: Alexandra Weissler, Tony Wells, and Crista Wichmann of the Wiener Library, London, for their help and kindness in finding books, documents, and photographs; Sara Halpéryn and Vidor Jacobsen of the Centre de Documentation Juive Contemporaine, Paris, who toiled on our behalf far beyond the call of duty; the University of Syracuse for the Dorothy Thompson Papers; the Leo Baeck Institute, New York; the Public Record Office, Kew; the Political Archives of the Federal German Foreign Office, Bonn; the Federal German Archives, Koblenz; the Central State Archives of the German Democratic Republic, Potsdam; the Prussian State Archives, Berlin; the staff of the London Library; the staff of the British Library Newspaper Library, Colindale.

We would like to offer a special word of thanks to Walter Lassally and

Andrew Wiseman, who took time out from their busy professional lives in films and television respectively, to help with the translation of various documents, pamphlets, books, etc.; and to Angela Cassidy of Syntax Wordprocessing for her usual swift and enthusiastic typing and penetrating questions.

And finally, we must, as always, give thanks to our wives, Rosemary Read and Barbara Fisher, for their unfailing support, patience, and understanding during the research and writing of this book.

Contents

Contents

KRISTALLNACHT

Prologue

The Spark

The weather in Paris was unseasonably mild on Monday, November 7, 1938. With temperatures in the low sixties, the city had been basking in an Indian summer for the past week: Men left their overcoats in the closet, girls wore light dresses, and cafés on the boulevards had not yet taken in their sidewalk tables, which had been out since early spring.

At exactly 8:35 A.M., a small, dark-haired young man in a khaki-colored raincoat arrived outside a shop called A La Fine Lame ("At the Sharp Blade") at 61 Rue du Faubourg Saint-Martin, a quiet street in the tenth arrondissement running northeast from the Boulevard Saint-Denis, across the Boulevard de Magenta, along the side of the Gare de L'Est, and ending at what is today the Place de Stalingrad.

The youth approached Mme. Carpe, wife of the owner, who was in the process of winding up the heavy iron shutters that protected the shop window at night—the merchandise sold at A La Fine Lame was mainly sporting and hunting equipment, including knives, guns, and ammunition.

"I want to buy a revolver," he said to her.

Mme. Carpe told him to see her husband, the gunsmith, inside the shop. The young man went in. M. Carpe was a small, stocky, middle-aged man with a mustache, looking rather like an English major gone slightly to seed. He was the kind of witness examining magistrates and police officers yearn for—a precise man able to give exact details about everything, including the time. Time, in fact, was his hobby—he frequently acted as timekeeper for sporting events—and he happened to be checking his watch at the moment the young stranger spoke to his wife.

The young man entered and repeated his request, seeming, according to M. Carpe, "very calm, correct, [and speaking] perfectly adequate French."

"Why do you need a gun?" the shopkeeper asked.

"I often have to carry large sums of money to the bank for my father,"

3

came the reply, "and I want to be able to defend myself if anyone should try to rob me."

Since he was only about five feet two inches in height and weighed little more than one hundred pounds—a weight most jockeys would envy—the young man's story seemed reasonable enough to M. Carpe, who saw no reason to refuse. In those days in France, the sale of firearms was virtually unregulated. Anyone was entitled to buy any kind of weapon from a revolver to a machine gun, provided he was "of sound mind," a condition that was left to the gunsmith to judge. All the law required was that the purchaser should provide proof of identity so the vendor could accurately record the sale, and that he should then register the gun with his local police station.

M. Carpe's customer knew nothing about guns. He was not sure whether he needed an automatic or a revolver, and the only caliber he had ever heard of was the .45, which he had seen in western movies. After some discussion, M. Carpe suggested a 6.35mm five-shot "hammerless" revolver, manufactured by several companies in Belgium and France, a small gun no larger than a starting pistol, which would fit into the palm of one hand. This was one of the most popular weapons of the period—there was even a special version called a Velo-Dog, for cyclists to use against fierce animals who tried to pull them from their bicycles.

In fact, it was designed as a "vest pocket" gun, small enough and slim enough to avoid spoiling the line of a suit, with no protruding parts to snag on clothing: The hammer was enclosed (hence the description "hammerless"), and the trigger had no guard but folded up into the body of the gun and had to be pulled down before it could be used. As the gun possessed no extractor mechanism, a special rod had to be used to push out each spent cartridge before reloading. The price of the gun was 210 francs, plus 35 francs for a box of twenty-five cartridges.

M. Carpe demonstrated how to load and unload, and how to ready the trigger mechanism for firing. Then, in accordance with the law, he asked for his customer's name and address, and for his identity papers. The young man told him he lived at 8 Rue Martel, only a couple of streets away—whether because he wanted to mislead any subsequent investigation or because he was nervous and made a genuine mistake is impossible to say, but this was an old address. In fact, he had recently moved to 6 Rue des Petites Ecuries, just around the corner from the Rue Martel. He also produced a Polish passport in the name of Herschel Grynszpan. It was a name that was to appear on the front pages of newspapers all over the world the next day.

M. Carpe filled out the proper declaration form for Herschel to hand in to the local police station in the Boulevard de Strasbourg, then wrapped the gun and the box of cartridges separately, using two sheets of paper for the gun, held firmly in place by rubber bands. This, he later told the examining magistrate, was his normal practice, to discourage customers from unwrapping a gun and loading it in the street.

Herschel picked up his two packages, bade a polite farewell to M. and Mme. Carpe, and walked out of their shop, turning left as though heading for the police station. He never reached it, changing direction at the next corner. Passing the Hôtel Idéal-Suez, where he had spent the previous night, and the cinema that occupied its ground floor, where, as a great movie fan, he was a regular customer, he crossed the Boulevard Saint-Denis and went into the Café Tout Va Bien, one of the establishments that he frequented with his friends. Downstairs in the basement toilet, he unwrapped his purchases, loaded five cartridges into the chambers of the revolver; then, with the gun in one pocket and the box of cartridges in the other, he mounted the stairs again and left the café.

The time was a fraction after 9:00 A.M.

The métro station Strasbourg-Saint-Denis was just outside the café. Herschel ran down the steps to the ticket office, where, incredible as it now seems, he tried to buy a cheap round-trip ticket. Could he really have believed he would be allowed to return to the Tout Va Bien to celebrate? But he was too late: The ticket-seller informed him he could not buy a round-trip ticket after 9:00 A.M., so he was forced to pay one franc, twenty-five centimes for a regular one-way fare. He took the métro to Solferino, a station on the Boulevard Saint-Germain. From there he walked to the nearby Rue de Lille. The time was now 9:30 A.M.

The Rue de Lille runs parallel to the Quai Anatole France, on the left bank of the Seine, which in due course becomes the Quai d'Orsay, traditional home of the French Foreign Office. Herschel stopped by a high wall with a lodge at either end and three gateways, the central, highest one surmounted by two stone eagles. Through the gates he could see an elegant four-story mansion with an Egyptian-style portico supported by two circular columns with ornate, gilded capitals. Above it, over the folded-back striped canvas awning, the scarlet, white, and black swastika flag of the Third Reich hung motionless in the morning air. Number 78 Rue de Lille housed the German embassy.

Herschel had never been to the embassy before, and did not know which was the public entrance. He approached one of the policemen on duty in front of the building, François Autret, and asked him which office he should go to, as he wanted to apply for a German entry visa. Autret told him he had come to the wrong place: Visas were issued from the

German consulate in the Rue Huysmans, off the Boulevard Raspail in Montparnasse. Herschel knew this very well—he had been to the consulate several times—but he persisted until the policeman directed him to the embassy concierge, Mme. Mathis, in one of the gatehouses. Like M. Carpe, the gunsmith, Officer Autret later said the young man had seemed "very calm and quite normal."

Mme. Mathis, too, was struck by the polite young man: "He made a very good impression on me," she later told the examining magistrate, also remarking how calm and normal he had seemed. Herschel, as he was himself to tell the magistrate, was making "a giant effort to control himself and give no sign of his great nervousness." He asked to see the German ambassador. As he did so, a casually dressed man in his fifties strolled past them on his way out of the embassy—Count Johannes von Welczeck, the ambassador himself. Although he overheard Herschel's request, Welczeck ignored it: There were plenty of staff on duty to handle such visitors, and in any case, he was off on his morning constitutional. His silence saved his life.

Mme. Mathis directed the nice young man across the courtyard to the door on the left of the main building, and from there he climbed the fifteen steps to the first floor, where he found one of the embassy porters, Henri Nagorka, acting as receptionist. Herschel had until then been speaking in French. Now, he switched to German, telling Nagorka, "I would like to see a person of some importance, who is *au courant* with German secrets. I have an important document to deliver." Nagorka offered to pass the document on, but Herschel insisted he must hand it over personally. The porter showed him into the waiting room, while he contacted the only official who was on duty at that hour, Ernst vom Rath, the third secretary. Vom Rath told him to bring the young man up to his office at the head of the staircase, one floor up.

It may seem surprising that a total stranger should have been able to walk in off the street and, with a minimum of formality and no apparent regard for security, be shown into the office of a relatively senior official. But the embassy staff were used to receiving visitors on mysterious errands: The Germans operated an active espionage and intelligence section from 78 Rue de Lille. It was, in fact, an uncle of vom Rath's, a previous ambassador to France, who had been responsible for setting it up several years earlier.

Ernst vom Rath was a tall twenty-nine-year-old man with a high forehead, neatly parted fair hair, and the earnest face of a young schoolmaster who might well have trouble keeping order in class. When Nagorka showed Herschel Grynszpan into the small, overcrowded room, he was seated at his desk facing the window, his back to the door, opening the morning mail. As Nagorka announced the visitor by name, then withdrew, vom Rath invited Herschel to take a seat in the leather-covered chair to the left, then turned his own chair so that he was facing his visitor. Vom Rath asked to see the important document Herschel was supposed to be carrying. For some seconds, Herschel did not reply. Then he reached into the inside pocket of his jacket.

"You are a *sale boche* [filthy kraut] and here, in the name of twelve thousand persecuted Jews, is your document!" he screamed.

Pulling out his revolver, he readied the trigger mechanism and fired five shots at the diplomat, at a range of less than two meters. "I aimed at the middle of the body," he later told Police Superintendent Monneret.

Vom Rath half rose from his chair, turning the left side of his body toward the gun in a pure reflex action. The first bullet entered below the rib cage. Traveling almost horizontally, it damaged the spleen, perforated the stomach, and lacerated the pancreas before finally lodging in the right thoracic cavity. The victim slumped sideways over the desk. The second shot entered his left side slightly above the entry wound caused by the first, passed through the thoracic cavity, and lodged in the right shoulder. Herschel continued firing until his gun was empty. But the three other bullets all missed their target and hit the wall behind the desk.

To the would-be assassin's horror, vom Rath was not dead. He staggered to his feet, clutching his abdomen and calling for help. Herschel rose to his feet, too, trembling violently. He made no attempt to reload his gun, or to move toward vom Rath, but just stood there.

Nagorka was nearest the third secretary's office when he heard the shots and the cries for help. Running down the corridor, he found Ernst vom Rath in the doorway of his office, holding both hands to his belly. "I am wounded!" he cried. The embassy's other porter, Krüger, appeared on the scene a few seconds later, and he and Nagorka seized Herschel. But by now a monstrous calm had descended on the young gunman. He seemed serenely indifferent to his fate.

"I don't intend to escape," he said. "I won't do anything more."

There was a sudden flurry of activity as more staff arrived. Medical help was summoned for vom Rath. The French police, in the person of Officer Autret, were called into the embassy to arrest the assailant. While Nagorka and Krüger excitedly explained what had happened, Herschel sat calmly in a chair seeming unconcerned and showing no remorse for his action. Indeed, when the two porters told Officer Autret that the victim was still alive, Herschel quietly remarked, "It's a pity he's not dead."

Ernst Achenbach, the ambassador's secretary, later recalled that when Autret frisked the young man to see if he was carrying other weapons, Herschel spoke almost kindly to the policeman. "Don't be afraid," he said. "I'll come with you." Only as he was being led away in handcuffs did he make a sudden, final gesture of defiance, screaming, "*Sales boches!*" at the Germans.

Autret led Herschel on foot to the police station at 2 Rue de Bourgogne, less than 500 meters from the embassy. As they skirted the Chambre des Députés, Herschel suddenly spoke again, announcing, as though to clarify the morning's events both for himself and for the policeman, "I've just shot a man in his office. I do not regret it. I did it to avenge my parents, who are living in misery in Germany."

Herschel's act of vengeance, however, was to be the spark that ignited a terrible explosion of hatred and violence throughout Nazi Germany, dramatically escalating the suffering of hundreds of thousands of innocent people just like his parents.

"Down with the November Criminals!"

For many people in France, and indeed throughout the world, there was a genuine fear that Herschel Grynszpan's five shots would prove as fateful as those fired by a Bosnian student, Gavrilo Princip, on June 28, 1914, in Sarajevo. Those shots, killing the archduke Franz Ferdinand of Austria, had been the spark that set off the explosion of the First World War. Barely a quarter-century later, in November 1938, it did not seem too fanciful to imagine that the assassination attempt in Paris might provide an excuse if not a trigger for the start of a second world war.

The international climate was fraught. Less than six weeks before, in the face of an imminent German invasion of Czechoslovakia, the French had mobilized their reserves to bring the number of men under arms to a million; the Russians had started massing troops on the western border of the Ukraine and providing the Czechs with military aircraft; and the British had put the Royal Navy on full alert. The Germans, for their part, had called up 750,000 reservists, while the Poles—at that time supporting Hitler—were themselves preparing to invade Czechoslovakia and grab the industrial region of Teschen. Smaller nations had watched and waited in great trepidation, for it had been a situation in which anything could happen, and all depended on the whim of one unstable individual, Adolf Hitler.

Fear of Hitler and of his resurgent Germany was the predominant factor in Europe throughout most of the thirties. And with the possible exception of Czechoslovakia, nowhere was the fear and distrust greater than in France, grievously wounded twice in forty-four years—first in 1870 and then in 1914—by German invasions. The terrible toll of the First World War, when France lost 1.5 million dead (more than 10 percent of her active male population) in the mindless slaughter of battlefields such as Verdun, the Marne, and the Somme, had left people and leaders alike with little appetite for another such conflict.

In the years immediately following 1918, the French had been determined to make the Germans pay dearly for the war they had started, and to ensure that they would never again be strong enough to mount another attack. At the Paris Peace Conference, they succeeded in having Germany stripped of her former colonies and forced to hand over large tracts of land in Posen and West Prussia to the newly restored Poland, the provinces of North Schleswig to Denmark, Malmédy and Eupen to Belgium, Alsace and Lorraine to France, the area around Teschen (Oderberg) to the new state of Czechoslovakia, and Memel to Lithuania, while the ancient German seaport of Danzig was declared a free city, linked to Poland.

The German Army was limited to one hundred thousand men, with no tanks, heavy artillery, or aircraft. The general staff was dissolved. The navy was to have no U-boats, and its heaviest vessels were to be no more than six battleships of ten thousand tons each. The fortifications on the island of Heligoland, protecting the approaches to the ports of Wilhelmshaven, Bremerhaven, and Hamburg, were to be dismantled. The entire Rhineland was to be occupied by the Allies for fifteen years, and was then to remain permanently demilitarized.

Economically, the penalties imposed on Germany for her guilt in starting the war were crippling. In addition to the payment of huge reparations of 134 billion gold marks, the equivalent of three times her annual income, Germany was to compensate France for the devastation of her northern industrial region and its coal mines by handing over to her the Saar district, complete with its heavy industries and coal mines producing 17.2 million tons of coal a year, for a period of fifteen years.

To make sure the Germans were properly humiliated, the French Army of Occupation in the Rhineland included large numbers of colonial troops from Morocco and black Africa; the local population was terrified by the blacks' very appearance, to say nothing of their reputation for rapacious brutality. And when Germany failed to fulfill her reparation payments in 1923, French and Belgian troops were sent in to seize the Ruhr, the industrial heartland of Germany, which had provided some 80 percent of the country's iron and steel production since the mines and mills of Upper Silesia had been given to Poland the year before.

The French action, and German attempts to meet reparation payments, helped provoke one of the most dreadful phenomena of those unsettled times in Germany, hyperinflation. The mark had in fact been slipping steadily since 1921, when it had fallen to seventy-five to the dollar, one tenth of its value on Armistice Day. During 1922, it had fallen to four hundred to the dollar, and by the time the French and Belgians marched into the Ruhr it was already down to seven thousand. But that was only the beginning: Within days of the occupation and the general strike that immediately followed, the figure rose to fifty thousand as the German government issued paper money as fast as the presses could print it, in a deliberate effort to frustrate the French and wipe out debts and reparation payments. Their cynical strategy was staggeringly successful—by August 1, the rate against the dollar hit 1 million, by November it was 4 billion, eventually reaching 215 trillion marks to the dollar, 43 trillion to the pound sterling, before everybody stopped counting.

The total collapse of the currency and the economy inevitably threw open the doors to political chaos, with uprisings and rebellions in various parts of the country. Extreme parties of both right and left thrived on the unsettled conditions, feeding on the bitterness of bourgeois and worker alike. Among them was the Nationalist Socialist German Workers' party, led by a former corporal with two iron crosses and a military cross for bravery in the war, who staged an unsuccessful attempt at a coup d'état in Munich in November 1923.

Adolf Hitler differed both from the other political agitators and from the governing parties in that he did not blame the French or the British for Germany's fate during and since the war. He saw the reasons for Germany's downfall much closer to home: "No—not down with France," he cried at public meeting after public meeting, "but down with the November criminals! That must be our slogan!" The "November criminals," those men who had overthrown the kaiser and sued for peace in November 1918, he identified as Jews and communists and their dupes. Since Hitler regarded Marxism as a Jewish conspiracy to destroy the Western nations, he therefore blaming the Jews for everything bad that had befallen Germany since 1914.

Hitler's attempted putsch was an abysmal failure. But it did turn him from a local Bavarian rabble-rouser into a national figure, and with Mussolini having succeeded in taking power in Italy earlier that year, the twin monsters of Fascism and Naziism began casting their shadows across Europe. The people of the democracies, however, were more concerned with the shadow falling from the east: The fear of bolshevism was already blinding many statesmen and their subjects to the dangers of right-wing dictatorship, a blindness that has plagued much of the free world for most of this century.

Fear of a total breakdown of the social order in Germany, creating ideal conditions for a bolshevik revolution, was one of the factors that led Britain and France to modify their attitudes to their defeated foe. But there were other factors, too, that were equally important. In Britain by the mid-twenties, there was a strong popular reaction against the vehemence of Versailles. Anger and the need for revenge had given way to a growing sympathy for the plight of the Germans. The innate desire among the British people for fair play led them to feel that the terms of the peace treaty had been unnecessarily harsh. They began to look for ways of helping Germany to recover.

The Locarno Treaty, signed on December 1, 1925, was largely the result of Britain's commitment to conciliation. It was hailed as the start of a new understanding between France and Germany, and indeed as ushering in a new era of peace and hopefully prosperity throughout Europe. The frontier between the two countries was confirmed, and guaranteed by Britain and Italy, the Rhineland was to remain demilitarized as a permanent buffer zone, while in the east, France reaffirmed her existing alliances with her two satellite states, Poland and Czechoslovakia, as a defense against any German aggression in that direction.

Shortly afterward, in 1926, Germany was admitted to the League of Nations, an organization devoted to maintaining peace, and thus was rehabilitated into the international community. The following year the Control Commission on German rearmament was withdrawn. In 1929, reparations payments were revised downward, and external controls of German finances ceased. In 1930, five years ahead of schedule, the armies of occupation were withdrawn from the Rhineland. On the surface, everything looked rosy for European harmony, despite the mounting international economic crisis. Beneath the surface, however, was another story.

Throughout the entire period between the two world wars, German leaders of every political shade were unanimous in one overriding aim: The repudiation and revision of the Treaty of Versailles and the restoration of Germany as the leading power on the continent of Europe. While he was acknowledging his country's frontiers with Poland and Czechoslovakia at Locarno, German foreign minister Stresemann also gave notice that Germany intended to "revise" them at some time in the future. And even while agreeing to abide by the terms settled at Locarno, Stresemann was renewing another pact, made three years earlier at Rapallo with the Russians, under which the two international pariahs agreed to help each other in various ways. The most noteworthy of these was also the most secret: The outlawed German general staff, thinly disguised as the Truppenamt, or Office of Troops, would provide staff college training for senior Soviet officers, most of whom had been no more than sergeants in the czarist army, and in return, the Soviet Union would provide sites for German armaments factories and training areas for infantry, tank, artillery, and air exercises safe from Western eyes. In this clandestine fashion, German rearmament had already started, backed by the numerous flying clubs, sports associations, and youth organizations that supplied hidden forms of military training.

For the moment, however, there was no overt threat to anyone, and as the twenties ended, the prospects looked good for a continuing peace.

The Great Depression of the early thirties threw Europe into confusion again. Economic hardship and financial instability began to create political unrest and encourage extremist policies and even revolution. As the stock markets of the world collapsed from 1929 onward—the French, incidentally, being the last major nation to suffer, not feeling the worst effects until 1932–33—the specter of war reappeared in Europe.

While their economy was recovering well from the miseries of 1923, helped by substantial loans from the United States and Britain, the German people as a whole were content to leave their grievances on the shelf. But as their shelves were emptied of goods and comforts, the grievances were all that was left to feed on. Politicians, inevitably, were not slow to seize on the people's resentment. Adolf Hitler, rapidly gaining popularity and strength as times grew harder, was only one of many to blame his country's ills on the unjust peace settlement of 1919. Unlike most other politicians, however, Hitler offered positive action to obtain redress. He promised not merely to restore Germany's fortunes and position in the world, but to raise her to new heights of power, prestige, and prosperity.

While Stresemann was negotiating the Locarno Treaty, Hitler had been writing the second volume of *Mein Kampf*, his political testament, setting out his own—and his party's—aims for Germany. Pouring scorn on his rivals' failure to capitalize on the people's resentment, he wrote:

> It happens sometimes that peace treaties whose conditions beat upon a nation like scourges sound the first trumpet call for the resurrection which follows later. How much might have been made out of the Treaty of Versailles! Each point of it might have been burnt into the brains and feelings of the nation, till finally the common shame and the common hatred would have become a sea of flaming fire in the minds of sixty million men and women; out of the glowing mass a will of steel would have emerged, and a cry: We will be armed as others are armed!

Hitler's aims did not stop at rearmament and regaining the territories lost through the peace treaty. Indeed, he stated:

The frontiers of 1914 mean nothing in respect of Germany's future. They were no protection in the past, nor would they mean strength in the future. They would not give the German nation internal solidarity, nor would they provide it with nourishment; from a military standpoint, they would not be suitable or even satisfactory, nor would they improve our present situation with regard to the other world powers, or rather, the powers that are the real world powers. . . . It is the duty of us National Socialists to cling steadfastly to our aims in foreign policy, and these are to assure to the German nation the territory which is due to it on this earth.

No nation on earth holds a square yard of territory by any right derived from heaven. Frontiers are made and altered only by human agency. The fact that a nation succeeds in acquiring an unfair share of territory is no superior reason for its being respected. It merely proves the strength of the conqueror and the weakness of those who lose by it. This strength alone constitutes the right of possession.

From the moment he took up office on January 30, 1933—perfectly legally, it must be remembered, and not through force—Hitler set about the task of fulfilling his stated promises. It was his single-minded ambition to restore German greatness and make the nation not simply a world power again but the most powerful nation on earth. Throwing off the shackles imposed at Versailles and creating a new army, navy, and air force equipped with the very latest weapons was an important part of this, of course. But what was even more important was the creation of a unified nation comprised of the entire German race, and only the German race, inside the frontiers of a single "Greater Germany." When the time was right, the invincible armed forces of the Reich would march eastward to destroy the Jewish canker of bolshevism, drive the inferior races of Slavs back beyond the Urals, and settle the vast, empty, fertile lands with Germans.

"If I had the Ural mountains," he proclaimed in 1936, "with their incalculable store of treasures and raw materials, Siberia with its vast forests, and the Ukraine with its tremendous wheatfields, Germany and the National Socialist leadership would swim in plenty!"

The idea of Hitler's smashing bolshevism and breaking up the Soviet Union was one that had great appeal to most Western leaders, who saw bolshevism rather than Naziism as the principal enemy. Yet surprisingly few of them took his dreams of conquering and colonizing the Ukraine seriously. As time went by, however, and he began to establish the Nazi regime more and more firmly, tightening his grip on the country year by year from 1933 onward, they were forced to face the disturbing prospect of a vast German land empire in their backyards.

To any British government this was, to say the least, unacceptable.

For generations their foreign policy had been based on maintaining a balance of power in Europe, with no single nation being allowed to gain supremacy. However, Britain herself was not a Continental power: most of her army was stationed abroad to protect the Empire. As always, the British relied on the English Channel to provide a *cordon sanitaire* against the political infections of the continent. Secure behind twenty-two miles of sea, the British felt they could afford to take a rather more relaxed view of German ambitions than the neurotic French. The French, on the other hand, lived cheek by jowl with Germany, and the bitter memories of 1870 and 1914–18 were still fresh in their minds. A resurgent Germany—a strong, confident, unified nation embracing all racial Germans—was in their eyes a beast very much to be feared. Inevitably it would come to dominate Europe.

Germany's existing population of around 70 million was already almost double France's falling total of 39 million. Any increase would disturb the precarious military balance. There was also an added threat in that several million of the racial Germans whom Hitler wanted to bring into his Reich lived in Poland and Czechoslovakia, the two countries that France was obliged by treaty to protect. And French confidence was not increased by Britain and the United States, who were trying to impose a general disarmament that would reduce the French standing army from its peacetime level of five hundred thousand men to two hundred thousand, while at the same time allowing the Germans to double the size of theirs to the same amount.

French nervousness grew with every step Hitler took as the decade progressed. Within days of his becoming chancellor, he started eliminating opposition by banning all meetings or demonstrations by the communists, his most formidable adversaries. Within a month, he and his cronies had organized the burning down of the Reichstag Building, using it as an excuse to arrest four thousand leading communists in advance of the elections he had promised the country. To no one's surprise, the Nazis and their allies won a controlling majority of the seats, and at the first meeting of the new Reichstag, Hitler was given complete emergency powers for four years. His first words, as the result of the vote was announced, were directed to the socialists: "And now I have no further need of you."

In October 1933, Hitler withdrew Germany from the Disarmament Conference—he had already given orders to prepare training grounds and arms factories in Germany itself to take over from those in the Soviet Union—and from the League of Nations. In 1934, on the death of President Hindenburg, he became president as well as chancellor, proclaiming himself *Führer*, or leader. In 1935 he denounced the Treaty of Versailles, and reclaimed the Saar, thus beginning the process of clawing back what Germany had lost in 1919.

On March 7, 1936, Hitler took his boldest step yet, by marching his troops into the Rhineland and repudiating the Locarno Treaty. It was an unashamed gamble by the führer, and a significant test of French resolve—the German troops were under orders to withdraw at the first sign of military resistance by France or Britain. There was none: The French generals told their government they were not prepared to fight. Dispirited and in disarray, France was still suffering the worst effects of the Depression, from which the other nations were already recovering. Her endemic political instability was at its worst, with governments changing as rapidly and regularly as partners in a square dance, and there was no one in any position of authority with the will to stand up to Hitler.

The British had at last started serious arms manufacture only two weeks before, in an effort, as Royal Air Force historians would later write, "to catch the electric hare of German rearmament," but the national mood was for peace at virtually any price. There was also a great deal of sympathy still for the Germans and very little for the French. So Hitler was allowed to get away with the first moves in his campaign. His next followed swiftly: In spite of an international agreement limiting new warships to a maximum size of thirty-five thousand tons, German shipyards started building two battleships, the *Bismarck* and the *Tirpitz*, of forty-five thousand tons each. Again, no one did anything to stop him.

Hitler's moves took place in an international climate that was becoming decidedly unsettled in other areas, too. Mussolini, seeking the prestige of an empire for Italy, annexed Ethiopia, which he had invaded the year before. As with the Rhineland incident, the League of Nations proved totally impotent. On July 17, 1936, a military insurrection led by General Francisco Franco started a civil war in Spain that was soon seized on by Hitler and Mussolini on the Nationalist side and Stalin on the Republican side as a great opportunity to try out new weapons and tactics under real battlefield conditions. There could be little doubt that for Germany and Italy this was not just an exercise, but a rehearsal for a future war, an impression that was strengthened later that year when the two nations signed a formal treaty of alliance, creating the Rome–Berlin "Axis."

Peace was a rapidly diminishing commodity in other parts of the world, too, notably the Far East. Internal struggles in China involving dissident warlords, the Nationalist forces of Chiang Kai-shek, and the communists of Mao Tse-tung were overshadowed by the threat of Japanese expansion. The Japanese, determined to establish themselves as a world power, had been fighting both the Chinese and the Russians intermittently since 1931, when they had invaded and occupied Manchuria. Now, they were becoming ever more belligerent in China itself in a string of incidents clearly pointing the way toward all-out war. In November, they forged their first formal links with Nazi Germany by signing the Anti-Comintern Pact, unsettling evidence, following so closely on the creation of the Axis, that the aggressive powers were aligning themselves for trouble.

Trouble duly followed in 1937, when the Nazi Condor Legion was unleashed in Spain, shocking the world in April with the first-ever mass air raid against a civilian target, the Basque city of Guernica. But the Japanese soon outstripped the Germans in the ferocity of aerial attacks, when they started a full-scale war against China in July.

Reports of the devastation caused by modern warfare in Spain and China created alarm and despondency in Western Europe, and a new and frantic desire to avoid war at all costs. Although Britain and France both continued to rearm, albeit slowly and reluctantly, they chose to try and buy Hitler off with ever-larger concessions, actively pursuing the policy of appeasement championed by newly appointed prime minister Neville Chamberlain in Britain and Foreign Minister Georges Bonnet in France.

Chamberlain and Bonnet have, quite rightly, been much blamed for their naïveté in trying to appease Hitler. But their policies were in line with public sentiment in their countries: Appeasement was popular, and those politicians who opposed it, such as Winston Churchill and Anthony Eden, were in a very small minority. The person who liked it best of all, however, was Hitler—it suited his purposes perfectly.

Encouraged by the signals that he could get whatever he wanted if he only threatened loudly enough, Hitler entered 1938 in a mood of total confidence, and got down to the serious business of fulfilling his dreams. He started by getting rid of the last few conservatives in positions of authority, firing the army chief and assuming an active role as Commander in Chief of all the armed forces, and filling other posts with compliant yes-men. The most notable of these was Joachim von Ribbentrop, a pompous ignoramus who replaced the skilled and experienced Baron Konstantin von Neurath as foreign minister. Hitler then turned his attention to Austria, the country of his own birth. While the rest of the world looked on, he applied more and more pressure on the Austrian government and then, on March 13, 1938, calmly marched in his troops and annexed the country without a shot being fired.

With Austria in the bag, swelling the Reich's resources with men, arms, industry, and mineral wealth, Hitler began turning the screw on his next victim, Czechoslovakia. During the spring, he worked to raise tension, aided by the 3 million Germans living in the Sudetenland, a horseshoe-shaped region encompassing the country's entire western frontiers. Unlike the Austrians, however, the Czechs were not prepared to give in without a fight. They had a well-trained and well-equipped modern army, which they proceeded to mobilize. They also called on France, Britain, and the Soviet Union to honor their obligations. Hitler's bluff was called. He was forced to back down—at least for the time being, for he was nowhere near ready for war.

The respite was only temporary, however—a few days later, he told his military commanders, "It is my unshakable resolve that Czechoslovakia shall be wiped off the map of Europe." Although he did not set a firm date for the operation, he ordered all preparations to be complete by October 1. Throughout the summer, he kept building up the pressure, fomenting trouble with the Sudeten Germans over grievances and atrocities both real and faked. He made speech after speech vilifying the Czechs and their leaders. He massed his troops along the border under the deliberately transparent cover of summer exercises. In September, the temperature of the crisis reached the boiling point. It seemed that war throughout Europe was inevitable. France mobilized her reserves, Britain put the Royal Navy on full alert, the Soviet Union—pledged to join France in aiding the Czechs—started moving the Red Army into position and persuaded the Romanians to allow Soviet troops and aircraft to cross her territory to Czechoslovakia.

In London, trenches were dug in Hyde Park, gas masks issued, schoolchildren evacuated from the capital, and hospitals cleared, ready to receive war casualties. In France, railways and roads were jammed with people fleeing Paris in fear of bombing. Thousands of Germans were reported to be scurrying out of the western frontier zone, away from the invasion they expected from France.

At the last minute, however, the spirit of appeasement won the day. Chamberlain hurried to visit Hitler and, with the agreement of French premier Edouard Daladier and Foreign Minister Bonnet, offered Hitler the Sudetenland. The result of this magnanimity with other people's territory was that Hitler immediately increased his demands, backing them with an ultimatum that if they were not met by October 1, he would invade Czechoslovakia. Again, Chamberlain, Daladier, and Bonnet capitulated, flying to Munich for a hurriedly arranged conference, with Mussolini acting as mediator. Britain and France withdrew their backing for the Czechs, and agreed that they should cede the whole Sudeten region, including the Czechs' defensive fortifications, starting the next day. All non-Germans were to evacuate the area immediately, leaving behind their homes and possessions. There would be no compensation. In return, Hitler promised that this was his last territorial ambition. He even agreed to sign a declaration with Chamberlain that their two countries would never go to war with one another again.

It seemed that by the sacrifice of part of Czechoslovakia, war had been averted and peace in Europe assured. Chamberlain and the French leaders returned home to rapturous receptions. The world breathed again. William Shirer, visiting Paris after reporting from Munich and Berlin, noted in his diary, "At Fouquet's, at Maxim's, fat bankers and businessmen toasting Peace with rivers of champagne. But even the waiters, taxi drivers, who used to be sound, gushing about how wonderful it is that war has been avoided, that it would have been a crime, that they fought in one war and that was enough."

The feeling of elation did not last more than a few days, however, especially in France, where the reaction set in during the very first week after Munich. On October 3, the vice-chairman of the Foreign Affairs Committee of the National Assembly, Ernst Pezet, wrote to a German acquaintance, "Already our people is coming to its senses after the animal joy—understandable and excusable—of having escaped war. And now it is getting a grip on itself and feels that it has been cheated . . . some even say betrayed. . . . It is already ashamed of having betrayed an ally. . . ."

In fact, France had done more than that. By forcing the Czechs to hand over their protective fortifications, Daladier had effectively destroyed France's military position and irrevocably upset the balance of power in Europe. With almost twice the population of France, Germany could always put a larger army into the field in the event of war. To counter this, France depended on keeping Germany squeezed between her own army in the west and those of her allies in the east, particularly the smaller but formidable Czech forces, backed by the vast Skoda complex, then one of the most advanced arms industries in the world. The amputation of the Sudetenland, however, effectively disarmed the Czechs by removing their vital shield. In consequence, France herself was more vulnerable—and the need for peace at any price became more pressing than ever.

In London, too, disillusion was beginning to set in as it gradually became clear that nothing had been achieved in the long term. A growing number of people throughout Europe were beginning to doubt the validity of Hitler's promises of no further territorial ambitions. Hitler himself was complaining to his inner circle that Chamberlain and Mussolini had deprived him of his excuse for war with Czechoslovakia—he desperately wanted to show off the might of his new Wehrmacht, to give his warriors their first taste of blood and of glory. Now, he would need to find another pretext. By mid-October, he was trying to persuade the Poles to join him in a crusade against the Soviet Union, to seize and share the Ukraine. At the same time, he was already starting to press Poland and Lithuania over the return to the Reich of the ancient port cities of Danzig and Memel. He was also picking a quarrel with the Poles over the number of Polish Jews living in Germany. Among them was the family of Herschel Grynszpan.

"Jews Not Wanted"

Hitler's hatred of the Jews was at the center of his entire philosophy. His obsession with eliminating them from Germany did not run parallel with his other ambitions—it was an essential element of every single one of them. To Hitler, the greatest obstacle to the fulfilment of his dream of creating the "Thousand-Year Reich" was the Jews. He saw them as a people with no land of their own, parasites sucking the lifeblood of their hosts wherever they settled, dominating the economic life of the world through an international conspiracy, seeking always to weaken other races, other cultures. In his eyes, and those of many other Germans, the Jews sought to pollute the unique purity of the German race: Unlike the French, British, Spanish, and others, this had never been mongrelized by the racially mixed forces of Imperial Rome, since Germany east of the Rhine had never been conquered by them.

Somehow the Jews could be blamed for just about all the ills of the world, and especially those of Germany. Jewish financiers had been responsible for the arms race that led to the First World War; the Jews had lost the war for Germany, through the *Dolchstoss*, the stab in the back, by the November criminals—who were themselves either Jews or Jewish puppets; it was the Jewish international financiers who had demanded crippling reparations payments, and who had been responsible for the economic crash; the greatest scourge of the time was, of course, a Jewish invention—were not Marx and Engels Jews? And was not bolshevism, therefore, nothing more in the last resort than another part of the Jewish conspiracy to destroy Germany and the other Western nations?

Hitler did not invent this attitude, or any of those theories. They were already deeply rooted in German thinking long before he began his political career—indeed, the idea of solving Germany's "Jewish problem" by means of genocide had been proposed as early as 1865 in a book entitled *The Value of Life*, by Eugen Duehring, a lecturer at Berlin University. By the late nineteenth century, a large and influential section of German society had become obsessed with theories of so-called scientific racism, and was growing increasingly anti-Semitic as a result.

In fact, there had been Jews in parts of Germany for some two thousand years, with few harmful effects. As craftsmen, merchants, soldiers, and sometimes slaves who were later freed there, they had followed the Roman legions northward. The first mention of a Jewish congregation in the Rhineland was in Cologne in the year A.D. 321, during the reign of the emperor Constantine. There, members of the Jewish community had owned property and even held office within the city itself. Jews had also prospered under the emperor Charlemagne—the Jew Isaac had been one of the party of three ambassadors he sent to Caliph Haroun al-Raschid of *Arabian Nights* fame, and the only one to survive the journey, bringing back an elephant called Abulabaz as a gift from the caliph.

It was not until the First Crusade of 1096, when Christian knights on their way to the Holy Land paused to sack Jewish communities, that Jews in Germany had to face the harsher realities of life under Christian rule. But things improved: Ninety-six years later, the Holy Roman Emperor Frederick I, Hitler's hero Barbarossa, placed Jews under his protection by incorporating them into his feudal system as part of the emperor's retinue. Frederick found them reliable and trustworthy—they did not get drunk or go whoring, they could read and write in a country where most of the population, even at the highest levels, were illiterate, and they knew the secret of long division, then closely guarded, which made them invaluable in financial dealings.

With the growth of the power of the papacy, the position of the Jews became less secure, but it was the Reformation that brought about a significant change in their status, thanks to Martin Luther. Luther has been called the father of modern Europe, but perhaps more important, he was the father of modern German. In translating the Bible into German, in order to give God's word directly to the people, he consolidated various dialects into a common language, and so created one of the principal tenets of German racism. Forever afterward, the definition of a German was to include anyone who spoke that language as his mother tongue—thereby binding Prussians and Austrians, Bavarians and Rhinelanders, Bohemians and Pomeranians into one race, no matter what the color of their hair or eyes, the tone of their skins, or the shape of their heads and bodies.

In the beginning, Luther was not anti-Semitic. In his pamphlet *That Jesus Christ Was Born a Jew*, published in 1523, he suggested that "since the Jews had treated us heathens in so brotherly a manner, we in our turn should treat Jews in a brotherly manner, hoping we might convert some of them." His hopes for the conversion of the Jews were to be dashed, however, and twenty years later, bitter and angry and a martyr to kidney stones, he turned on them with two pamphlets as savage and anti-Semitic as any passage in *Mein Kampf.* He now made a distinction between the people Moses led out of Egypt, whose patriarchs were greater men than any living in his day, and what he called "Caesar's Jews"—a phrase he derived from the passage in the Bible when Jesus, having been scourged and wearing a crown of thorns, was brought before the priests and the people. When Pilate said to them, "Behold your king!" the chief priests answered, "We have no king but Caesar."

For such creatures, Luther believed, no fate was too harsh, no punishment too severe. "I'd tear their tongues out of their throats!" he raged. Elsewhere he let loose a diatribe that was to prove uncannily prophetic, a model for later years:

> First, their synagogues or churches should be set on fire, and whatever does not burn up should be covered or spread with dirt so that no one may ever be able to see a cinder or stone of it . . . their homes should likewise be broken down and destroyed . . . they ought to be put under one roof or in a stable, like gypsies, in order that they may realize that they are not masters in our land, as they boast, but miserable captives . . . passport and traveling privileges should be absolutely forbidden to the Jews . . . all their cash and valuables of silver and gold ought to be taken from them . . . everything that they possess they stole and robbed from us through their usury . . . We must drive them out like mad dogs.

It all has an eerily familiar ring.

Luther's most celebrated pamphlet, *Against the Jews and Their Lies,* written in 1543, was regarded as excessive even at a time not noted for its delicacy in matters of controversy, and was suppressed in Strasbourg. But the infection had entered the body of German thought and was to remain there.

Throughout the nineteenth century, and the first two decades of the twentieth, the process of Jewish assimilation proceeded slowly, in fits and starts, made more difficult by the periodic influx of "foreign" Jews from the east, mostly fleeing the pogroms of the czars. But in the cities, where most Jews lived, those who were middle class and upwardly mobile worked hard to make themselves a part of German society. Many of them came to believe that they had succeeded, that they were totally assimilated, totally integrated, thinking of themselves as Germans first, rather than Jews.

On January 30, 1933, that belief was shattered as Hitler was appointed chancellor of Germany. On March 5, national elections gave the Nazis and their allies a majority of eighty-one seats in the Reichstag. Hitler was on his way to absolute power, and the long nightmare for the Jews began. On the streets of Berlin, his strong-arm squads, the brown-shirted storm troopers of the SA, the *Sturmabteilung*, went into action without fear of any authority. Working in gangs of between five and thirty men, they beat up individual Jews, in public, until, as the *Manchester Guardian* reported, "the blood streamed down their heads and faces, and their backs and shoulders were bruised. Many fainted and were left lying on the streets."

On April 1, the party organized a nationwide boycott of Jewish businesses, stores, cafés, restaurants, lawyers, and doctors. In each *Gau**, lists were printed and distributed detailing every Jewish business. Committees were established in every district to coordinate and control the boycott, and all other forms of Jew-baiting. Unsigned notices were to be posted in the streets, giving the names and addresses of those who continued to purchase from Jewish stores, and "pointing out to the miscreant members of the nation the shamefulness of their deeds, making them aware of the shame to which they would be subjected if they were proceeded against publicly." Female clerks working in Jewish stores were to be recruited "with the greatest secrecy" to pass on the names of people who bought from them.

Party orders demanded that members constantly remind their friends and neighbors that no German should buy from a Jew, and that they must break off friendships with anyone who continued to do so. "It must go so far," the orders continued, "that no German will speak to a Jew if it is not absolutely necessary, and this must be particularly pointed out. German girls who go with Jews are to be made aware of the shamefulness of their actions. A member of our party must have nothing whatever to do with such a person."

There were demands for the removal of Jewish students from German schools and colleges—a new law laid down that they were to be treated as foreigners. Many distinguished scholars and professors, including Albert Einstein, were forced into exile. On April 7, Hitler issued an order for the dismissal—euphemistically called "retirement"—of all civil ser-

* The Nazis divided Germany into thirty-two administrative regions known as *Gaue*, each governed by a party *Gauleiter*. Each *Gau* was divided into districts known as *Kreise*, headed by a *Kreisleiter*. Within these districts, party organization was further broken down into *Ortsgruppe* (local groups), *Zelle* (cells), and *Blöcke* (blocks).

vants "who were not of Aryan descent." The division of the nation into racial groups, "Aryan" and "Non-Aryan," became a reality.

A succession of decrees followed, all designed to isolate Germany's half-million Jews. The Star of David was painted on Jewish shopfronts, along with the word *Jude* ("Jew"), swastikas, and slogans such as JEWS OUT!, PERISH JUDAH!, GO TO PALESTINE! Books by Jewish authors, together with others considered to be "degenerate," were burned on May 10 in a massive bonfire outside the Opera House, opposite the main entrance to Berlin University. Jewish artists were excluded from the Academy exhibitions. Thousands of Jews were among those arrested and thrown into the newly opened concentration camps as opponents of the regime. Individual beatings and brutal murders became commonplace—by the end of 1933, some thirty-six Jews had been killed.

Throughout 1934 and 1935, the campaign against the Jews continued to gather momentum. Signs saying JEWS NOT WANTED appeared not only on cafés, hotels, stores, and sports stadiums, but also on roads leading into villages and small towns. Jews were driven out of entire towns and districts, to make them *Judenfrei* ("Jew free"), or *Judenrein* ("pure of Jews"). The Nazi press, particularly such rabid publications as *Der Stürmer*, a paper created by Julius Streicher, gauleiter of Franconia, specifically to attack the Jews, launched wave after wave of scurrilous propaganda. The Jews were accused, in the most lurid details, of every manner of evil, including the ritual murder of Christians. The "Elders of Zion" were said to be conspiring together to crush Germany.

After two and a half years of mounting terror and hostility, the racial hatred was formalized in two comprehensive new laws, known as the Nuremberg Laws since they were enacted in that city during the party rally on September 15, 1935. The first of these defined Reich citizenship, which could only be held by "a national of German or kindred blood." The second, the Law for the Protection of German Blood and German Honor, forbade marriages between Jews and Germans and finalized the disenfranchisement of the German Jews by declaring them to be noncitizens.

A month later, a first decree of the National Law of Citizenship was published, defining the term "Jew" and setting out various degrees of *Mischlinge*, mixed-blood status, depending on how many Jewish parents or grandparents someone had. Only Aryans were allowed to hold official posts. Under the first decree of the second law, marriages between Jews and second-generation *Mischlinge* were prohibited. Sexual relations between Jews of any grade and Germans was forbidden. Jews were forbidden to fly the German flag, which had officially become the swastika under a third law passed at Nuremberg on September 15.

By making life as unpleasant and as difficult as possible for the Jews, the Nazis hoped that more and more would be forced to emigrate, so that eventually the whole of Germany would be *Judenfrei*. In fact, this policy was partially successful: From 1934 to 1937, the rate of Jewish immigration rose to about twenty-five thousand a year. By 1938, over a quarter of all Jews had gone, leaving about three hundred thousand, excluding Christians of Jewish descent and *Mischlinge*, who either obstinately refused to go, or who could not find a country prepared to take them.

But at that rate, as Reinhard Heydrich, deputy chief of the SS, pointed out, the solution to Germany's Jewish "problem" would take anything from ten to fifteen years to complete. Hitler was not prepared to wait that long. Something more had to be done.

Nineteen thirty-eight was to be the great watershed year for Hitler and the Nazis. After five years in office, Hitler finally consolidated his power by removing the last non-Nazis from his government, replacing the foreign minister, the economics minister, and various others, including all his principal ambassadors, with his own people. He also fired the army chiefs, and took over the role of Commander in Chief of the armed forces himself, in addition to his existing role as Supreme Commander, which he held automatically as head of state. With compliant puppets in charge of the country's armed forces, finances, and foreign affairs, the way was now clear for him to set out in earnest on his road to destiny.

Inevitably, that involved dealing with the Jews once and for all. During 1936, the persecution had calmed down considerably, since Berlin was hosting the Olympic Games and therefore needed to show a more pacific face to its visitors. This winding down in the level of violence had continued during much of 1937, prompting both outsiders and many German Jews to believe that things were improving after the excesses of the new regime's first three years. Perhaps, some dared to hope, the wilder elements had been allowed to have their fling, but would now be more controlled as the party became more responsible.

Such hopes were, of course, totally unfounded. With his power consolidated and his confidence growing every day as the Western powers' nervousness and fear of him increased, he was ready to start moving forward again. First, he needed to reradicalize the party, to relight the fires that had been damped down for nearly two years of rearmament and building. And the best fuel for this was increased activity against the Jews.

Soon there was another, more pressing reason for stronger action. On March 12, the German Army marched into Austria, unopposed. The next day, Hitler announced the *Anschluss* ("union") of the two countries. Austria had ceased to exist as a separate country, its population incorporated into the Reich. But the population of Austria included nearly two hundred thousand Jews—which meant that in a single day, the number of Jews in Germany had reverted to almost exactly what it had been when Hitler came to power in 1933. All those who had been forced to emigrate had been replaced.

As it happened, however, as well as providing a new problem, Austria itself demonstrated one way of tackling it, in Vienna. At the time of the *Anschluss*, Vienna possessed the third-largest Jewish community in Europe, after Warsaw and Budapest. According to the 1934 census, the last to be taken before Hitler's invasion, the Jewish population of Austria numbered 191,000, of whom some 90 percent, about 170,000, lived in the capital. This represented 10 percent of the city's population, but that 10 percent played a disproportionately important role in the city's cultural, professional, and business life. Freud, Schnitzler, Kafka, Mahler—the list of eminent Viennese Jews went on and on. Thanks to them, since 1900 Vienna had been one of the most intellectually exciting cities in the world, rivaling Paris in its ferment of new ideas. In the professions, over half the doctors and dentists were Jewish, as well as six out of ten lawyers and a quarter of all university professors—a figure that rose to 45 percent in the medical faculty. In the city's business life, whole areas of commercial activity, such as the scrap-metal business, advertising, and furniture, were in predominantly Jewish hands.

Austrian anti-Semitism was every bit as virulent as the German variety—Hitler had first been infected in his home country, after all. But until the *Anschluss*, it had been kept in check, physically at least, by government disapproval. On Friday, March 11, when it was known that the Germans would march in the next day, the need for restraint vanished. Austrian Nazis went on the rampage through the streets of Vienna in an outburst that lasted for days.

Any Jew, or anyone looking remotely Jewish, caught on the streets was attacked and beaten. Jewish shops were pillaged, windows smashed, goods stolen. Clothing stores and delicatessens were favorite targets for looters, since their contents could so easily be carried away. Many Jewish households kept considerable sums of money on hand in order to bribe the SA gangs and thus escape unharmed. "Jewellery, furs and even furniture were all acceptable," noted G.E.R. Gedye, the London *Daily Telegraph* correspondent, who was himself almost attacked by a mob because of his appearance. "All motor cars without exception, of course, were immediately stolen from their Jewish owners, the plunderers demanding at the same time either a lump sum or regular contributions 'to buy petrol.' One optimistic Jew I knew, thinking that one day he might get his own car back, volunteered to act as chauffeur for several weeks to the gang which took it." Incredible as it seems, the offer was accepted—on condition that he keep the gang in food and drink and other goodies until they no longer needed his car.

Throughout the first days of Nazi occupation, the Viennese mobs continued to run riot, while the police did nothing, standing by while Jews and supporters of the deposed chancellor, Schuschnigg, were attacked in the street. They looked on as people were seized and given brushes and water or paint stripper and forced to scrub off pro-Schuschnigg slogans that had been painted on pavements and walls all over the city. Gedye saw his first "cleansing squad" at the Praterstern: an old Jewish man dragged through the screaming crowd by storm troopers and forced to remove the portrait of the former chancellor that had been stenciled on the base of a statue. "Work for the Jews at last! Work for the Jews!" the mob howled. "We thank our führer for finding work for the Jews."

No Jew was safe, however exalted. The chief rabbi of Vienna was dragged out into the streets and forced to scrub pavements, as was General Pick, a distinguished ex-soldier and a veteran of the First World War, as well as previous head of the Jewish community in Austria. Jews were forced to clean out latrines in SS barracks while wearing their sacred prayer bands on their arms, and to suffer many other similar indignities. Hundreds of Jews committed suicide, unable or unwilling to face the horrors of mob rule. Thousands more fled from the city and the country, into neighboring states. Those who could headed further afield, to France, Britain, or the United States.

The example set by the Viennese Nazis was not lost on the party in Germany. The weekly newspaper of the SS, the *Schwarze Korps*, praised their enthusiasm, saying, "They have managed to do overnight what we have failed to do up to this day in the slow-moving, ponderous north. In Austria, a boycott of the Jews does not need organizing—the people themselves have instituted it with honest joy." Over the following months, the Austrians devoted their "honest joy" to trying to achieve in weeks what had taken their German brothers five years, in downgrading, humiliating, and persecuting their Jewish citizens.

In April, to coordinate and supervise the business of driving the Jews out of the country, Heydrich sent a newly promoted SS *Untersturmführer* called Adolf Eichmann to Vienna to organize and run a special bureau, the Central Office for Jewish Emigration. Setting up his headquarters in a commandeered Rothschild palace, Eichmann went to work to make Austria completely *Judenfrei* in as short a time as possible. He was soon establishing new records for the expulsion of Jews by ordering his men to dump them across the border, any border, anywhere.

Eichmann's methods were brutal and simple. On one occasion, he evicted fifty-one men, women, and children from their Austrian village on a Saturday—the Nazis were making a habit of choosing the Jewish Sabbath for their actions—put them into small boats and pushed them into the Danube, leaving them stranded on a sandbank in midstream near the Czech village of Theben. They were discovered on the Sunday by a Czech border patrol, who heard their plaintive cries for help.

The Czechs gave them food and shelter overnight, but the next morning put them across the Hungarian border. The Hungarians did not want them, either, and managed to force thirty-five of them back across the Austrian border. The remaining sixteen found shelter aboard an old French barge anchored in the river. There they stayed for five months, until the Hungarian authorities ordered them to leave, whereupon they slipped their anchor and drifted downstream aboard their decrepit little ark, into oblivion. We do not know what became of them after that.

In Germany, meanwhile, the pressure on the Jews was being stepped up. On April 26, Göring decreed that all Jewish holdings valued at more than five thousand Reichsmarks must be registered, so that he would have a complete record of all Jewish wealth. Six weeks later, he ordered all remaining Jewish businesses to be marked as such. On May 28, the Jews of Frankfurt-am-Main, one of the oldest communities in Germany, were subjected to a day of intimidation and abuse, similar to one held a month before in Vienna when Jews had been dragged into the Prater amusement park, made to eat grass, climb trees, and twitter like birds, then forced to run in circles until they collapsed. Some had been strapped into the coaches of the Prater's roller coaster and sent around and around at top speed until they lost consciousness. Many had suffered heart attacks, and several died.

In Frankfurt, there were similar "pleasure hours," as the Nazis called them, and also a repetition of the scenes that had taken place in Berlin in April 1933. The British consul general, R. T. Smallbones, reported to London, "On the windows of Jews' shops various caricatures of Jews were painted, such as Jews hanging from gibbets, with insulting inscriptions." Gangs of SA men went around to Jewish homes, telling the families "to leave Germany quickly as, next time, quite different measures would be taken against them."

On June 9, there was an ominous new development, when the main synagogue in Munich was burned down. The next day, in his capacity as gauleiter of Berlin, Goebbels made a secret speech to members of the city's police, telling them, "In the coming half year, the Jews must be forced to leave Berlin. The police are to work hand-in-hand with the party in this." As though to reinforce his words, more than two thousand Jews throughout Germany were arrested on charges of "race pollution." The British chief passport-control officer, and head of station in Berlin for the Secret Intelligence Service, Captain Frank Foley, reported to London that it was "no exaggeration to say that Jews had been hunted like rats in their homes, and for fear of arrest, many of them sleep at a different address overnight." Those who were taken were thrown into Dachau or the recently opened concentration camp at Buchenwald, near Weimar, where they were made to slave for fourteen to sixteen hours a day, breaking and hauling stones in the "quarries of death."

During the summer and early autumn, the inmates of Buchenwald and Sachsenhausen, the camp near Berlin, were put to work enlarging their camps to receive thousands more prisoners. At Dachau, near Munich, the workshops were turned over to the sewing of Stars of David on thousands of striped uniforms. Every Jew was aware that something sinister was brewing, but no one knew what it would be, or when it would happen.

Still the pressures continued to build. On August 10, violence flared again, with the torching of another major synagogue, this time in Nuremberg. A week later, on August 17, a new decree ordered all Jews to take the names Israel or Sarah before their existing first names. On September 27, Jewish lawyers were forbidden to practice in Germany. On October 7, all German passports belonging to Jews—which already had to have the letter *J* stamped on them in red—were withdrawn and invalidated, to be replaced by special identity cards.

On October 14, Göring signaled that the time was approaching for still more drastic action when he told a meeting of his colleagues, "The Reich must eradicate doubtful elements from the population—namely the last remaining Jews." Drastic action was clearly needed, since there were still nearly half a million of them in the expanded Reich. Although most were desperately anxious to escape, there were still those who refused to accept what was happening, clinging to the hope that the storm would pass, somehow, sometime. Those stubborn souls needed to be convinced that there was no hope. So, too, did other countries, which were growing increasingly alarmed by the flood of emigrants pouring out of Germany and seeking refuge with them.

Many nations were starting to close their doors rather than open them. Soon there would be nowhere for those half-million Jews to go. If the Nazis were not to find themselves stuck with them, therefore, they would have to take action quickly. The problem was finding the right opportunity, the right time, and the right stimulant to mobilize all their forces to deliver one enormous, shattering blow.

That opportunity was unwittingly handed to them, with near-perfect timing, by that seventeen-year-old youth in Paris, Herschel Grynszpan.

A Postcard from Poland

Herschel Feibel Grynszpan was a Jew, of somewhat confused nationality. He was born on March 28, 1921, at 36 Burgstrasse, Hanover, Germany. His parents were Polish, but had started life as Russian citizens, having been born in eastern Poland at a time when it was under Russian rule: Herschel's father, Sendel Siegmung Grynszpan, at Dmenin in 1886, his mother, Rifka, the following year at Radomsko. Their lives followed a similar pattern to those of thousands of other Jews in Central and Eastern Europe in those years.

After completing his compulsory military service in the Russian Army—probably four years, in view of the fact that he could read and write—Sendel Grynszpan started in business, like Tevye in *Fiddler on the Roof*, as a milkman, later becoming a tailor and dealer in secondhand clothes. He married Rifka Silberberg in Radomsko in April 1910. A year later, they fled to Germany in fear of their lives, terrified that the outrages then being perpetrated in the neighboring Ukraine would spill over into Poland. The Ukraine was in ferment, with Ukrainian nationalism, in Neal Ascherson's phrase, "well established, angry and ambitious." It was anti-Polish, anti-Russian, and anti-Semitic. The Grynszpans' move was timely and wise, for the threat did not diminish: By 1918, when the Ukrainian nationalists and the White Russian armies fought for possession of the country during the Russian civil war, Jews were slaughtered like cattle, dying in thousands.

The Grynszpans settled in Hanover, where Sendel found work initially as a plumber, before being able to return to tailoring and set up his own business in 1918. It did not provide a good income at the best of times, and by 1929, when the Depression hit small businesses all over Europe and worst of all in Germany, he was forced to give up his shop and try to make a living as a junk dealer. From July 1933 to October 1934, things were so bad that he had to eke out his modest earnings with welfare assistance until the beginnings of an economic revival under Hitler's rule enabled him to return to tailoring once more.

By this time, eight children had been born to Sendel and Rifka, four boys and four girls. Only three survived, however: a daughter, Ester Beile (known as Berta), born January 31, 1916; a son, Mordechai Eliese (known as Marcus), born August 29, 1919; and Herschel. Such a high mortality rate was unusual even for families living in the poverty and squalor the Grynszpans suffered for most of their lives. A possible clue is to be found in the report of the French doctors who examined Herschel after his arrest: This states that his teeth showed what is known as the Hutchinson characteristic—being more widely spaced than normal, and crenated, or notched—a classic symptom of hereditary syphilis.

The effects of this unpromising family background on Herschel must have been increased by the surroundings in which he grew up. Burgstrasse, where the Grynszpans lived, was in an old, run-down part of Hanover, near the sham-Gothic bulk of the railway station. It was a sleazy area, where the squalid Scheiber Market flourished—thousands of little stalls selling everything from dubious delicacies to stolen goods—and where whores, muggers, pickpockets, and thieves pursued their various trades. Hanover itself was a center of homosexuality: There were no fewer than 500 male prostitutes on the police books in 1918, and the chief criminal inspector put the number of homosexuals in the city at about 40,000, out of a total population of some 450,000. The Grynszpans' neighborhood earned particular notoriety during the early years of Herschel's childhood through the activities of one Fritz Haarman, known as "the Butcher of Hanover," who picked up his victims, mostly adolescent boys, in the railway station, and took them home to 27 Cellarstrasse, just around the corner from Sendel's shop. When he had finished with them, he strangled them, butchered their corpses, and sold the flesh as meat. He was executed in 1925.

Herschel was educated at Public School Number 1, a few doors from home in the Burgstrasse, from the age of six until he was fourteen. In the opinion of his teachers, he was of above-average intelligence but incurably lazy, and consequently passed no examinations and received no diploma, leaving in 1935 with nothing more than the usual *Abgangzeugnis*, in effect a final report card that said little more than that he had attended that particular school. Herschel claimed his unimpressive scholastic record was due to the teachers taking no interest in their Jewish students, who were, he told the French examining magistrate, "relegated to the back of the classroom and treated as outcasts."

Much of Herschel's time immediately after he left school was spent in trying to find a way of getting out of Germany. His father made him register with the Palestinian Service in Berlin, an organization that sent Jews to settle in Palestine—but unfortunately they were only interested in those who were over eighteen and fit and healthy enough to withstand the rigors of the harsh life they would have to face. Herschel was neither. Sendel then sent him to enroll with the Misrachi, a Zionist group in Hanover, who paid for him to go to the rabbinical seminary, the Yeshiva, in Frankfurt-am-Main. There he studied Hebrew for a year, being described by his teachers as a student of "average aptitude and intelligence."

By the time Herschel returned home on April 15, 1936, at the end of his studies, the Nazis' racial laws were hitting the Jewish community increasingly hard, and the Grynszpan family was in desperate straits once more. The two elder children managed to find some kind of work, though it was very poorly paid, but Herschel does not seem to have shared their determination, leaving job-hunting to his father. "My father searched everywhere," he told the French examining magistrate. "They asked him what his religion was. When he said, 'I am Jewish,' they answered, 'The devil take the Jews. Nothing doing.' " He went on to complain that he was persecuted in the street by Nazis: "I was kicked more than twice a day, even by little boys, who called me 'dirty Jew.' "

Herschel was not entirely without talent—he was good with his hands, loved tinkering with things mechanical, and wanted to become a plumber, an electrician, or a mechanic. But he lacked any sense of the urgent need to find work, and was content to loaf, his head full of impossible dreams. It was an old watchmaker who planted a new dream in his mind, which was to lead him to his nemesis. Meeting him in the synagogue one day, the old man advised him to leave Germany.

"A boy like you can't stay here under such conditions," he told him. "In Germany, a Jew is not a man, but is treated like a dog."

The watchmaker suggested Herschel go to France, and offered to speak to Sendel about it. Sendel had a brother, Abraham, a tailor like himself, who had been living in Paris since 1923. Sendel wrote to him. Abraham Grynszpan and his wife, Chawa, who were childless, replied immediately, not only agreeing to take Herschel in, but also offering to adopt him.

Before Herschel could go to Paris, he had to get his papers in order. He began by applying to the Polish consulate in Hanover for a passport: Although born in Germany, he was technically a Polish citizen. The passport was issued on June 3, 1936, and five weeks later Herschel went to the Hanover police headquarters to obtain an exit visa and—most important in case his plans did not work out—a reentry visa so that he could return to Burgstrasse and his parents.

The journey to Paris was an adventure in itself, and somehow typical of Herschel's character. He did not travel directly to the French capital, but took a circuitous route with stopovers on the way at the homes of two of his father's many brothers: Uncle Isaac, at Essen, in the heart of Ruhrland, and Uncle Wolf, who lived at 37 Rue des Tanneries, Brussels. Uncle Wolf turned out to be less hospitable than his brother in the Ruhr, who had housed and fed Herschel for several days. He swiftly made it clear that he was not running a hotel and did not want penniless relatives sponging on him. After a few days, Herschel moved out and went to stay with a neighbor, a man called Zaslawski, who was also vaguely related to the family. Zaslawski agreed to put Herschel up for a few days, provided he did not regard the arrangement as permanent and that Uncle Wolf and his family fed him.

Herschel suddenly found himself facing a serious problem. Although he was desperate to get to Paris, where Uncle Abraham and Aunt Chawa awaited him, he could not get into France. First, he needed an entry visa, which cost fifty francs, and second, the French police at the border were turning back Jews who could not prove that they had sufficient funds to live on. Unfortunately, Herschel had no money, and neither Uncle Wolf nor Zaslawaski were prepared to lend it to him—they were both, of course, living on the poverty line, with wives and families of their own to support, and probably did not have fifty francs to spare. Herschel's luck changed at last when Zaslawski's sister, a Mme. Rosenthal, arrived in Brussels from her home in Paris to spend a short holiday with her brother. She clearly felt sorry for the waiflike fifteen-year-old boy and, being a resourceful woman, quickly devised a scheme to smuggle him into France.

On September 15, 1936, Herschel left the Rue des Tanneries with Mme. Rosenthal and boarded a train to Quiévrain on the Belgian–French border, about twenty kilometers from Mons. There she put him on a tram to Valenciennes, the nearest large town on the French side. The tram was much used by Belgian workmen with jobs in France, and during the rush hour the passports of passengers without baggage were rarely checked. The ruse worked. Herschel was in France at last—but he was an illegal immigrant and would have to live by stealth. Once he had arrived safely in Valenciennes, he contacted Uncle Abraham in Paris, who came to collect him and take him to his new home.

The sign on the front door of the cramped, two-roomed apartment at 23 Boulevard Richard Lenoir read MAISON ALBERT. It sounds like a down-market hairdresser's, but in fact was the name of Abraham Grynszpan's one-man tailoring business. It was not much of a business: Abraham made clothes, basically as a subcontractor, for various large stores in Paris. Overheads were high—the rent alone was five thousand francs a year—and competition was fierce, even cutthroat, but Abraham was a hard worker and managed to earn five hundred to six hundred francs a week, enabling him and his wife to enjoy a certain degree of comfort. They welcomed Herschel to their small home at the end of September 1936. He was in a pitiful state, exhausted and depressed after his experiences, but Chawa put up a bed for him in the living room, and he quickly settled into his new life.

The Boulevard Richard Lenoir runs from the Place de la Bastille to the Boulevard Voltaire, in the eleventh arrondissement on the edge of Belleville, the largest of the Jewish ghettos in Paris. Jews who had emigrated from Eastern Europe tended to congregate there, and Herschel would have felt at home immediately: He had simply exchanged life in one ghetto for life in another. Even the language was the same—not French but Yiddish, with German as the second language. Local newspapers and magazines were printed in Yiddish or German: Yiddish dailies such as the *Pariser Haint* and the communist *Di Naye Presse*, and German papers such as the *Pariser Tageblatt*. The smells and sounds and street cries of the area would have seemed familiar; most of the shop signs were in Yiddish, and Jewish restaurants and kosher butchers abounded. Indeed, there were so many Jews living in the area that the four local public schools in the fourth arrondissement closed on Saturday, the Jewish Sabbath, rather than on Thursday, the traditional closing day for French schools.

From this base, Herschel soon discovered Paris. His uncle was generous and gave him thirty to forty francs a week pocket money, in return for which the boy was supposed to run errands and make himself generally useful. This was not a large sum, but it was enough for him to be able to go to the odd dance and to buy a coffee or a *jus d'orange* in some café and, all in all, to feel himself to be quite the boulevardier. It was hardly a life of luxury, sleeping on a made-up bed in Aunt Chawa's living room, but no doubt it was considerably better than he had been used to in Hanover. The domestic situation improved slightly when Abraham and Chawa moved to another apartment at 8 Rue Martel in the tenth arrondissement, one of those vast nineteenth-century Parisian apartment blocks, towering floor after floor above two inner courtyards like something out of a Zola novel. In the early autumn of 1938, they moved again, just around the corner to 6 Rue des Petites Ecuries.

While living in the Rue Martel, Herschel made one of his few friendships with someone of his own age in Paris, Nathan Kaufmann, the son of a tailor like Uncle Abraham, who lived across the street. Together, Herschel and Nathan wandered the boulevards, often in the company of the son of another neighbor, Solomon "Sam" Schenkler. As often as he could afford it, Herschel went to the movies, mostly to the local movie houses the Saint Martin and the Globe, sometimes with his friends, sometimes alone, and regularly once a week with his uncle and aunt. His favorite subjects were war films and love stories, notably *Morocco*, the Gary Cooper–Marlene Dietrich vehicle; *Ben Hur*, the Biblical epic; *Michael Strogoff*, a fast-paced Czarist Russian adventure story based on a Jules Verne novel, starring Anton Walbrook and Elizabeth Allen; and *Dark Eyes*, with Harry Bauer and Simone Simon.

Herschel also enjoyed dancing, going fairly regularly to a hall on the Boulevard Strasbourg called the Eldorado and to a Polish-Jewish sports club, L'Aurore, which organized country outings during the summer in association with a Jewish newspaper, *La Nouvelle Presse*, to places such as Noisy-le-Grand on the banks of the Marne. Outside of these activities, Herschel's spare time was spent hanging out at the Café Tout Va Bien with a bunch of youngsters of his own age. Much of the time, they were all too broke to go inside and order anything, so simply congregated on the pavement outside. There is no record that Herschel ever had any dealings with girls, except as dancing partners—indeed, after his arrest he confided to one of his lawyers that he was still a virgin. His only vice seems to have been cigarettes, of which he smoked three packs a week.

Like many boys of his age, Herschel was not overfond of work. One of the reports made on him after his arrest declared quite bluntly that he was lazy: "He didn't work in Hanover, he didn't look for work in Brussels, and he didn't work in Paris, either. He always has an excuse. In Germany he didn't find work because he was Jewish; in Brussels because his relatives were disagreeable; in Paris, he was such a law-abiding stickler for rules and regulations that he wouldn't work without a work permit." Herschel later explained to the examining magistrate that he could have found work if he had wanted to, "but I didn't want to put myself in an illegal situation."

In fact, Herschel had been trying to escape from his "illegal situation" during the whole of his time in France.

Three or four weeks after his arrival in Paris in October 1936, his father signed a legal document that made his brother Herschel's legal guardian. The first thing Uncle Abraham did was to try to legalize his nephew's status with the French authorities. This was a matter of some urgency: Not only was Herschel an illegal immigrant with no entry visa or visitor's permit, but the German reentry visa on his Polish passport was due to expire on April 1, 1937—though they managed to get this extended to June 1937—after which he would find himself with nowhere to go except Poland. Herschel had no wish to go there: It was a totally alien country to him, he did not speak the language, and he knew no one—though inevitably he had relatives there, living at Radom.

Uncle Abraham began by seeking the help of the Central Committee for the Assistance of Jewish Emigrés, making a formal application through them for a French identity card for Herschel. For some reason, the committee did not send off Herschel's application to the Ministry of the Interior until January 29, 1937, nearly three months later, when Herschel was given a receipt that in effect provided him with a temporary French residence permit while he awaited the outcome of his application.

In the meantime, hoping to stay on the right side of the law, Uncle Abraham took Herschel's Polish passport down to police headquarters and made a clean breast of things, confessing that the boy had entered the country without permission. He was fined one hundred francs and had to sign a guarantee undertaking to support his nephew and teach him a trade.

As the months dragged by with no decision from the Ministry of the Interior on Herschel's application, the extended time limit for his German reentry visa approached its end. On May 24, 1937, with one week to go, Herschel or someone in the family had a brainstorm. That day, he presented himself at the Polish consulate with the story that his passport had either been lost or stolen. After checking that he was in fact a passport holder, the consulate supplied him with a new one, valid for six months, until January 7, 1938. Armed with this clean document, Herschel applied to the German consulate for a new reentry visa.

More weeks passed, and Uncle Abraham and Aunt Chawa clearly began to grow weary of supporting the work-shy youngster. The entire Grynszpan family, including Herschel's father, came to the conclusion that it would be best if he returned to Germany. The Hanover authorities, however, thought otherwise: They refused to renew his visa. Shortly afterward, on August 11, 1938, the French authorities ordered him to leave France within four days.

Herschel was now in a desperate situation. Germany was closed to him. He was not considered strong enough to go to Palestine. Poland was a foreign country, and in any case there was no guarantee he would be admitted, since a recent law gave the government the right to revoke the citizenship of anyone who had lived abroad for more than five years— Herschel, of course, had never even set foot inside the country. Now that France had rejected him, he had become a nonperson, trapped inside a nightmare.

Unable to leave France as ordered, Herschel went into hiding, in a maid's room on the fifth floor of their old apartment block at 8 Rue Martel. When the police came looking for Herschel at 6 Rue des Petites Ecuries, Abraham was able to say quite truthfully that his nephew was not there—though he was forced to lie when asked if he knew where he was now.

Searching vainly for some way out of his predicament, Herschel hit on a fantastic new idea: He would join the French Foreign Legion. Ignoring the fact that he was both too young and too frail, he persisted in this dream for some time—he even went on a hunger strike until Uncle Abraham gave him two hundred francs "to take the necessary steps" to join the Legion. But he put off going to the recruiting office. "I intended to enlist," he later told the examining magistrate, "but I hesitated because of my parents, who had already lost five children." His friend Nathan Kaufmann said that he also talked of suicide at this time.

Herschel may well have contemplated suicide, for he was now under pressure from every direction. In addition to worrying about his own safety in Paris, he was increasingly concerned about his family in Hanover. Every fresh piece of news from Germany seemed merely to be the prelude to something worse, and there was no shortage of news. Practically every day the *Pariser Haint*, the Yiddish daily paper that his uncle took, published reports and articles on the plight of Jews in Germany. On October 1, it carried a report on measures the German government proposed to take against Polish Jews to force them to leave the country and return to their homeland. On October 29, the first news appeared of the expulsion of Polish Jews from Berlin and Cologne. The following day there were more reports of expulsions from Leipzig, Munich, and Nuremberg. On October 31, the *Pariser Haint* reported that twelve thousand Polish Jews had been deported from Germany. It went on to say that the Polish government had authorized those whose papers were in order to enter Poland, where local Jewish charitable organizations could minister to their needs.

What was happening to Herschel's mother and father, brother and sister? On November 3, he received a postcard from his sister Berta that confirmed his worst fears. The card, which was found in his wallet by Officer Autret at the time of his arrest, read:

"You have undoubtedly heard of our great misfortune. I will give you a description of what happened.

"On Thursday night there were rumors circulating that all Polish Jews of a certain city had been expelled. However, we refused to believe them. On Thursday night at 9:00 P.M., a Schupo [local policeman] came to our house and told us we had to go to the police headquarters with our passports. We went just as we were, all together, to the police headquarters, accompanied by the Schupo. There we found almost our entire neighborhood already assembled. A police wagon then took us at once to the Rathaus [town hall]. Everyone was taken there. We had not yet been told what it was about, but we quickly realized that it was the end for us. An expulsion order was thrust into our hands. We had to leave Germany before October 29 (Saturday). We were not allowed to return to our homes. I begged to be allowed to return home to get at least a few essential things. So I left with a Schupo accompanying me and I packed a valise with the most necessary clothes. That is all I could save. We don't have a cent."

The next day, Herschel read a report in the *Pariser Haint* from the small Polish border town of Zbaszyn—or Zbonszyn, as it was known in Yiddish—which substantiated everything Berta has said in her postcard:

> Critical situation of Polish Jews deported from Germany. More than 8,000 persons have overnight been made stateless. They were rounded up and deported, largely to Zbonszyn, in no-man's-land between Germany and Poland. Their living conditions are uncomfortable and distressing. Twelve hundred of them have fallen ill and several hundred are without shelter. As there is a risk of epidemic, Red Cross doctors with the help of doctors from the OSE [Oeuvre de Secours aux Enfants, a children's charity] have distributed typhus vaccinations and 10,000 aspirin tablets. A number of cases of insanity and suicide have been reported.

It was this news from Poland that finally pushed Herschel Grynszpan over the edge.

The Making of a Martyr

Jews had been settled in Poland for hundreds of years: The earliest records show Jewish communities in the area between the rivers Oder and Vistula as far back as the tenth century. They were joined during succeeding ages by waves of immigration from the east, and although considerable numbers left for the New World in the late nineteenth and early twentieth centuries, the population census of 1931 established that there were 2.7 million Jews in Poland—almost certainly an underestimate—making up no less than 8.5 percent of the entire population. By 1939, this figure had grown to around 3.25 million. In Warsaw and several other cities and large towns, they accounted for a third of all inhabitants.

The position of Jews in Poland fluctuated according to the circumstances of contemporary history: At times they were badly treated, at other times less so. In 1643, for example, the merchant class was divided by law into three categories—Poles, foreigners, and Jews—which meant Polish Jews did not enjoy the same rights as their fellow Poles but were lumped with such outsiders as Scots, Armenians, and Lithuanians, or with other non-Christian groups such as Turks and Tartars. A hundred years later, however, William Coxe, an English traveler, wrote that in Poland Jews "enjoy privileges which they scarcely possess in any other country except England and Holland."

In more recent times, the fluctuations in Jewish fortunes were even more marked. For a brief period following the rebirth of an independent Polish state after the First World War, Jews enjoyed a remarkable degree of business and artistic freedom. The Jewish press flourished, publishing in both Polish and Yiddish. The Yiddish theater reached new heights of artistic excellence, especially in the cities of Warsaw and Wilno—otherwise known as Vilnius or Vilna—the former capital of Lithuania seized by the Poles in 1920. And there was a thriving Jewish film industry that turned out scores of movies in Yiddish.

With the death of Marshal Józef Pilsudski in 1935, however, Jewish circumstances deteriorated rapidly. Pilsudski, the de Gaulle of Poland, architect of the new republic and its dictator since 1926, had not been personally anti-Semitic, recognizing the Jews as an integral part of Poland's heritage. In reflection of this, *Opinia*, a Zionist weekly published in Warsaw, was able to describe him in its obituary notice as "one of those personages created in the measure of gods."

Pilsudski's successors fell far short of such standards in most respects, and not least in their attitude to the Jews. In March 1935, the short-lived civilian government that followed him introduced legislation to restrict Jewish ritual slaughter of animals. The military government that took power in 1936 passed new and even more restrictive laws against the Jews. Known as the "government of the colonels," though most members of the junta were now generals, the new rulers turned the country into what has been described as a "national-totalitarian state." Though not quite as totalitarian as those in Poland's two mighty neighbors, Germany and the Soviet Union, the new regime was distinctly authoritarian and extremely nationalistic, and the increased influence of the Polish Fascist parties insured that anti-Semitism became one of the pillars of its political program. In fact, it was only this anti-Semitic stance that held the Polish right together.

The new laws that were passed almost immediately when the colonels came to power extended far beyond the question of ritual slaughter: They included various means of restraining Jews from practicing different trades and professions—an echo of events in Nazi Germany. As is so often the case, this downgrading of Jews to second-class citizens was initially due to economic factors. Poland's economy in the thirties was in a desperate state, partly because of the country's chronic instability, partly as a result of the world Depression, from which she was unable to recover as quickly as her neighbors since she was industrially underdeveloped. Inevitably, the Jews were the obvious scapegoats, who could be blamed and punished for Poland's ills. By denying them work, the Poles could keep what little there was for themselves.

In 1936, with unemployment standing at 466,000, the economic situation did, in fact, slowly begin to improve. But the persecution of the Jews continued in various forms, to some extent encouraged by the Catholic Church, which had long set its face against the so-called murderers of Christ. The Church did not officially preach anti-Semitism—though many individual priests were openly anti-Semitic—but it did not object when, for example, Catholic associations for the legal, medical, and other professions were among the first in Poland to require of their members pure Aryan blood.

Against a background of steadily increasing anti-Jewish activity, the first pogrom in modern Poland took place on March 9, 1936, in the village of Przytyk, to the south of Warsaw near Radom, where Sendel and Rifka Grynszpan came from. A mob of Polish peasants attacked Jewish houses in the village square, smashing windows and furniture, killing a Jewish shoemaker and his wife and severely beating their children. The Jews of Przytyk fought back—some had filled bottles with benzine ready to throw—and a twenty-year-old religious Jew called Shalom Lasky produced a revolver and shot dead one of the attackers.

The violence increased sporadically throughout Poland during 1936 and 1937, mostly on a small scale, unpleasant and frightening but with few deaths, culminating in a much larger pogrom in the city of Brest-Litovsk on May 13, 1937, under the slogan "We owe our troubles to the Jews!" In August 1936, in another echo of Nazi practice, the Polish government ordered all shops throughout the country to include on the shop sign the name of the owner as it appeared on his birth certificate. This served to identify Jewish-owned shops, and painted graffiti soon began to appear on them, daubs mirroring in Polish those that were already so common in the German Reich: JEWS OUT!, DON'T BUY AT JEWISH SHOPS, and GET OUT TO PALESTINE!

Polish Jews began to question their future in a country governed by the generals and colonels of the ruling junta. They tried to flee in ever-increasing numbers, but already doors were starting to close. In 1936, a record 11,596 men, women, and children from Poland, nearly 2,500 more than from Germany, arrived in Palestine. But in 1937, the Palestinian Arabs began a revolt against Jewish immigration into their country. The numbers that year were cut to 3,636 as the British imposed tighter restrictions, vainly attempting to reduce the troubles and the number of deaths: Between April 1936 and the end of 1937, 113 Jews had been killed by Arabs, and 15 Arabs by Jews in reprisal raids.

By 1938, with stricter quotas being imposed by countries such as Britain itself, the United States, France, Switzerland, and Brazil, which until then had all taken relatively large numbers of refugees, the prospects of escape were fading fast for the 3.25 million Jews in Poland.

The situation in Poland was bad news for all those Polish Jews resident in Germany—many of them, like the Grynszpans, since before the First World War. Since 1935, the Nazis had been steadily tightening the screws on German Jewry, determined to force Jews out and making it abundantly clear that they did not care where they went. This naturally alarmed the

Polish and Eastern European Jews living there, considerable numbers of whom began to investigate the possibility of returning "home."

Such a development was not to the Polish government's liking. The last thing they wanted was an exodus in reverse, a mass return of Jews from abroad: They were trying to find ways of getting rid of their indigenous Jewish population. The counselor of the Polish embassy in London, M. Jazdzewski, put the matter quite bluntly during an official call at the British Foreign Office later that year. "Poland's Jewish question," he said, "is more than pressing. It is becoming intolerable. It is not a question of any responsible person in Poland wishing to get rid of the Jews because they are unpopular, but simply that their numbers are now so great and are increasing so rapidly that it is becoming impossible to find livelihoods for all of them." After pressing Britain to find homes for Polish Jews in Northern Rhodesia—present-day Zambia—Jazdzewski concluded by repeating that "for Poland the question of finding an outlet for her Jews is one of vital necessity."

While "finding an outlet" for Jews from inside Poland posed insurmountable problems, preventing the return of those who had already gone could well be feasible. It would have to be handled with a certain delicacy, to avoid upsetting either the Western democracies or the Germans, but this, too, could surely be achieved. On March 12, 1938, however, the matter suddenly became more urgent, with the Austrian *Anschluss*. Many of Austria's Jewish population came originally from Poland. Thousands fled across the border to escape the wave of violent anti-Semitism that was unleashed in Vienna and the rest of Austria. Clearly, something would have to be done, and done quickly.

On March 31, 1938, the Polish government passed a law giving it the right to revoke the nationality of any Polish citizen who had been living abroad for more than five years. There was no specific mention of Jews in the new law, and the government vehemently denied that it was intended to apply only to them. But no one was fooled—not the Germans, and certainly not those Polish Jews living in Germany. In April 1938, like many of her compatriots, Herschel Grynszpan's mother, Rifka, made the first of several trips to see members of her family in Radom to find out what could be arranged if she and Sendel and their children returned there.

Further action by the Polish government was postponed for the outcome of a world conference at Evian, Switzerland, called by President Roosevelt in July to attempt to find a solution to the refugee problem. But with the failure of the Evian conference, swiftly followed by further

German advances, this time into Poland's immediate neighbor to the south, Czechoslovakia, after the Munich settlement, they soon gave another turn to the screw. On October 6, they announced a decree stating that all Polish passports must bear a new control stamp, without which they would be considered invalid.

This seemingly innocuous contrivance—which again made no mention of the Jews—threatened to have far-reaching consequences. In the future, Polish citizens whose passports did not bear the new stamp could be refused reentry: anyone who failed for any reason to comply with the new regulation would be unable to return to Poland and could find that he or she had become a stateless person overnight. Those living in Germany would have no right of domicile in either country.

The German authorities had no illusions about the purpose of this latest measure: "By this decree," Heinrich Himmler, Reichsführer of the SS and chief of German police, reported in a memorandum to Hitler, "the Polish government obviously intended to make it impossible for the numerous Polish Jews living abroad—particularly in Germany—to return to Poland. Practically, this would mean that some 70,000 Polish Jews in Reich territory would have to be tolerated permanently in Germany."

The decree was due to take effect on October 30, 1938, leaving the Germans just two weeks in which to persuade the Poles to withdraw or amend it. Their reaction was swift and positive. Hans Adolf von Moltke, German ambassador in Warsaw, was instructed to inform the Polish government that unless it withdrew the decree, so that it would "in no way affect the obligations of the Polish government to admit holders of Polish passports into Poland immediately . . . even if their passports do not bear the inspection stamp," all Polish Jews would be expelled from the Reich "immediately, on the shortest possible notice."

On October 29, the Poles replied, again denying that the decree was specifically aimed at the Jews, and refusing to halt it. By then, the Germans had already started rounding up some fifteen thousand Polish Jews throughout the Reich, from Berlin to Vienna, from Hamburg to Graz. Parents were taken from their homes, children were arrested as they came out of school and taken to the police station, their school bags still in their hands. As the operation continued throughout October 28 and 29, men, women, and children were even dragged out of bed and herded to railway stations without being allowed to pack.

In Hanover, the Grynszpans were among the first to be taken. In his evidence to the Eichmann trial in Jerusalem in 1961, Sendel gave a firsthand account of the treatment they received:

It was a Thursday, October 27, 1938. A policeman knocked at our door at eight o'clock at night and told us to report to the police station with our passports. He said, "Don't bother to take anything else, you'll be right back." When we reached the police station, my wife, my daughter, my son Marcus and myself, we saw a large number of people, some were sitting, some standing. People were weeping. The police inspector was shouting at the top of his voice, "Sign, sign, sign! You are being deported." I had to sign, like everyone else. One of us did not. His name, I believe was Gershon Silber, and he was made to stand in the corner for twenty-four hours.

They took us to the concert hall beside the river Leine, and there, there were people from all the areas of Hanover, about 600 people. There we stayed until Friday night; about twenty-four hours. Then they took us in police trucks, about twenty men in each truck, to the railway station. The streets were black with people, shouting, "The Jews out to Palestine!"

The stationmaster of Hanover was later able to report to the Gestapo that everything had gone without a hitch:

Special train SPECIAL HANOVER 4199 made up at 19:30—about two hours before departure. Consisting of 14 well-lit carriages each with 55 seats, of which 35 or 40 were occupied. The departure of the Jews, carrying large quantities of hand luggage, proceeded from platform 5, which had been closed to the public before the train was assembled. The Jews were allowed to purchase food and tobacco. The special train departed on schedule at 21:40 from track 11, platform 5.

Special Hanover 4199 arrived at Neubenschen on the German–Polish border punctually next morning. Sendel Grynszpan takes up the story again:

It was Shabbat morning—Saturday morning. When we reached Neubenschen at 6:00 A.M. there came trains from all sorts of places, Leipzig, Cologne, Düsseldorf, Essen, Bielefeld, Bremen. Together we were about 12,000 people.

When we reached the border, we were searched to see if anybody had any money, and anybody who had more than ten marks, the balance was taken from him. This was the German law. No more than ten marks could be taken out of Germany. The Germans said, "You didn't bring any more into Germany and you can't take any more out."

The SS were giving us, as it were, protective custody, and we walked two kilometers on foot to the Polish border. They told us to go—the SS men were whipping us, those who couldn't walk were beaten until the road was wet with their blood. They tore away their little baggage from them, they treated us in a most cruel and barbarous fashion—this was the first time that I'd ever seen the wild barbarism of the Germans.

They shouted at us "Run! Run!" I myself was hit and I fell in the ditch. My son, Marcus, took my hand and said, "Come on, Papa, run. They'll kill you if you don't."

Total confusion reigned on the border itself. "The Poles had no idea why we were there," Sendel Grynszpan recalled, "or why there were so many of us." Although the new decree did not come into force until October 30, the Polish border police still refused to accept them. At one point, a brutal game seems to have developed, with the Germans pushing groups of Jews across the open, or "green" frontier, and the Poles pushing them back again further along. At the main crossing point, the Jews were faced by Polish border guards with fixed bayonets. "Go on!" the Germans shouted. "Don't worry. They wouldn't dare shoot you." Using their rifle butts, they drove the Jews forward, like cattle, toward the Polish bayonets. The Polish troops fired a volley into the air. Panic-stricken, the Jews stampeded across the border into no-man's-land, where they stayed, refusing to budge, huddled in the near-freezing rain and mud for three hours, until 10:00 A.M.

"Then a Polish general and some officers arrived," said Sendel Grynszpan. "They examined our papers and saw that we were Polish citizens, that we had special passports. It was decided to let us enter Poland. They took us to a village of about 6,000 people, and we were 12,000. The rain was driving hard, people were fainting—some suffered heart attacks. On all sides one saw old men and women. Our suffering was great. There was no food—since Thursday we had not wanted to eat any German bread."

The village was Zbaszyn, forty miles southwest of Poznan. There the Jews were left to find what shelter they could—Sendel recalled being put into stables still dirty with horse dung. Rosalind Herzfeld, a British woman working for one of the Jewish charities, described how she found "thousands crowded together in pigsties. The old, the sick and children herded together in the most inhuman conditions." Things were so bad, she said, "that some actually tried to escape *back* to Germany and were shot."

The French-Jewish journal *L'Univers Israelite* reported on the scene:

Many parents can no longer find their children, and many children no longer know where to find their parents. The post office at Zbaszyn receives numerous letters addressed to the refugees. The letters are not distributed since it is impossible to find the persons to whom they are addressed. Money orders, some sent by cable from the U.S., await the discovery of the addressees.

The local population is very much distressed by the misery of the refugees and is doing everything to alleviate the situation. Even the German inhabitants of Zbaszyn are offering to help the afflicted.

Thirty-seven Jewish refugees, whose papers were not in order, were sent back to Germany by the Polish authorities. The German customs refused to admit them. The unfortunate persons find themselves caught between two closed borders. In this group there are some women, one child and one old man of 65.

Of the fifteen thousand Jews dumped on the frontier, or pushed over it, the Polish government refused to admit nearly half of them. Seven thousand were stranded in Zbaszyn—it was not until July 1939, only a matter of weeks before the outbreak of war, that the government finally relented and permitted those still surviving to proceed into Poland proper.

The Grynszpans were lucky. They were able to leave quite soon, having found accommodation with relatives in Lodz, the center of the Polish textile industry, a city to the southwest of Warsaw with a population of some six hundred thousand, one third of whom were Jewish. Life in Lodz was fraught with danger for any Jew: Since 1934, the city council had been dominated by a coalition of anti-Semitic parties who were doing their best to purge the city of its Jews—an operation that was to be taken over on September 8, 1939, by the SS after the German Army had taken the city within a week of the invasion. Nevertheless, in November 1938 it was a vast improvement on Zbaszyn.

While they were still in Zbaszyn, however, and before they knew they would be allowed to leave, Berta Grynszpan wrote another postcard to her brother in Paris, describing their situation. "We are very poorly fed," she wrote. "We sleep on straw sacks. We have received blankets. But, believe me . . . we won't be able to stand this much longer. Since we left, we have not been able to undress. Aunt Sura [Sendel's sister] stayed behind. She is considered 'of undetermined nationality.' Aunt Ida [Rifka's sister] is here. Uncle Schlojma [Ida's husband] is in the hospital. He has had an eye operation and stayed there." Berta asked Herschel to send money, and concluded, "We can't go any further."

Living as a fugitive in a strange country, while the family he loved had become refugees, there seemed nothing Herschel could do to help. He had no money to send them. He could not even go to Poland to share their misery. Torn between rage, despair, and guilt, he even talked— with some relish, it must be said, since at a young seventeen he was of an age to enjoy self-dramatization—of suicide, telling Aunt Chawa that he intended to throw himself into the Seine. He said much the same thing to Aunt Chawa's brother, Bernich Berenbaum, and to her brother-in-law, a man called Laufmann, telling him he wanted to die and be buried in the same grave as his parents. His despair, however, did not prevent his going to see a movie with his friend, Nathan Kaufmann, that evening, Saturday, November 5, at the Scala Cinema, 48 Rue du Faubourg Saint-Martin—almost exactly opposite M. Carpe's gun shop.

The next day, Herschel had a violent row with Uncle Abraham at the dinner table, accusing him of ignoring the plight of his family in Zbaszyn and refusing to send them money. Abraham protested that there was no point in sending money since they had no address for Sendel and the others. Furthermore, he added, he was a poor man and had little enough to send in any case. Voices were raised, the argument grew more and more heated, and finally Abraham shouted in a fury that if Herschel didn't like living under his roof, he could leave. Herschel turned to go. Aunt Chawa and Nathan Kaufmann, who had arrived toward the end of the quarrel, tried to calm it down, and for a moment it seemed as if they had succeeded. But then something more was said, the row flared up again, and Herschel slammed out of the apartment. Nathan, who hurried after him, said later that he had the impression Uncle Abraham had actually shown Herschel the door. When he tried to persuade Herschel to return, Herschel replied, "I will not go back. I'd rather die like a dog than go back on my decision."

The argument on November 6 was not the first time Abraham and Herschel had fallen out over money. There was a mystery that not even the examining magistrate was able to resolve, though he questioned every member of the family after Herschel's arrest, over the sum of three thousand francs (or marks—the currency varies in different accounts) that Herschel's father was said to have sent to Abraham to cover the boy's expenses in Paris. No amount of questioning ever managed to establish whether the money had actually been paid to Abraham, or whether it was an amount to be disbursed by him to be repaid by Sendel later. Certainly, however, Herschel had six hundred francs in his possession on November 3, to buy a new overcoat. And at some point in the argument on November 6, before Herschel flung out of the apartment, Abraham either gave him or threw at him two 100-franc notes. It was this money that Herschel used the next morning to buy the gun.

After leaving the apartment, Herschel and Nathan went off to a dance at L'Aurore sports club. Herschel was still in a black mood, however, and wouldn't join in any of the fun. When Nathan tried again to persuade him to go back home and make things up, he again refused, saying he would not spend the night under his uncle's roof and was going to a hotel.

The two boys left the dance at about 7:00 P.M. and walked up the Rue de Turenne toward the Place de la République, separating near the municipal offices of the tenth arrondissement on the corner of the Rue du Château d'Eau and the Rue du Faubourg Saint-Martin. They arranged to meet later that night, at 9:00 P.M., at the Tout Va Bien. Nathan arrived at the appointed time, but there was no sign of Herschel. When he failed to turn up, Nathan grew worried and eventually set off to look for him. Failing to find him, Nathan decided to go back to the Grynszpans' apartment at 6 Rue des Petites Ecuries. Herschel was not there.

By now, Abraham had calmed down. When Nathan arrived, he was, in fact, discussing Herschel with his wife's brother-in-law, Jacques Wykhodz. When he learned that Herschel was missing, Abraham became alarmed—the boy had, after all, been talking about committing suicide. He put on his coat and went looking for his nephew. He never found him.

When he parted from Nathan, Herschel had wandered down the Rue du Faubourg Saint-Martin to the Tout Va Bien on the Boulevard Saint-Denis, where he had a sandwich and something to drink for ten francs. A little before 8:30 P.M., he left the café, crossed the Boulevard Saint-Denis, and walked a couple of hundred yards up the Boulevard de Strasbourg. At number 17, above a cinema, was the small Hôtel Idéal-Suez—both are still there, but today the hotel calls itself the Cosmotel. Herschel went up to the reception desk on the first floor and booked a room for the night, paying twenty-two francs, fifty centimes in advance. He registered in the name of Heinrich Halter, salesman, birthplace Hanover, age eighteen, but did not fill in the green registration card that all foreigners were required to sign. He told Mlle. Laurent, daughter of the proprietor, who spoke to him in German, that he had left his documents in his luggage, which was still at the station. Since the German express had just arrived at the nearby Gare de L'Est, no one questioned his story.

Immediately after booking in, "Herr Halter" left the hotel again, saying he would return about midnight. The porter assumed he was going to collect his luggage from the station. He returned shortly after midnight—still without luggage—and was shown to his room. Thanks to an electric control board on the first floor, to the right of the landing, the night porter was later able to testify that Herschel kept the light on in his room far into the night.

"I had a very restless night," Herschel subsequently told the examining magistrate. "I dreamed a lot. In my dreams I saw my parents mistreated and beaten, and the dream made me suffer. In my dreams I also saw

Hitlerites who grabbed me by the throat to strangle me. I also saw boycott demonstrations such as those I had experienced in Hanover, where, for example, I saw Germans mistreated and spat upon when they went into a store owned by a Jew. Demonstrators screamed at them: 'You are damned! You are selling the German people to the Jews!' I was obsessed by that question. Again and again I asked myself, 'What have we done to deserve such a fate?' And I couldn't find any answer."

Later, when he was being examined by the medical authorities, he told a similar, if rather less graphic, story: "I did not sleep well because of the bad dreams I had. I saw myself going into the gun shop. I also had visions of my family's plight. I woke three times during the night. Each time, my heart was beating fast. To make it calm down, I put my hand on my chest."

The following day was Monday, November 7. At 7:30 A.M., Herschel got up, washed, and dressed. At 7:45, he ordered breakfast—*café complet*, at five francs—which was served in his room. Before he left, he took a photograph out of his wallet—a picture of himself, the sort of thing taken by street photographers at fairs—and wrote a message on the back to Uncle Abraham and Aunt Chawa. First, in Hebrew, he wrote the words "with God's help." The rest of the message was in schoolboy German, with one grammatical and two spelling errors: "My dear relatives, I couldn't do otherwise. God must forgive me. My heart bleeds when I think of our tragedy and that of the 12,000 Jews. I have to protest in such a way that the whole world hears my protest, and this I intend to do. I beg your forgiveness. Hermann." (In German, Herschel became Hermann.)

Leaving the Hôtel Idéal-Suez, Herschel went straight to M. Carpe's gunshop at 61 Rue du Faubourg Saint-Martin, where Mme. Carpe was winding up the heavy iron shutters. He was calm, collected, and polite.

"I want to buy a revolver," he told her.

After the shooting of Ernst vom Rath, the German ambassador was nowhere to be found—he was, of course, still enjoying his morning constitutional, totally unaware of what was happening in his embassy. In his absence, his secretary, Ernst Achenbach, whose office was next to vom Rath's, and Dr. Kurt Bräuer, the counselor, took control of the immediate crisis, calling the police to arrest Herschel Grynszpan, and one of the embassy's physicians, Dr. Claas, to attend to his victim.

Claas quickly examined the wounded man, then summoned an ambulance to rush him to the nearest medical facility, the Alma Clinic, a private hospital about one kilometer away at 155 Rue de l'Université. He also telephoned Professor Baumgartner, one of the finest surgeons in France, who hurried to the clinic to take charge of the case. Their first plan was to transfer vom Rath to the more famous and better equipped American Hospital at Neuilly, but he was suffering severe internal hemorrhaging, due to the lacerations of his spleen, and his condition had become critical. He could not be moved again. If Baumgartner were to have any hope of saving his life, he had no alternative but to operate immediately, at the Alma Clinic.

Only one of the two bullets that hit vom Rath had caused really serious injury: the first shot, which had damaged the spleen and pancreas and perforated the stomach. Baumgartner removed the spleen and pancreas and sutured the stomach. The patient was also given a massive blood transfusion under the supervision of a well-known specialist, Dr. Jobé. As this was before the days of blood banks, this involved contacting various voluntary donors with the right blood type, who then had to come into the clinic to give blood on the spot. Among them was a remarkable former Parisian restaurateur by the name of Thomas, a First World War veteran, holder of the Croix de Guerre and the Médaille Militaire, who had already given blood 107 times during the preceding eight years.

By the time Count von Welczek, the ambassador, returned from his walk, everything that could be done was already being done. He telephoned the clinic, and discovered the prognosis was not good—no one held out much hope for vom Rath's life—then dashed around the corner to the Quai d'Orsay to see the French foreign minister, Georges Bonnet.

"I have just had a narrow escape!" he announced dramatically, forgetting for a moment that his third secretary had not been so lucky. In his opinion, he said, the shooting was a deliberate attempt to put an end to "the tentative political rapprochement between France and Germany," which he and Bonnet had worked so hard to achieve with a proposed Franco-German friendship treaty.

Bonnet was appalled by the news, and by its potential effect on Franco-German relations. After asking Welczek to convey his profound regrets at the tragic incident to the German government, he sat down with the ambassador to discuss the political implications of Herschel's action. But while Bonnet, an even more ardent appeaser of Hitler than British prime minister Chamberlain, feared these could prove extremely serious for France, neither he nor Welczek seems to have even remotely foreseen the actual consequences in Germany. Certainly, it was some consolation for Bonnet to learn that the would-be assassin was a Polish and not a French Jew—it was bad enough that the shooting had occurred on French soil, albeit in the German embassy, but since Herschel was a foreigner, the blame could not be laid at the door of France. With Hitler in a rampant mood after the Munich settlement only five and a half weeks before, that, at least, was a blessing.

Hitler, who had just arrived in Munich after addressing a Nazi party rally in Weimar, was immediately informed of the shooting. His initial re-action was to promote vom Rath to the rank of counselor of embassy, several steps up the diplomatic ladder. He also ordered his personal physician, Dr. Karl Brandt—a man who was to be condemned to death in 1946 for supervising experiments on concentration-camp victims—and Professor Georg Magnus, director of the surgical unit at the University of Munich, to go at once to Paris to attend to the wounded diplomat.

The two doctors boarded a three-engined Junkers 52 airplane at Nuremberg at 1:44 A.M. on November 8. They arrived at Paris's Le Bourget Airport at 5:13 A.M. to be met by Kurt Bräuer, who took them to their hotel for a few hours' rest before he and Ambassador Welczek called to drive them to the Alma Clinic. They arrived there at 10:30 A.M. and conducted a thorough and careful examination of vom Rath, who had had a disturbed and restless night. When they had finished, they issued a statement to the press: "The condition of Counsellor vom Rath is regarded as serious in view of the wound in the stomach. Considerable loss of blood due to the lacerations of the patient's spleen has been treated with transfusions. The excellent surgical and medical treatment given by Professor Baumgartner of Paris allows us to hope for an improvement."

The conclusion of the statement must have been especially welcome to vom Rath's parents and his younger brother, Gunther, who had just reached Paris on the Nord Express from Cologne. The two men went straight to the clinic, but Frau vom Rath waited until next day, when she took with her an overnight bag, clearly intending to stay at her son's bedside for as long as was necessary. The wounded man was delighted to see his family, but he was so weak, they begged him not to talk.

The vom Raths were an old, conservative East Prussian family. The father was a pious man, a retired government adviser to the Cologne police—during the Second World War he was to be recalled to duty to become head of the Berlin police. He had three sons, two of whom were destined to become lawyers. Ernst was the eldest.

After attending the universities of Bonn, Munich, and Königsberg, Ernst had passed his law examinations at the age of twenty-one, a few months before Hitler came to power. It was a period of intense nationalistic fervor at the University of Königsberg, as it was indeed throughout the whole of East Prussia, a province that was separated from the rest of Germany by the Polish Corridor—"that strip of flesh cut from our body," as Hitler himself described it in an article written for the British *Sunday Express*—a band of territory giving Poland her only access to the Baltic Sea. Ernst vom Rath joined the Nazi party that year—automatically becoming what was called an *Alter Kampfer*—literally an "old fighter"— because he joined before the party came to power.

In the following year, 1933, he joined the SA, the *Sturmabteilung*, becoming a storm trooper, though in view of his never very sturdy physique, it is most unlikely that he ever did any fighting, or even took part in any of the activities that made the Nazis so hated. Indeed, he does not seem to have been a particularly keen party member, and even appears to have had a Jewish girlfriend while in college (though that was in no way unusual at that time even for the most ardent members). However, according to one of his embassy colleagues in Paris, at no time did he ever demonstrate any strong opposition to Nazi policy regarding the Jews, saying he believed it "to be necessary for the good of the German nation." His father later declared that his son "was in complete accord with his government and with the cause of National Socialism, to which he was entirely devoted."

The truth is, that like so many of his generation, Ernst vom Rath probably joined the party partly from a sudden access of nationalistic fervor, and partly from the cool calculation that it was the best means of advancing his career; afterward, as far as possible, he shut his eyes to any excesses carried out in the party's name.

During the next three years, he worked as a lawyer in the magistrate's court at Zinten, near Königsberg, and later as a magistrate himself in the Berlin lower courts, where he tended to specialize in financial cases. But a career in diplomacy beckoned—it was quite common for members of the German Foreign Office to qualify as lawyers and gain experience in the courts before joining the service. Ernst was helped by the fact that he had a family connection: A maternal uncle, Roland Köster, was a distinguished diplomat who was then German ambassador in Paris, one of the plum postings of the day.

After the standard six-week training and probationary period, Ernst officially entered the German Foreign Office on April 13, 1935. He was sent as an attaché to the Paris embassy, where his uncle made him his personal secretary and head of protocol, but this stay was to last only a few months: His uncle died at the end of 1935, and shortly afterward Ernst returned to Berlin. He was then sent to Calcutta, but the climate did not agree with him, and he fell ill with severe dysentery. Shipped back to Germany, he spent some time in the hospital and was then discovered to have contracted a mild case of pulmonary tuberculosis. He did not recover his strength until the summer of 1938, when he was posted back to Paris. There, he had the misfortune on Monday morning, November 7, to be the only official available to see a polite young man in a khaki raincoat who claimed to be delivering a secret document.

While Ernst vom Rath was fighting for his life in the Alma Clinic, his attacker was being questioned by the French authorities. Herschel had been taken first to the police station at 2 Rue de Bourgogne, where he submitted calmly to the routine preliminaries—name, address, identity card, and so on. When he turned out his pockets, there was little enough in them—just thirty-eight francs in loose change, the box of cartridges he had bought from M. Carpe (with five now missing), his new Polish passport, number 758686, series 1, issued by the Polish embassy in Paris on August 7, 1938, and his wallet. In the wallet, the police found a certificate of domicile at 8 Rue Martel, dated November 5 and signed by the concierge, a Mme. Corbin, and the uncompleted document given to him by M. Carpe for registering the gun with the police. There were three invitations to a dance at L'Aurore, the fateful postcard from his sister in Zbaszyn, and the photograph of himself with the message he had written on the back.

The preliminary investigation was conducted by Inspector Monneret. Herschel was cooperative and talked quite freely. "From the moment I read my sister's postcard on Thursday, November 3," he told the inspector, "I decided to kill a member of the embassy." He still had no idea of the identity of the man he had shot, and did not seem particularly interested in finding out. He did, however, make a serious attempt to avoid incriminating Uncle Abraham and Aunt Chawa, telling the inspector he had left their apartment on August 11, and that they had not hidden him when his visa expired. They knew nothing of what he planned to do, he said, and were in no way involved.

Halfway through the interrogation, an official from the German embassy named Lorz arrived at the police station and asked to be present while Herschel was being questioned. Astonishingly—for it was quite contrary to the rules of criminal procedure—Inspector Monneret agreed. It is not clear whether he was under pressure from above or whether he acted on his own initiative, but he even went so far as to allow Herr Lorz to conduct part of the interrogation himself. No doubt out of courtesy to Monneret, the German questioned Herschel in French:

LORZ: Why did you shoot the embassy secretary?
GRYNSZPAN: To avenge persecution by the filthy Germans.
LORZ: Why did you feel it was your duty to do this?
GRYNSZPAN: Because the deported Poles are of my religion.
LORZ: Are you Jewish?
GRYNSZPAN: Yes.

Later that afternoon, Inspector Monneret began the task of reconstructing the crime. He had Herschel brought face-to-face with Uncle Abraham, with Mlle. Laurent, the receptionist at the Hôtel Idéal-Suez, and also with M. Carpe—all of whom, naturally, identified him. But when the inspector tried to take Herschel into the German embassy, to the scene of the shooting, the boy refused to go, convinced that the Nazis would either kidnap or kill him.

Shortly before midnight, Herschel was taken by police car to the Quai des Orfèvres, headquarters of the Sûreté, the Criminal Investigation Department. There, he faced another interrogation, this time at the hands of Inspector Badin, before being escorted, handcuffed, on the afternoon of the next day, November 8, to the Public Prosecutor's Office in the Palais de Justice.

Herschel's attempts to protect Uncle Abraham and Aunt Chawa from the consequences of his action came to nothing. Judge Tesnière, the examining magistrate who began his first interrogation of the boy later that day, chose to order their arrest on the ground that they had knowingly harbored an illegal immigrant. This constituted a misdemeanor punishable by a sentence of from one month to one year in prison, plus a large fine.

Clearly, Judge Tesnière chose to arraign the elder Grynszpans simply in order to remove them from the case, since they were not accomplices, nor had they influenced their nephew in any way. Tesnière succeeded in convincing the public prosecutor, M. Frette-Damicourt, that there was no conspiracy, no plot, merely a distraught youth who had sought revenge for what his family had suffered in Germany and Poland. For the French government, such a conclusion had the great virtue of simplicity: one victim, one would-be assassin. The possibility of political fallout was reduced to a minimum.

By the morning of November 9, there had been no improvement in the condition of Ernst vom Rath. At 9:30 A.M., the indomitable M. Thomas was summoned to give blood yet again, and when Professor Baumgartner left the clinic at 11:30 A.M., he was not optimistic. One of the journalists who swooped on him as he emerged from the door suggested that vom Rath must have at least a fair chance of recovery, if only because of his youth. The professor shrugged his shoulders.

"If there had been only one wound . . ." he said. "But there are three." Presumably he was referring to the damage to the spleen, stomach, and pancreas.

The two German doctors, Brandt and Magnus, arrived shortly afterward in an embassy car. When they left, they could add little to what Baumgartner had told the reporters: "We can say nothing except that the condition of the patient is still very grave," they said. "We will undoubtedly return during the course of the day."

They did return, shortly after lunch, to join the vom Rath family at the bedside. There was nothing more they could do: By then, it was clear that the patient was sinking fast. Shortly after 3:00 P.M., he went into a diabetic coma, due to the pancreatic damage. He died at 4:25 P.M.

That night at 10:30 P.M., the coffin containing the body of the dead diplomat was placed in a hearse and driven slowly to a mortuary chapel in the Rue de Lille, close by the German embassy. The cortège was followed by most of the embassy staff, led by Count von Welczek, Dr. Brandt, and Professor Magnus, and by nearly two hundred members of the German community in Paris. The beatification of Ernst vom Rath as a Nazi martyr had begun.

"The SA Should Be Allowed to Have a Fling"

Herschel Grynszpan's timing for the shooting of Ernst vom Rath could hardly have been worse. November 9, the day vom Rath died, was the holiest day in the entire Nazi calendar, and in 1938 it had a special significance for the party faithful. It was the twentieth anniversary of what Hitler called "the greatest villainy of the century"—the infamous "stab in the back" by the "November criminals" who had forced the kaiser to abdicate, declared Germany a republic, and agreed to sign an armistice. It was also the fifteenth anniversary of the "Beer Hall Putsch," which had failed to bring Hitler to power in 1923 but had catapulted him to national prominence.

For the dedicated party member, it was the second of these anniversaries that was now the more emotive. Fifteen years before, on the evening of November 8, 1923, Hitler had invaded a political mass meeting that was being addressed by the state commissioner and virtual dictator of Bavaria, Gustav von Kahr, in Munich's Bürgerbräukeller. Amid much waving of pistols and machine guns, the Nazi führer had proclaimed a new national government with himself at its head, and the legendary war leader General Erich Ludendorff as Commander in Chief of the army.

The putsch had been ill-conceived and inadequately planned, and had run into trouble immediately. After a night of confusion, everything had fallen apart. At 11:00 A.M. on November 9, Hitler had set out in desperation, with Ludendorff at his side, leading some three thousand armed followers in a march on the city center. Their aim was to free a detachment of Nazi SA storm troopers besieged in the old Bavarian War Ministry, and then to take over the city as a base from which to topple the national government in Berlin. Ludendorff had been certain the army and police would join them and fight under his orders, as they had done during the war. But he was wrong. The army failed to rally to the Nazi cause. The police stayed loyal to the Bavarian and national governments.

At noon, as the marchers advanced, singing, along the narrow Residenzstrasse, heading for the broad expanse of the Odeonsplatz and the War Ministry, they were faced by a solid cordon of about one hundred police armed with carbines outside the Feldherrnhalle, the memorial to Bavaria's war dead. Someone fired a shot—no one is certain who, some say Hitler, others one of his leading henchmen, Julius Streicher—killing a police sergeant. The police opened up in reply. In less than sixty seconds, the revolution was all over. Sixteen Nazis and three policemen lay dead; many others, including Hermann Göring, then chief of the SA, were wounded. Hitler, his left shoulder dislocated as he dived or was pulled to the ground, was the first to flee. He was hustled into a car and driven away to take refuge in the country home of his friend Putzi Hanfstaengl, whose wife nursed him until he was arrested there two days later.

Hitler was subsequently tried and sentenced to the minimum possible term of five years imprisonment in Landsberg Castle, where he lived in some comfort, enjoying privileged status, receiving unrestricted visitors, and eating so well he started getting fat. He spent much of the time profitably writing the first volume of a book called *Four and a Half Years of Struggle against Lies, Stupidity and Cowardice*—a title that his more commercially minded publisher Max Amman, changed to "*My Struggle*," i.e., *Mein Kampf*. On December 20, 1924, Hitler was released on parole after serving less than nine months of his sentence. Two months later, he reconstituted the Nazi party, abjuring armed revolution in favor of achieving power through the ballot box. The party's principal aims, however, remained the same as Hitler's charge to the Bürgerbräukeller audience: "Fight Marxism and Judaism not according to bourgeois standards, but over dead bodies!"

Hitler had set about creating the myth of the Munich Putsch by marking its first anniversary with a speech to the other inmates of the Landsberg prison, and he continued the process on his release. He was banned from public speaking in Bavaria for two years, but in 1927, when the ban was lifted, he returned to the Bürgerbräukeller on November 8 to make an emotional speech in memory of the events of those two days in 1923, and of the sixteen "martyrs" who had been gunned down outside the Feldherrnhalle. The gathering of the old fighters in Munich to hear Hitler's speech became an annual event, growing in importance and further embellishing the legend with each passing year.

The tenth anniversary had conveniently fallen during the party's first year in power, and from then on, the celebrations assumed even greater status as semistate occasions. In 1935, they reached a peak of carefully controlled hysteria when the bones of the martyrs were exhumed to lie in state in the Feldherrnhalle in sixteen bronze sarcophagi, surrounded by brown drapes and flaming braziers. Amid all the pomp that the Nazis stage-managed so well, Hitler paid solemn homage to the remains, which were then reinterred in two specially constructed neoclassical temples in the Königsplatz. The ceremonies of 1935 became the model for the following years, a two-day festival that completed the transformation of a squalid and utterly botched putsch into a golden myth of fallen heroes dying for a noble cause. Like most Nazi rituals, it was a hollow sham, epitomizing the whole phony philosophy of the movement. But also like most Nazi rituals, it was a highly intoxicating occasion.

Each year, Hitler made his speech in the Bürgerbräukeller on the evening of November 8. Each year, he and Göring and the old comrades of the original march led a procession of thousands along a route lined with hundreds of masts from which hung dark red pennants bearing the names of the fallen heroes in golden letters. The old fighters wore brown shirts or "historic" uniforms—gray windbreakers and model 23 ski caps—supplied by the "Bureau for November 8–9." Loudspeakers blared the "Horst Wessel Song," a memento of another so-called martyr, who had died in a street brawl in 1930.

At the Feldherrnhalle, representatives of the armed forces joined the marchers—a symbolic change from the events of 1923—while a sixteen-gun salute boomed out over the city. There was a respectful silence as Hitler laid a huge wreath at the memorial plaque, and then the whole procession moved off between lines of flags dipped in salute, accompanied by the strains of "Deutschland über Alles" played at a mournful tempo, to the Königsplatz. At the twin temples, a roll call of the dead was intoned, with the crowd answering "Present!" to each name. It was an occasion that could be guaranteed to recharge the religious fervor of the faithful. For those who could not be there, the ceremonies were broadcast and reported throughout the Reich.

It was against this background that the news arrived of the attempted slaying in Paris. The first sensational press reports hit the streets on the morning of November 8, as the old comrades gathered in Munich for the start of the celebrations. Goebbels, who rejoiced in the title of Reichs minister for public enlightenment and propaganda, had seized on the shooting with undisguised glee as a heaven-sent opportunity to inflame anti-Jewish feeling. He had issued a directive, telephoned by his ministry to all newspaper editors, ordering that the attack on vom Rath, by a Jew, "must completely dominate the front page." The papers had responded well.

The *Völkischer Beobachter*, the Nazi party's own newspaper, led the pack, coming straight to the point with the headline JEWISH MURDER ATTEMPT IN PARIS—MEMBER OF THE GERMAN EMBASSY CRITICALLY WOUNDED BY SHOTS—THE MURDERING KNAVE A 17-YEAR-OLD JEW. Giving the signal for a new wave of anti-Semitism, the article continued, "It is clear that the German people will draw their own conclusion from this new deed. It is an impossible situation that within our frontiers hundreds of thousands of Jews should control our shopping streets, places of entertainment, and as 'foreign' landlords pocket the money of German tenants, while their racial comrades outside call for war against Germany and shoot down German officials."

The first results came that evening, in the provinces of Hesse and Magdeburg-Anhalt, where Jews were attacked, their businesses damaged and synagogues set on fire. The next morning, while vom Rath's life still hung in the balance, the *Völkischer Beobachter* kept up the temperature with the banner headline THE SHOTS IN PARIS WILL NOT GO UNPUNISHED! Pointing the way for the rest of the Reich, it reported the previous night's disturbances: "In answer to the provocation from Paris, the cowardly Jewish murder, substantial spontaneous demonstrations have occurred in Kurhessen by the population against the Jews." Goebbels's own newspaper, *Der Angriff*, meanwhile declared more wordily, "From this vile deed arises the imperative demand for immediate action against the Jews, with the most severe consequences." Every other newspaper throughout the Reich carried similar provocative messages.

While the Nazi papers ranted and raved, the Jews were denied any opportunity to comment. All Jewish newspapers and magazines were banned until further notice. At the same time, another decree barred all Jewish children from German schools. It was confidently forecast that the first official ghettos in Europe since the last one was closed down in Rome in 1870 would soon be established in German cities. A Jewish businessman in Munich, J. Littner, wrote in his diary:

> The circle of non-Jewish friends will be smaller from day to day, and a picture begins to develop in which we shall soon be living in an invisible ghetto . . . the mood for November 9 grows worse . . . massive penalties will be demanded, massive penalties from us, which we ourselves fear. We Jews now fear November 9, the great feast day of the party . . . the excited atmosphere of the incited national passions. . . . On the evening of the 9th, the radio broadcast extracts from the people's demonstrations against the so-called Jewish murdering rabble, and from the loudspeakers came voices like the howling of rabid dogs.

News of vom Rath's death was brought to Hitler as he sat at dinner in Munich's old Rathaussaal, the town hall chamber. Shortly before 9:00 P.M., an adjutant entered and handed him a message. He pushed back his plate, turned to Goebbels, who was sitting next to him, and spoke to him quietly and intently. According to Goebbels's testimony to the party inquiry later, they spoke of the previous night's anti-Jewish riots in Hesse and Magdeburg-Anhalt. Hitler, he said, told him that although the party was not to organize such demonstrations, it should do nothing to stop them if they occurred "spontaneously." Others present reported that they heard Hitler say, "The SA should be allowed to have a fling." He then rose and left the meeting, without making the traditional closing speech. Whatever happened next, the head of state of the Greater German Reich could claim to know nothing, nor to have given any specific orders. That, together with the closing speech, was left to Goebbels—and Goebbels made the most of the opportunity.

After a rousing beginning, he paused, and waved a piece of paper at his audience. "I have news here for you tonight, to demonstrate what happens to a good German when he relaxes his vigil for one moment," he declaimed. "Ernst vom Rath was a good German, a loyal servant of the Reich, working for the good of our people in our embassy in Paris. Shall I tell you what happened to him? He was shot down! In the course of his duty, he went, unarmed and unsuspecting, to speak to a visitor at the embassy, and had two bullets pumped into him. He is now dead."

Allowing the full effect of this news to sink in, he banged his fist on the table and raised his voice still further. "Do I need to tell you the race of the dirty swine who perpetrated this foul deed? A Jew! Tonight he lies in jail in Paris, claiming that he acted on his own, that he had no instigators of this awful deed behind him. But we know better, don't we?"

Pandemonium broke out in the hall, as the old comrades yelled for vengeance. Goebbels quieted them again, and continued, "Comrades, we cannot allow this attack by international Jewry to go unchallenged. It must be repudiated. Our people must be told, and their answer must be ruthless, forthright, salutary! I ask you to listen to me, and together we must plan what is to be our answer to Jewish murder and the threat of international Jewry to our glorious German Reich!"

The opportunity for action against the Jews on a shattering scale, vital to the success of Hitler's plan for a *Judenfrei* Reich since the *Anschluss* had raised Jewish numbers again, had presented itself with miraculous timeliness. The murder of vom Rath was the perfect pretext, at the perfect moment—and Hitler, with his unerring sense of occasion, was clearly resolved to take the fullest advantage of it. Already, Goebbels told the audience in the Rathaus, there had been anti-Jewish riots in various parts of Germany. Similar "spontaneous" demonstrations must be organized immediately; but the party itself must not appear to be responsible.

The action report of the leader of the SA Group Nordmark describes what happened immediately after the Goebbels speech:

> At about 10:00 P.M. on November 9, the requirement for the operation was put to a number of gauleiters in the Munich Hotel Schottenhammel by an unnamed member of the Nazi party's Reich directorate. I thereupon volunteered the services of my SA Group *Nordmark* to the gauleiter [of Schleswig-Holstein], Heinrich Lohse. About 10:30 P.M., he telephoned his chief of staff in Kiel: "A Jew has fired a shot. A German diplomat is dead. In Friedrichstadt, Kiel and Lübeck there are entirely superfluous places of assembly; and these people are still trading in stores in our midst. We don't need either of them. There is to be no looting. There is to be no maltreatment, either. Foreign Jews are not to be molested. If there is any resistance, use your firearms. The whole operation is to be in plain clothes, and is to be over by 5:00 A.M.

Similar messages from other gauleiters and SA leaders spread the word throughout the country that it was not just Herschel Grynszpan who was to blame for the murder of Ernst vom Rath, but the whole of Jewry, and that the whole of Jewry must therefore be made to pay. Within a short time, the witches' sabbath was sparking into life.

While the storm troopers of the SA were gearing themselves for their "fling," SS Standartenführer (Colonel) Heinrich Müller issued an urgent teleprinter message from his Gestapo Headquarters in Berlin's Prinz Albrechtstrasse to every state police bureau in the Reich, alerting them to the fact that "demonstrations against the Jews, and particularly their synagogues, will take place very shortly." The Gestapo were not to interfere, but were to cooperate with the regular police to prevent looting "and similar excesses." They were also to secure any important archive material found in synagogues—Gestapo in Cologne were reminded that there was "especially important material" in the synagogue there, which was to be seized immediately—and to prepare for the arrest of some twenty thousand to thirty thousand Jews. Primarily, the order stated "*well-to-do Jews* are to be selected." More detailed instructions would be issued during the course of the night.

"If, during the actions about to take place, Jews are found in possession of *weapons*," the final paragraph stated, "the most severe measures are to be applied. The special task units of the SS as well as the general SS may be employed for all phases of the operation. Suitable measures are to be taken to ensure that *the Gestapo remains in control of the actions under all circumstances. . . ."*

The police had, in fact, already taken precautions to ensure that the Jews could not fight back effectively. On November 8, they had begun disarming Jews, removing anything that could be used for protection from every Jewish household. They claimed their haul in Berlin alone already totaled 2,569 daggers and swords, 1,702 firearms, and 20,000 rounds of ammunition.

The further instructions that Gestapo Müller had promised were put on the teleprinters at 1:20 A.M. by Reinhard Heydrich. The delay was due to his having to be roused from his bed at Munich's luxurious Hotel Vier Jahreszeiten and then having to check with Himmler, who in turn had to check with Hitler. Heydrich's orders confirmed the Gestapo chief's first message, and elaborated on the details:

FLASH MUNICH 47767 10.11.38 0120 SECRET
TO: ALL REGIONAL AND SUBREGIONAL GESTAPO OFFICES

TO ALL SECURITY SERVICE DISTRICT AND SUBDISTRICT HQs FLASH URGENT
SUBMIT AT ONCE!

SUBJECT: MEASURES AGAINST THE JEWS THIS NIGHT

On account of the attack on Legation Secretary v. RATH in Paris, demonstrations against the Jews are to be expected throughout the Reich in the course of this night (9 to 10.11.38). The following directives are issued for dealing with these events:

1. Immediately on receipt of this teleprint directors of Gestapo offices or their deputies must communicate by telephone with their regional party directorates—*Gauleitung* or *Kreisleitung*—and arrange a conference with them to discuss and agree upon the implementation of the demonstrations. The proper inspector or commander of the regular police is to be called in. In the course of the meeting the political leaders are to be notified that the German police have received the following instructions from the Reichsführer SS and chief of police and that measures taken by the political agencies are to be in accordance with them:
   a. Only such measures are to be taken that will not endanger German lives or property (e.g., the burning of synagogues only to be carried out if there is no danger of the fire spreading to the surrounding district).
   b. Businesses and residences of Jews may be destroyed but not looted. The police have been directed to supervise the execution of this order and to arrest looters.

   c. Particular care is to be paid in business streets that non-Jewish businesses are to be protected from damage under all circumstances.

   d. Foreign subjects are not to be molested—even if they are Jews.

2. Assuming that the directives given under No. 1 are complied with, the demonstrations are not to be prevented by the police, but only watched to see that the directives are adhered to.

3. Immediately upon receipt of this telegram, the police are to seize all archives from all synagogues and offices of Jewish community organizations, to prevent them from destruction in the course of the demonstrations. This refers to material of historical importance, not to recent taxation lists, etc. The archives are to be handed over to the competent SD [Security Service] offices.

4. The direction of all security police measures with regard to the demonstrations against the Jews is in the hands of the Gestapo, insofar as the inspectors of the security police do not issue orders. Officials of the criminal police as well as members of the SD, the special task units and the general SS may be brought in for carrying out the security police measures.

5. As soon as the events of this night make it feasible for the officials concerned, they are to arrest as many Jews—especially wealthy ones—in all districts *as can be accommodated in existing cells.* For the time being, only healthy male Jews of not too advanced age are to be arrested. After the arrests have been carried out, concentration camps in the region are to be contacted immediately, to make arrangements for the transfer of the Jews to the camps as quickly as possible. Particular care must be taken that Jews arrested on the basis of this directive are not mistreated.

6. The contents of this order are to be forwarded to the competent inspectors and commanders of the regular police as well as to SD district and subdistrict HQs with the statement that the Reichsführer SS and chief of German police [Himmler] has ordered these police measures. The chief of the regular police has issued corresponding instructions to the regular police, including the fire fighting police. The closest cooperation between the security police and the regular police must be maintained in carrying out the measures ordered.

   Receipt of this teleprint is to be confirmed by the directors of the Gestapo or their deputies by teleprint to Gestapo head office for the attention of Standartenführer Müller.

Signed: Heydrich
SS *Gruppenführer*

All night, the messages flashed to and fro to the SA, SS, SD, Gestapo, criminal police, security police, regular police, party offices, all the complex components needed to keep the totalitarian machine operating. The instructions were confirmed, refined, defined. The aim was clear: The Nazi state did not want the Jews, but it did want their remaining wealth. While the Jews were to be forced out, their businesses were to be preserved as intact as possible, ready for seizure. At 2:16 A.M., the chief of the security police in Munich flashed an urgent signal to Gestapo offices in Augsburg, Nuremberg, and Würzburg:

> Plainclothes agents of the Gestapo and Kripo [criminal police] are to move around in the demonstrations and are to prevent the permissible destruction of Jewish stores and apartments from leading to looting. They will remain with the groups of demonstrators and at the end of the demonstrations the uniformed *Ordungspolizei* [regular police] are to seal and secure the destroyed stores and apartments. Furthermore, in all police districts only existing places of detention are to be occupied by prisoners.

Forty minutes later, an order was issued from the office of Rudolf Hess, then Hitler's deputy führer, to all gauleiters, stating, "On explicit orders from the very highest level, there is to be no arson against Jewish businesses or the like, whatsoever, under any circumstances." Synagogues and Jewish community centers, it seemed, were to be burned to the ground wherever possible, but business premises and homes were to remain standing.

While the police and the SD were under specific instructions on what they could or could not do, the SA were given no such orders inhibiting their actions. They were under the impression that they had been given a completely free hand.

This dichotomy was not accidental. The official report on the affair, drawn up for the Supreme Tribunal of the Nazi party three months later, states, "It was normal practice to give hazy, unspecific instructions for any action which the party did not wish to appear to instigate." The result, it continued, was that many party members "acquired the habit of overstepping the bounds of their instructions . . . particularly in arranging illegal demonstrations."

Individual SA commanders interpreted their orders differently. In the Bremen area, for instance, the Nordsee SA group were instructed to wear their uniforms while destroying Jewish property. After the job had been done, guards were to be posted over the smoldering ruins, so that no objects of value could be removed. The Nordsee SA obviously believed it was a pity to waste a good pogrom on the Jews alone. Their orders concluded with an instruction that they could "also be extended to include Freemasonry."

At one minute to midnight on November 9, the Munich city fire department received its first alarm call. Demonstrators had smashed the display window of a textile business in the Augustenstrasse and set fire to the display. The entry in the fire service's records notes the cause of the fire as "Anti-Jewish demonstration." Three minutes later came the first major alarm—the city's first synagogue was ablaze.

The pogrom had begun.

The Pogrom

In the early hours of November 10, the terror spread rapidly throughout the length and breadth of Greater Germany as party thugs backed by hordes of ordinary Germans went on the rampage. Otto Tolischus, for *The New York Times*, described it as a wave of destruction unparalleled in Germany since the Thirty Years' War. "Beginning systematically in the early morning hours in almost every town and city in the country," he wrote, "the wrecking, looting and burning continued all day. Huge but mostly silent crowds looked on and the police confined themselves to regulating traffic and making wholesale arrests of Jews, 'for their own protection.' "

The Berlin correspondent of the London *Daily Telegraph*, Hugh Carleton Greene, reported later in the day:

> Mob law ruled in Berlin throughout the afternoon and evening and hordes of hooligans indulged in an orgy of destruction. I have seen several anti-Jewish outbreaks in Germany during the last five years, but never anything as nauseating as this. Racial hatred and hysteria seemed to have taken complete hold of otherwise decent people. I saw fashionably dressed women clapping their hands and screaming with glee, while respectable, middle-class mothers held up their babies to see the "fun."

The "fun" involved more than the wrecking of a few shops. During the twenty-four hours of Germany's first organized pogrom since the Middle Ages, at least 7,500 stores, 29 warehouses, and 171 houses were destroyed; 191 synagogues were razed by fire and a further 76 physically demolished; 11 Jewish community centers, cemetery chapels, and similar buildings were torched and another 3 gutted; at least 30,000 Jewish men were arrested and thrown into concentration camps. Seven Aryans and three foreigners were also arrested—"for their protection."

The death toll was given on November 11 in a report from Heydrich to Göring as thirty-six, with the same number severely injured—all of them Jews. Not surprisingly, these figures had to be revised: By January it was admitted that the number killed during those twenty-four hours was officially put at ninety-one. The true figure was at least 236, among them 43 women and 13 children, with more than 600 permanently maimed. Hundreds more died in concentration camps during the next few months.

The first "spontaneous demonstration" of the night took place within a few minutes of the announcement of vom Rath's death, even before Goebbels had spoken, in the town of Dessau, one hundred kilometers southeast of Berlin. By midnight, as we have seen, synagogues and stores in Munich were already ablaze, and by 1:00 A.M. on November 10, reports were coming in to police and party headquarters of killing and looting at Lesum, a village outside Bremen, and of similar activity in Potsdam. Elsewhere in the Reich, however, both the timing and the nature of the action depended very much on local conditions, varying widely from place to place.

At Baden-Baden, for instance, the fashionable spa town in Württemberg-Hohenzollern, the start of the pogrom was delayed until 7:00 A.M. so that it would not disturb the sleep of late-season visitors. And in the Cologne SA group, a storm trooper called Letting upset the program's efficiency by refusing to turn out at 5:00 A.M. on the grounds that he had to be at work early and he knew his boss would never accept the action as a reason for his absence. Not only would he lose a day's pay, he might even lose his job, too. In the end, Letting's superior officer had to promise to fix things with the boss and to make up any loss of pay out of SA funds. Only then did the pragmatic storm trooper agree to play his part.

Some of the most barbarous incidents occurred in Austria and the Sudetenland, newly absorbed into the Reich and anxious to show the strength of their allegiance. And inevitably, as the birthplace of Naziism, Bavaria distinguished itself in the violence shown to the Jews: nine murders and ten suicides, half of them women, were recorded in Nuremberg alone on November 10.

In Berlin, as one would have expected, the pogrom was meticulously organized. The start was delayed until 2:00 A.M., to allow time for police squads to isolate Jewish buildings, cut telephone wires, switch off electricity supplies and heating to Jewish shops and businesses so as to prevent untoward accidents, and set up road barriers to divert traffic away from the areas where the mobs were to be let loose. Only when everything was prepared did they give the signal for action to commence, allowing the storm troopers to do their worst, while the fire department stood by, just in case.

By dawn, nine of the twelve synagogues in Berlin were burning. Outside the biggest, in Fasanenstrasse, Davidson, the reader of the synagogue, appealed to the captain of a fire crew who were watching the blaze with professional interest, begging him to turn on his hoses. The man refused. It was against orders. "We've come to protect the building next door," he explained.

In Prinzregentenstrasse, the caretaker of the synagogue, together with all his family, was reported to have died in the flames. Around the corner, two Jews pursued by a mob to the second floor of an apartment block jumped from the window and crashed onto the pavement below, mortally injuring themselves.

With daylight, the mobs swarmed down the Unter den Linden, the Kurfürstendamm, and Tauentzienstrasse, where the biggest and most fashionable stores were situated, smashing plate-glass windows, hauling out furs, jewelry, furniture, silver—but only from Jewish-owned businesses. In Leipzigstrasse and Friedrichstrasse there was more devastation, spreading eastward in the direction of Alexanderplatz. Here, the destruction was even worse, because there were more Jewish shops in the area. "In Friedrichstrasse in downtown Berlin," reported the *Washington Post*, "crowds pushed police aside in their hunt for plunder. Late in the afternoon fire broke out in Israel's department store near Alexanderplatz, but firemen soon extinguished the blaze."

The sacking of Israel's was particularly symbolic, for the store was a Berlin institution that was even mentioned in Baedecker. Founded in 1815, shortly after Napoleon's escape from Elba, N. Israel was the first and oldest Jewish-owned department store in Berlin, the first, indeed, of all the great Jewish business houses in the city. It was always advertised as *"Das Kaufhaus in Zentrum,"* the store in the center of the city, though by 1938 that claim was no longer true. Over the years, the main shopping district of Berlin had moved steadily westward toward the Kurfürstendamm. The high-class stores had followed, as stores will, leaving Israel's beached like some great art-nouveau whale on the corner of the Rathausplatz in the Brandenburg district. But as far as Israel's was concerned, it was still at the center, still serving its traditional clientele: landowners of the Brandenburg district, army families, the Berlin upper classes on whose linen the Israel seamstresses embroidered personal monograms, the poor nobility.

A brigade of smartly uniformed doormen opened the doors for customers, and a horde of shopgirls and frock-coated floorwalkers hastened to serve them. At the far end of the great central hall, where the linen department was situated, rose a grand stairway worthy of any opera house. Above, three floors up, an arched glass roof ran the length of the hall, while on each floor around the hall, galleries lined with showcases led to spacious showrooms. Israel's was a model of its kind, a stodgy Berlin Harrods, a firmly middle-class Macy's.

Unlike most other large stores, Israel's was not part of any chain, but remained independent and privately owned. On July 7, 1938, with Nazi pressures becoming intolerable, the Israel family sold out to one of their Aryan competitors, Emil Köstrer's Family Emporium. Considering the times, they got a reasonable price. But the Economics Ministry, then headed by the frightful Walther Funk, a notorious drunk and a homo-sexual, refused to ratify the sale. The store was therefore in a kind of racial business limbo, neither Jewish nor Aryan.

In the afternoon of November 9, Kurt Liepart, a buyer in the carpet department and the new Nazi *Betreibsrat* (head of the works committee), went to see the boss, Wilfrid Israel, to warn him not to open the store the following day. But Israel had friends high up in the police. Believing that this was protection enough to guarantee the safety of the store, he chose to ignore Liepart's warning.

On the morning of November 10, the heavy iron shutters protecting the store's windows were raised, and N. Israel was open for business as usual. At the same time, as if by a miracle, a number of police appeared in the Rathausplatz and discouraged anyone from wreaking their ven-geance on the inviting shopfronts of the firm. Israel's must have been the only Jewish business in Berlin with a police guard. It seemed that Wilfrid's connections were willing and able to protect his business. So confident was he, in fact, that in the course of the morning he left the building to go to the offices of the *Reichsvertretung der Deutschen Juden*, the central organization that represented the whole of the Jewish com-munity. But at 2:00 P.M. the police were just as suddenly and mysteriously withdrawn. Shortly afterward, a mob of young men, armed with clubs and iron bars, shoved the doormen aside and entered the store. They were followed by uniformed SS men. Once inside, the job of destruction began.

While the SS men rounded up as many of the Jewish staff as they could, the mob went to work, wrecking display cases, tearing down lengths of silk from the stands, and trampling clothes and materials underfoot. Floor by floor, they smashed their way through the store, scattering frightened employees, hurling furniture and other goods from the galleries into the main stairwell and typewriters and equipment from the administrative offices on the top floor through the outside windows. When the destruction was finished, a detachment of police mysteriously reappeared, but made no attempt to arrest anyone, or to restore order. They simply kept the crowds back from the windows, in case they injured themselves on all the broken glass.

Elsewhere in Berlin, the storm troopers were turning their attentions to private homes, too. In the fashionable suburb of Dahlem, where many party notables, including Foreign Minister Ribbentrop, had their houses, they battered their way into the mansions where richer Jews still lived, dragged off the able-bodied men, stripped and humiliated older men, and in at least fifteen cases dragged wives and daughters into bedrooms to rape them.

Franz Rinkel had a fine house at No. 2 Brückenhalle, filled with priceless antiques and art treasures. He had rented out part of the house to U.S. consul Raymond H. Geist, but Geist was away when the mob arrived. They locked Rinkel's family into a room upstairs and began to beat Rinkel himself. They were interrupted by two uniformed SS men and a Nazi lawyer called Dr. Lilienthal, who had previously offered to buy the house for half its value—an offer that Rinkel had angrily refused. Now, the lawyer was back, with a bill of sale already prepared. It was for one fiftieth of his previous offer. He held out the document to Rinkel, inviting him to sign it.

"Think of your womenfolk," he said. "Think of your own life if that mob comes back. But you will come to no harm if you sign this paper."

Rinkel signed. Then he was dragged away to the local jail, and from there to the Sachsenhausen concentration camp. A fellow prisoner there was Eugene Garbaty, owner of one of Germany's largest cigar factories. He was forced to sell his factory for one million marks, one tenth of its value, and had his country house near Dresden seized. The million marks did not go far—he had to pay half a million in fines, and the other half million to Count von Helldorf, chief of police in Berlin, as a bribe in order to obtain an exit visa.

In spite of the troubles during the night, many Jews—like the employees of Israel's department store—tried to carry on with their normal lives on the morning of November 10. Many, of course, were not yet aware of what was going on, and certainly did not appreciate the scale or the severity of the pogrom. Ruth Schemel and Selma Ginsberg were two of the children who went to school as usual, but as the troubles continued, their teacher, Dr. Barschauer, decided to close down for the day, telling his students to go straight home and not to attract attention to themselves.

On their way in, through Müntzstrasse and Rosenthalerplatz, Ruth and Selma had witnessed scenes of almost insane vandalism. They had seen Jewish shops broken into, shop windows and display cases smashed, stock dragged out and left in the middle of the street—along with broken furniture and pianos. On their way back home, they saw something that horrified them even more—a group of storm troopers held a Jewish man, while others daubed his bald head with red paint. The girls were standing in Bülowplatz talking about what they had just seen when a passer-by shouted at them, "Why don't you go to Jerusalem?"

Incensed, Ruth shouted back, "We can't get the permit!"

When she told her mother about it, she got a slap for being so stupid. She should have kept her mouth shut, bitten her tongue.

The Schemels had been forced to leave their comfortable flat in Lessingstrasse, near the Tiergarten, for a house in Prenzlauerstrasse. To make ends meet, they let off a room to a middle-aged man, who was not only a Nazi party member but also in the SA. When a mob appeared outside their house, shouting for the Schemels, their lodger leaned out of the window and shouted, "Go away! There are no Jews here!" The sight of the familiar brown uniform was enough for the crowd—they moved on. He later told the Schemels, "I am in the SA, but I don't like what is going on here." Nevertheless, after the incident, it was clear that he could no longer stay with them. He moved on to new lodgings shortly afterward.

Inge Fehr was the niece of a former chancellor of Germany, Gustav Stresemann, leader of the People's party (National Liberals), who as foreign minister had negotiated and signed the Locarno Treaty in 1925. When Hitler came to power, she was eleven years old and at school in Berlin, where a new subject was added to the curriculum—daily lessons in "racial knowledge." In an original version of Darwinian theory, the children were taught that while the rest of the human race were descended from monkeys, Germans and Scandinavians were descended from blue-eyed geese. Jews, the teaching went, were racially related to Negroes. It came as something of a shock to little Inge to discover that her beloved father, Professor Oscar Fehr, head of the ophthalmic department of the Rudolf Virchow Hospital, must be a Negro, since he was a Jew. Inge herself was a *Mischling*, of mixed blood, for her mother was Christian and her father had converted. She had been confirmed in the Lutheran Church—but in the end that made no difference.

Her religious teacher at school, a local minister named Hauk, had a flair for creative theology, teaching the children that Christ was not, after all, a Jew—that was a Biblical error—but actually an immigrant into Palestine of impeccable Aryan descent. Hauk later achieved a certain degree of notoriety in religious circles when he came to blows with a brother minister after insisting on placing a photograph of Adolf Hitler on his church altar.

On November 10, 1938, Inge Fehr was hurrying to school when she noticed a column of smoke rising above the city. But she had no time to investigate this. She was in English class—appropriately, they were studying Shakespeare's *Macbeth*—when the headmistress burst into the classroom to tell the girls that they must leave the school immediately by the back door and go straight home. A pogrom had begun.

On her way home, Inge followed the column of smoke and discovered that it came from the synagogue in Fasanenstrasse, which had been set on fire. Crowds stood on the pavement on the opposite side of the street watching the blaze. A couple of streets further on, in Tauentzienstrasse, which joins the Kurfürstendamm at the Kaiser Wilhelm Memorial Church, she saw crowds smashing the windows of Jewish shops and jeering at the owners as they tried to salvage their stock.

But worse was to come. On the pavement outside her own house, she found written in red paint the words FEHR, JUDE ("Fehr, Jew"). The sloganeer was an ex-employee of her father's—Gerhard Brode, a keen SA man who had sometimes even worn his uniform to work. Brode had worked for Dr. Fehr ever since 1927, originally as a chauffeur, but after the doctor learned to drive, he had been kept on as a doorman for the surgery. When the Nazi racial laws made it almost impossible for a Jewish doctor to practice, Dr. Fehr had been forced to let Brode go. As a result of his pavement handiwork, the man also lost a job with an Aryan family next door to the surgery. Brode pursued his vendetta against Dr. Fehr— he extorted one thousand Reichsmarks from him after threatening to betray him to the Gestapo.

The Freyhans had an apartment opposite the synagogue in Levetzow-strasse, which is in Tiergarten near the river Spree. Both the Freyhans were teachers, and although she was already seven and a half months pregnant, Kate Freyhan was still teaching at the Jewish girls' primary school in nearby Auguststrasse. When she came home from school on November 10, she found hordes of schoolchildren bombarding the synagogue with stones. She stood at the window of the apartment, watching as the children tore up cobblestones and threw them through the windows of the synagogue. The children were there all afternoon: The vandalism went on for hours. The police just stood around and watched, making no attempt to interfere.

When Kate Freyhan went to the corner shop to get some milk, she found it full of people watching the stone-throwing. Many of them shook their heads in silent disapproval. The young woman who owned the shop was indignant: It was disgraceful, the police just standing there and doing nothing to stop it. "After all, it is private property," she declared.

While most people in Berlin and elsewhere disapproved of what was going on but stayed silent and did nothing, the pogrom provided many Germans who were not Nazis and who detested the regime with an opportunity for positive action. For many, it was no doubt their first, and perhaps only, act of defiance; for some, it set them on the dangerous course of actively working against Hitler.

The Sinzheimers were a well-to-do Jewish family with two children who lived in a large apartment in Uhlandstrasse, just by the corner of the Kurfürstendamm. Uhlandstrasse is a long street, and for much of its length runs parallel to the Fasanenstrasse. Just by the Sinzheimers' apartment was a flower stall run by Herr Müller, a communist who made no bones about his political loyalties and who was frequently in and out of concentration camps. Frau Sinzheimer always bought her flowers from him: They had known each other for years.

Herr Sinzheimer was away on business in Paris when the pogrom began. His secretary and his wife phoned him and advised him to stay there until it had all blown over—in spite of the fact that his wife and two children, an elderly cook, a Turkish maid, and a nanny would be on their own and unprotected in Berlin.

The night of November 10 promised to be as bad as it had been in the early hours of the morning. The women and children sat together in the apartment, while outside there was shouting in the streets, the sound of smashing glass, and sudden inexplicable bursts of shooting. Suddenly, at 9:00 P.M., the doorbell of the apartment rang. Fearing the worst, Frau Sinzheimer opened the door to find Herr Müller the flower-seller outside, a bottle of brandy in one hand and a large revolver in the other. He informed his old friend that he had come to stay the night to protect them. If any of "those bastards" laid a hand on the family, he declared, he would shoot them. It might have been the brandy talking—and in any case it is debatable if a known communist armed with a gun was a wise choice of bodyguard for a Jewish family—but Frau Sinzheimer was grateful for his presence. He sat up all night, drinking brandy and playing cards, and at 6:00 A.M. left the apartment to go to the flower market to get his stock for the day.

As he was leaving, they heard over the radio an announcement that any Jew found in possession of a firearm would be shot at once. That was when Frau Sinzheimer remembered that her husband had a hand-gun, for which, of course, he had a license, though that was hardly liable to placate the SA if they found it. The gun was hidden in a secret drawer in his desk. The only trouble was that she did not know how to open the drawer.

However, she refused to admit defeat, and being a resourceful woman, telephoned her friend the refrigerator repairman to ask him if he would help. He came over almost immediately, ostensibly to repair her refrig-erator, broke into the desk, and found the gun and license. But the next problem was how to get rid of it safely without its being traced back to the family.

Frau Sinzheimer put on her street clothes and, picking her way among the wreckage and rubble of the previous two nights' destruction, went to her husband's favorite tobacconist's on the Kurfürstendamm and bought a large box of cigars. Back home, she removed the cigars, placed the gun and license at the bottom of the box, then filled up the top layer of the box again with cigars. She then made her way to the local police station on the Kurfürstendamm and asked to see a sergeant, whom she knew well, about taking on a new cook. German law required the local police to be notified about any change or addition to household staff. Frau Sinzheimer presented her friend the sergeant with the box of cigars. At her suggestion, he opened the box—and found the gun license. Inves-tigating further, he came across the gun itself. He lit up one of the cigars, using the license as a taper, and when no one was looking, dropped the gun in his wastepaper basket. "Hurry home, Frau Sinzheimer," he said, "before you give me a heart attack!"

Richard Stukerts was a chauffeur employed by Dr. Carl Loesten of Berlin. He persuaded his parents to hide his Jewish employer in their home at Wittenau during the pogrom. In another case, a postman spent the night walking up and down the street in front of the home of two elderly Jewish ladies, his uniform successfully affording them protection.

Colonel (later General) Hans Oster was chief of staff to Admiral Can-aris, head of the Abwehr (German Military Intelligence). Oster and his family lived in the same Berlin apartment block and on the same floor as the Meumanns, a well-to-do Jewish family. Herr Meumann was a lawyer. The two families were friends.

On the afternoon of November 9, Frau Oster called on Frau Meumann to warn her that she had heard the Jews were being arrested all over Berlin. She offered to hide Herr Meumann in the Osters' apartment, should the Gestapo call to arrest him. There were two staircases in the apartment block, one for tradespeople that connected with the back doors of the various flats, and one for the residents. Frau Oster suggested if the Gestapo knocked at the Meumanns' front door, Herr Meumann could slip out of the back door of his apartment and across to the back door of the Osters'.

Though grateful for the offer, in the end the Meumanns decided it was too risky for both families—particularly the Osters, who had everything to lose if they were caught sheltering a Jew in their apartment. Instead, Connie Meumann, the daughter, was sent out on her bicycle to arrange a hiding place for her father with one of her girlfriends.

However, it was the first time that the Meumanns were made aware that Hans Oster was prepared to work actively against the Nazis. Later, as one of the leaders of German resistance, he was to pass information to the Allies about Hitler's plan to invade Holland, Belgium, and Denmark. In 1943, he was dismissed from the Abwehr for using its "front organizations" abroad to help Jews escape to safety. Implicated in the 1944 July plot to assassinate Hitler, Oster died hanging from a piano-wire noose in the Flossenbürg concentration camp.

Bremen is Germany's oldest port. With Hamburg and Lübeck, it was one of the big three in the Hanseatic League in the Middle Ages. Over the years, Bremers—the inhabitants of Bremen—developed a reputation for being correct but cold in their dealings with outsiders. For centuries Jews lived in Bremen, and for centuries the Bremers maintained the same frigid politeness towards them. "Jews were not received in society here," T. B. Wildman, the British consul, reported to the Foreign Office in London, "and while the Bremer would treat the relatively few local Jews, who were in business, in a correct manner, he would never invite them to his house."

What little politeness remained after nearly six years of Nazi rule ended abruptly at about 10:30 P.M. on November 9, when the *Gruppenführer* of the SA Group Nordsee, based in Bremen, telephoned from Munich immediately after leaving the meeting in the Hotel Schottenhammel, to pass on the orders for the pogrom. His chief of staff, Roempagel, may have made a mistake in taking down what he heard over the phone, or his *Gruppenführer* may have misunderstood the original briefing. "All Jewish stores are to be destroyed at once by SA men in uniform," was the message written down—which was in direct opposition to Goebbels's instruction that uniforms were not to be worn, in case anyone should get the idea that the attacks were not an act of spontaneous indignation by the German people as a whole, but preplanned nationwide vandalism by the SA.

The rest of the instructions dictated by the *Gruppenführer* were clear enough, however. "After the destruction, SA guards will be posted with the task of ensuring that no objects of value are removed. SA administrative leaders will ensure the safety of all objects of value, including money," he ordered, adding that the local press should be invited along to witness the SA's triumph over the Jews. After the usual orders regarding the burning down of synagogues, and protecting only Aryan property from the fires, he went on to say that "Adjacent Jewish houses are also to be protected by the fire services, though Jews must leave, as Aryans will move in during the next few days."

The orders continued with instructions that the SA must liaise with the municipal authorities, so that Jewish shops and businesses, including Jewish peddlers and street traders, could be correctly identified. Even the question of the graffiti to be painted on Jewish shops and synagogues was covered. Approved texts included: REVENGE FOR THE MURDER OF VOM RATH, DEATH TO INTERNATIONAL JEWRY, and NO DEALINGS WITH NATIONS UNDER THE SWAY OF THE JEWS.

"The police must not intervene," the *Gruppenführer* stated. "The führer desires that the police do not intervene."

Some idea of what happened next in "correct" Bremen can be gleaned from Consul Wildman's report. The burgermeister of Bremen, SA Gruppenführer Heinrich Böhmcker, whom Wildman described as a typical Nazi drunkard and bully, decided that he did not have enough storm troopers to carry out the job in an appropriate manner, so he bused men in from the surrounding country districts. They started work at 2:00 A.M. The burgermeister had also arranged for a detachment of the local fire department with three engines and seventeen escape ladders to be standing by at numbers 6 and 7 Gartenstrasse, where the synagogue and its administrative building, the Roseneckhaus, were situated, hoses at the ready in case the blaze looked about to spread.

Once the synagogue was burning nicely, the storm troopers then turned their attention to the administrative building next door and thoroughly ransacked the place. A party of them also set fire to a funeral chapel at the Jewish cemetery in Hastedt, a suburb of Bremen, tore up tombstones, and desecrated a number of graves.

At about 4:00 A.M., storm troopers turned their attention to Jewish shops and businesses in the city itself. In one instance, they used a truck to smash the windows of a number of shops. After these had been looted and stripped of everything of value, they put up their prewritten placards bearing the approved slogans.

At about 5:00 A.M., they began to arrest Jews, both men and women and even children. "In some special cases where the women were very old and infirm they were allowed to remain in their houses. The rest, however, were taken off to the Misslerhaus, a former hostel for emigrants . . . and to a building in the Dechanatstrasse and the Lloydheim." Two hours later, the women and children were released. One Jew, a man named Rosenberg, resisted. He was shot dead. There were also reports of a number of suicides.

Later that morning, in a grotesque spectacle, the Jews who had been arrested, most of them still in their nightclothes with just an overcoat thrown over their shoulders, were made to file past Burgermeister Böhmcker in a long column.

The following day, Friday, crowds of sightseers went to gaze at the damage in the Obernstrasse, the Oxford Street or Fifth Avenue of Bremen, which runs from east to west through the Altstadt. According to Wildman, the people seemed stunned, astonished at what had happened. The local newspaper, the *Bremer Nachrichten*, was sure that "[e]very citizen expressed satisfaction that here in National Socialist Bremen, Judah has received the justified answer for the underhand murder carried out by their compatriot, Grynzspan . . . Bremen's population, and, with it, the whole German people have shown that they are not going to look on patiently when German men are murdered by Jews."

The *Osnabrücker Tageblatt* expressed similar sentiments. It also reported that the synagogue in Rolandstrasse in Osnabrück, which lies some 130 kilometers to the south of Bremen, had been set on fire some time after midnight on November 10. Part of the interior of the synagogue and the roof were destroyed. Similar incidents were reported from Delmenhorst and Bremerhaven. Only Oldenburg, home of the Visbecker Bridegroom, Germany's Stonehenge, seems to have missed out.

As a postscript to a report he sent to the British embassy in Berlin on November 30, nearly three weeks later, Consul Wildman—with evident glee—was able to report that "the authorities in Berlin are not at all pleased at the way the SA and SS men carried out the pogrom in Bremen. It appears that it was intended that men in civilian clothes should smash the shops up and then SA men in uniform should be placed as sentries on the damaged property." Unfortunately, someone seems to have got the orders wrong. Everyone turned up in uniform. First they wrecked the shops, then they stood guard over them.

The error about the wearing of uniforms in Bremen was compounded when the orders worked their way through to smaller places like Lesum, a nearby village, where SA Company 411 was based. The commander, Truppführer Seggermann, phoned the local burgermeister, Hauptsturm-führer (Captain) Koester, the moment he received his orders, asking if he had also received instructions. Koester had heard nothing.

"The SA is standing by throughout Germany to carry out reprisals for the murder of Ernst vom Rath," Seggermann explained. "By tonight there must be no Jews left in Germany. The Jewish shops must also be destroyed."

Koester asked what was to happen to the Jews.

"Destroy them!" Seggermann told him.

Distinctly uneasy at this, which went much further than anyone had ever dreamed, Koester went to inform his superior officer, Sturmbann-führer (Major) Roeschmann, of the news. He found him at home, asleep in bed. The two men talked the situation over and decided to check with SA Group Headquarters in Bremen before taking any further action. The phone was answered by the duty officer, a man called Gross. Roeschmann queried the order he had received: Was it correct?

Gross replied, "Yes. In Bremen 'The Night of the Long Knives' [sic] has begun. The synagogue is already on fire."

Roeschmann: "Is that official?"

Gross: "That is official."

At the Café Wendt in Lesum, the leaders of Standarte 411, plus Kreisleiter Kuehn, the local party boss, met to discuss the matter. It was clear to everyone that the party had decided to solve the Jewish problem once and for all. As so often in the past, the party's orders were not specific, but it was obvious what they wanted done, so long as it did not create bad publicity for the SA.

Very few Jews lived in the village itself, but Scharführer (Staff Sergeant) August Frühling and Rottenführer (Corporal) Bruno Mahlsted knew what had to be done. Armed with pistols, they broke into the home of the Goldbergs and shot Herr and Frau Goldberg in their beds. They later murdered another Jew, named Sinsohn, in his house.

Not all German cities seem to have shared the same zeal for the destruction of Jewish property. For whatever reason, some authorities were less than enthusiastic about what was planned for November 9–10. Hamburg, founded by Charlemagne and for centuries Germany's greatest port, standing at the mouth of the River Elbe, was one such place. It was rumored, according to the British consul general, L. M. Robinson, that Berlin was worried that the action might not be carried out in Hamburg with "the thoroughness desired." Therefore, in order to insure the appropriate degree of rigor, they drafted in a number of SS men specifically to direct the operation.

One of the consul's informants lived on the central square of Hamburg, the recently renamed Adolf Hitler Platz. He (or she—there is no indication as to sex) reported seeing a large number of men in civilian clothes being paraded in front of the Rathaus by uniformed SA officials in the early hours of Thursday morning. The men were split into groups, each under the command of a different leader, and then they marched off. The time was 1:00 A.M. on November 10. The window-smashing began promptly at 3:30 A.M.

One of the streets to suffer was the Neuerwall, the principal shopping street in Hamburg, and only a short walk from the splendid nineteenth-century Rathaus. Another eyewitness told Robinson that they had seen trucks loaded with stones and rocks draw up outside various Jewish shops on the Neuerwall. They watched as "raiding parties" armed themselves with missiles from the trucks and set about smashing windows.

"The fears of the Berlin authorities . . . that Hamburg would not be drastic enough in carrying out orders seem to have been justified, since the action taken here appears to have been far less violent than in many other parts of Germany, judging by press reports. . . ." Robinson had heard of no attacks being made on Jewish homes in the city.

Those Jewish shopkeepers who had not fled into hiding were arrested, and their businesses placed in the hands of government-appointed trustees, pending the ultimate Aryanization of the firm. The trustees "have received instructions that in the event of the release of the owners, the latter are not to be allowed to resume management, nor is any money to be paid to them. Jewish employees who have not been arrested—and these are chiefly female assistants—have been given six weeks' notice; Jewish male employees under arrest are dismissed without notice on the ground that they have 'absented themselves from their employment.'

"The general local reaction among all classes is one of shame and disgust. Expressions of despair about the future are frequently heard." A number of arrests of Aryans who were incautious enough to voice their feelings in the street were made by Gestapo agents, who mixed with the crowds outside the wrecked shops. In all, about three hundred arrests of non-Jews were made, but only about thirty people were detained and sent to the concentration camps.

In all, about twenty-five hundred Jews were arrested in Hamburg as a result of the morning's work. The majority of them were sent in two trainloads on the nights of November 10 and 11—approximately seven hundred per trainload—to Fürstenwalde near Berlin, the station for the Oranienburg concentration camp. Other, similar parties followed later.

Elmshorn is a small town some thirty-four kilometers northwest of Hamburg and not far from Blankenese. On November 9–10, 1938, Lore Boas, a young Jewish woman who was about to emigrate to Australia—she was one of the lucky ones—was visiting relatives in Elmshorn with her mother to say her farewells to the rest of the family before leaving Germany for good. Her father had stayed behind at their home in the small country town of Güstrow in Meckenlenberg, near Rostock.

In the middle of the night, the household was woken by a loud knocking at the front door. There on the doorstep they found a group of storm troopers. The men said that they had come to protect them from the mob. The Germans, they said, were so incensed against the Jews for their involvement in the assassination of Ernst vom Rath in Paris that they were burning synagogues, destroying Jewish property, and so on. In order to protect Jews from the fury of the mob, the local authorities had ordered the SA to take all Jewish males into custody. The only male in the household happened to be the uncle. He was marched off by the SA. The women dressed and went down to the town center to see what was happening, and true enough, they found the local synagogue in flames.

Later, Lore's mother phoned her husband in Güstrow, advising him to come to Hamburg immediately. The following day, Lore was due to leave from the main Hamburg railway station for Holland, the first stage of her journey to Australia. They arrived early, hoping the father would get there before her train left. They waited on the station for hours. There were police and storm troopers everywhere, manning the platforms, searching each train that arrived for Jewish men who had escaped the net. As the hours went by, the two women realized that the father must have been picked up in Güstrow. When Lore's train pulled out of the station, there was still no sign of him.

Later it transpired that he had indeed been arrested and taken to the Sachsenhausen concentration camp, where he was held for several weeks. He was released on the understanding that he would leave Germany within a month. It was not until February 1939 that Lore's parents managed to escape from Germany—their destination was Shanghai, the only place that would take them.

Before the war, Leipzig was one of those quintessential German cities, one of the great cultural launching pads for German genius. Goethe had studied there; Johann Sebastian Bach had worked there in the Thomas Church; Schiller wrote his "Ode to Freedom" in a small farmhouse in one of the Leipzig suburbs, and—appropriately enough—Richard Wagner had been born there 125 years before.

In 1938, David H. Buffum, the American consul in Leipzig, wrote a report to his superiors in Berlin describing what he had personally witnessed. The proceedings, he said, began with a bizarre ritual—"rites held on one of the principal squares of the city on the night of November 9, 1938 in commemoration of fallen martyrs to the Nazi cause prior to their political takeover in 1933." The bodies of those so-called martyrs—"five-year-old remains of those who had been considered rowdyish violators of law and order"—had been exhumed from their graves to be displayed in ornate coffins in the Altermarkt. Meanwhile "the entire market place had been surrounded with wooden latticework about ten yards high. This was covered with white cloths to form the background for black swastikas at least five yards high and broad. Flame-spurting urns and gigantic banners completed a Wagnerian ensemble." The centerpiece of the display was a great urn in which flames burned, like the eternal flame on the Tomb of the Unknown Soldier. Eventually, "amid marching troops, flaring torches and funeral music," the coffins were returned to the local Nazi cemetery.

The crowds, curiously enough, do not seem to have been grateful for the display. "Judging from a few very guardedly whispered comments, the populace was far more concerned over the wanton waste of materials in these days when textiles of any kind are exceedingly scarce and expensive, rather than being actuated by any particularly reverent emotions. On the other hand for obvious reasons, there were no open manifestations of disapproval."

The pogrom began after this barbaric ceremony in the early hours of Thursday morning, November 10, with the shattering of shop windows and the looting of their wares. All of the local crowds observed were obviously benumbed over what had happened and aghast over the unprecedented fury of Nazi acts that had been or were taking place with bewildering rapidity throughout the city.

A twenty-five-year-old Dutch Jew, Wim van Leer, who was visiting relatives in Leipzig, was walking along a street when the action erupted around him. He watched in horror as a truck drew up a few houses further on from him, and "some twenty louts jumped down," rang doorbells, smashed the glass windows in the doors if there was no reply, and broke into Jewish homes. "Suddenly," van Leer wrote later, "the third-floor balcony doors were flung open, and storm troopers appeared, shouting to their pals below. One yelled something about all blessings coming from above, and, in expectation, that part of the pavement beneath the balcony was cleared. Next, they wheeled an upright piano over the edge. It nose-dived onto the street below with a sickening crash as the wooden casing broke away, leaving what looked like a harp standing in the middle of the debris."

After the SA and the mobs had finished smashing up Jewish property, throwing furniture and goods into the streets, they turned on individual Jews—men, women, and children. "In one of the Jewish sections [of the city]," Consul Buffum reported, "an eighteen-year-old boy was hurled from a three-story window to land with both legs broken on a street littered with burning beds and other household furniture and effects from his family's and other apartments."

But it was not just violence for its own sake—there was also widespread looting of cash, silver, jewelry, and any other valuables. And above all, the symbols of Jewry were destroyed. "Three synagogues of Leipzig were fired simultaneously by incendiary bombs and all sacred objects and records desecrated or destroyed, in most instances hurled through the windows and burned in the streets. No attempts were made to quench the fires, functions of the fire brigade having been confined to playing water on adjoining buildings. All of the synagogues were irreparably gutted by flames."

As for the commercial quarter of the city, the Jews were eradicated there, too. "One of the largest clothing stores in the heart of the city was destroyed by flames from incendiary bombs, only the charred walls and gutted roof having been left standing. As was the case with the synagogues, no attempts on the part of the fire brigade were made to extinguish the fire, although there was a certain amount of apprehension for adjacent property, for the walls of the coffeehouse next door were covered with asbestos and sprayed [with water]. . . ."

As an additional turn of the screw, "the owners of the clothing store were actually charged with setting the fire and on that basis were dragged from their beds at 6:00 A.M. and clapped into prison."

Buffum went to the zoological park and saw storm troopers throwing Jews into the stream that ran through it. They ordered the crowd that had gathered "to spit at [the Jews], defile them with mud and jeer at their plight." If anyone in the crowd expressed any sympathy for the victims, then the SA turned on them, too. According to Buffum, the crowd was horror-stricken, but also too afraid to do anything to prevent it—lest they, too, should end up knee deep in the stream and covered with mud.

This sport went on during the whole morning of November 10. At no time did the police intervene.

It was not only big businesses like the Bamberger & Hertz clothing store—the one mentioned by Consul Buffum—where the owners were accused of burning down their own property. The family of Abraham Rose, who owned a modest menswear and shoe shop, the Britania Stores, in Borna, a small country town twenty-nine kilometers southwest of Leipzig, was among many others who faced similar charges.

Abraham's son, Siegfried, who today lives as Frederick Rose in Canada, vividly recalls what happened to him as a seventeen-year-old in the pogrom:

> In the notorious November week in 1938, my father was ill and confined to our Leipzig apartment. My uncle Carl lived on the second floor over the store, so he could deputise for my father in charge of the business. To help my uncle, I had taken a day off and travelled out to Borna. In the afternoon, we heard a rumour through a neighbour that in the evening the Britania Stores would be smashed up and set on fire, like many more businesses in Leipzig.
>
> My uncle locked up at once, and let down the steel roller blinds over the display windows. A short time later, a crowd gathered in front of the store and started throwing stones and bottles. My uncle and I were cut off from the house at the back, where my aunt and her three children were, on the second floor. They could not leave the house without being molested.
>
> With the coming of darkness, we heard ax blows, and shortly afterwards the rear entrance from the garden was broken in. A commando of about eight men in jackboots stormed up the steps, shouting: "Out with the Jewish swine!" They broke down the bolted apartment door and threatened us with their revolvers, forcing us to unlock the entrance doors and open all the shutters and windows. All the display windows were immediately smashed and the goods pulled out. Meanwhile, my uncle and I were held in the store and beaten with a broken chair until we both had bloody heads.

After the whole of the fittings had been smashed, men brought cans of gasoline and splashed it on the walls and on the clothing stock, and in the storeroom on the first floor. They then dragged Siegfried and his uncle Carl out through the front door, where they were beaten up again by the mob. After that, they were arrested, but were released the next day.

"We began at once to search for my aunt and the children," says Rose, "and heard later that they had been rescued from the apartment by a brave, friendly family, and kept hidden. We found the store completely burnt out, including the little apartment and the storeroom. After three hours of freedom, an order apparently came to the Borna police from Leipzig, to arrest us both, on a charge of arson."

The next morning, Siegfried Rose and his uncle, along with other arrested Jews from the surrounding districts, were taken to the Jewish collecting point in the Leipzig exhibition halls. There, the two men were separated. The next day, in spite of his youth, Siegfried was taken to the Sachsenhausen concentration camp, where he was forced to sign a confession that he had set fire to his father's property.

"Fortunately," the local newspaper, the *Bornaer Tageblatt*, reported, "the local fire department was on the scene quickly, and was able to prevent the fire from spreading to the Aryan-owned businesses on either side." What was more, the paper continued, by 8:00 P.M., peace and quiet were restored to Borna, "thanks to our SA."

Another survivor from Leipzig, Alfred Glaser, remembers the traumatic experience of going into the city center the next morning:

> Everywhere, there were crowds of men, standing there, some sympathetic, others indifferent. I rushed across the market square, leaving the broken window glass behind me. I wanted to get to my girlfriend. In the Nord-, Gerber- and Humboltstrasse, men were hunting. Broken furniture lay in the street. And then I saw how SA and SS men were leading groups of Jews, all in lines. . . . I went no further, but returned to the market, to Grimmai-schestrasse. Then along came the driver for the fish merchants Grospitsch, where I worked. He drove to the edge of the curb and called to me to get on board. That was very dangerous for him, a non-Jew. He took me home.
>
> In Reudnitz, one was hardly aware of the tumult, but my mother stood waiting outside our house, and anxiously asked me why I had stayed out so long. The Gestapo had already been there, asking for me. I told my mother that I would leave Germany illegally, as I had no passport. Naturally, she started to cry her eyes out, as did my youngest sister, but she agreed that that would be best. I had taken all my savings out of the savings bank at the market, and my mother gave me something, too. I never saw her again.

At an isolated Jewish educational farm near Gräfenheinichen, Bitten-feld, in the flat farm country about sixty kilometers north of Leipzig, a group of young Jews, mostly teenagers, were undergoing training to prepare them for life on an agricultural kibbutz in Palestine. Around midnight on November 9–10, the still of the cold winter night was broken by the sound of several trucks turning into the farmyard. The trucks were filled with SS and SA men. They stormed into the boys' dormitory and dragged them into the farmyard in their nightclothes. There were shots, much shouting, cries of "Where are the girls?"

Two of the girls had been woken by the noise and had managed to slip through a back window and, wearing only their nightgowns, had fled through the dark to the safety of the flat fields and the wood beyond. There they were eventually found, barefoot and shivering with cold, long after the intruders had gone.

One of the Jewish boys had been shot. Apparently, he had been slow to answer questions put to him by one of the overexcited SA or SS men, and the man had fired his revolver. Perhaps he had only meant to scare the boy into answering, or perhaps he had been overcome by rage that the boy, confused, frightened, half-asleep, could not or would not reply. At any rate, the boy now lay dead.

The shooting seems to have worried the local authorities, because on the morning of Friday, November 11, the Gestapo arrived at the farm accompanied by the local village policeman. They found the place pretty much as the SA left it—littered with the debris of destruction: torn Hebrew prayer books, the Torah scroll slashed with knives, personal belongings ripped and broken.

The Gestapo interrogated each of the youngsters separately, but they seemed less interested in getting answers to their questions than in intimidation. Again and again, they reiterated that the shooting had not been intentional—it had been an accident. They said that each and every one of the youngsters would "face dire consequences if ever a word of it reached the outside world." Then they gave the boys half an hour to get ready and took them away in trucks to the Sachsenhausen concentration camp, leaving the girls behind.

One bizarre detail remains unexplained. Lili, the girl responsible for the catering at the farm, had made a large quantity of dough for baking bread. This seemed to worry her interrogator. He ordered her to dig a hole and bury it in the garden.

As for the shot boy, his corpse was taken away and buried at Gräfenheinichen. Only one Jewish girl was allowed to be present. The girls asked that his body be taken to Leipzig for burial in the Jewish cemetery there and that his parents be informed, but their request was refused.

They were forced to stay at the farm for five days, and each day a Gestapo man called to make sure they were all still there. On the fifth day, they were all interrogated once again, then released. It was only when Lili was sitting in the waiting room at the Leipzig station waiting for her connection to Breslau that she overheard people talking about what had happened throughout the Reich. Until then, she had thought the incident at the farm was unique.

It came as a shock to many Jews to discover that the vandals who destroyed their homes and businesses were not faceless strangers but people they knew, people they had always thought of as friends.

Charlotte Singer was the wife of a doctor who had been in practice in Neisse, a town eighty-two kilometers southeast of Breslau. Her husband was away in Berlin, attending a special course for Jewish doctors who were planning to emigrate. Mrs. Singer was still in Neisse because she was trying to collect the backlog of fees that were still owed to her husband. She was lodging with the Holzes, a well-to-do Jewish family in the town.

On Friday morning, November 10, she was woken by a crash. Her immediate thought was that her host's large and exuberant dog had knocked over the breakfast table, which he was always threatening to do. But then she heard the shouts of a large crowd and realized it was something more serious. Like many Jews who were completely integrated into German society, she had always believed that her fellow citizens of Neisse, ordinary respectable Germans, would never turn on her and her family. If the Nazis were going to persecute the Jews in Neisse, then they would have to import thugs from outside to do their dirty work for them. But she was wrong. The man who now entered her bedroom carrying an ax was Erich Brückner, one of her husband's patients, the son of a local plumber who had done a lot of work for the Singers.

Ignoring her, he proceeded to smash up the furniture in her room, overturning her writing table and spattering the carpet with ink. "To set fire to this place would be best!" he shouted to some friends outside. But they apparently could not be bothered—at any rate, they did not set fire to the house.

Later, as she was sweeping up the broken glass, Charlotte saw a second mob approaching. This one contained a number of women, about twenty in all—the other had been all-male. The second mob found at least one room in the house untouched—the kitchen—which they proceeded to wreck with great glee, finishing the job by breaking every last pane of glass in the house.

News came that all Jewish homes in Neisse had suffered the same treatment. Moreover, it seemed that the mobs were planning to return during the night and set fire to all Jewish property in the town.

They obviously could not stay any longer at the wrecked house. Mrs. Singer thought of Anna Krautwald, who had once worked for her as a parlor maid. Perhaps she could put them up. Like practically everyone in Neisse, Anna was a Roman Catholic. She now lived outside the town with her parents on their small property. Mrs. Singer went to see her, hoping to persuade Anna to allow herself, her son, and Mrs. Holz to sleep in one of the barns. But Anna did better than that: She talked her parents into letting the three Jews sleep in the house in the two spare beds. There was only one proviso—they had to promise to leave the house by 6:00 A.M., before it was light, in case Anna's brother discovered them. He was a member of the Nazi party and would give them away.

"In Düsseldorf and elsewhere," Consul Bell wrote, "reports indicate that anti-Jewish measures have been even more drastic than in Cologne." Düsseldorf, the capital of the state of Northern Rhineland-Westphalia, was the birthplace of Heinrich Heine the poet; Brahms, Schumann, and Goethe all lived there at one time or another. So did Kerry Weinberg, a young Jewish woman. She rented a studio apartment on the third floor of a large house overlooking a park. The house, which had an ornate wrought-iron fence in front, belonged to the widow of a judge, who, to augment her income, rented out half a dozen rooms in her mansion.

The girl was woken by her landlady at 3:00 A.M. It was still pitch dark outside. The landlady warned her to expect trouble. In the house next door, they could hear screams and banging. The screaming grew louder. Suddenly, shots rang out. A woman cried out, "My God, he's dead!" But who? The girl never discovered.

The judge's widow, her housekeeper, and Kerry tiptoed down to the big kitchen, where they sat in the darkness, expecting the mob to break in at any moment. But nothing happened. At dawn, the housekeeper, as tiny and fragile as a bird beside her employer, who was built on distinctly Wagnerian lines, made coffee.

When it was light, the girl decided to go for a walk to see the extent of the destruction. It seemed safe enough. The park was deserted, the streets quiet at last. She took the precaution of disguising her non-Aryan looks as best she could, with the aid of sunglasses and her hair tucked inside a large hat. A few blocks away, she came across a huge crowd standing opposite a Jewish school, watching it burn.

When she got back to the house where she lodged, another crowd awaited her. This one, however, was watching the SS in action. They were busy removing the widow's furniture, lifting it over the wrought-iron fence and throwing it into the street beyond. The crowd roared with delight when the feet of the landlady's grand piano—she was a noted musician—caught on the railings, and the instrument hung there, like a huge butterfly supping at a flower.

At 4:00 A.M., a gang of SA men smashed down the door of a Jewish hospital and ordered all the patients out of their beds. When the staff protested, the SA insisted on examining the patients themselves. In the end, only those who had just had operations were allowed to remain. The rest had to get up out of bed, dress, and go home.

Twenty-four kilometers east of Düsseldorf, in the cutlery-manufacturing town of Solingen, twelve-year-old Francis H. Schott was worrying about his father, who was trying to make a living as a private physician after being dismissed from his post as chief of the municipal hospital. Dr. Schott, an assimilated Jew and baptized Christian, had not yet told his children that under the latest Nazi decree he would have to cease practicing altogether by January 1, 1939. He had applied for a United States visa, but it would be "a long and uncertain wait." Already, they had lost their house, which went with the doctor's job at the hospital, and had had to move into a long, narrow apartment in the town.

"Even a twelve-year-old boy can tell that hatred against the family and himself is meant to be almost physical," Francis Schott recalls. "Everyone in a Nazi uniform—and there are more of them every day, worn by fellow schoolchildren and oh-so-big men—is strutting. What might they do to us besides making it impossible to stay in Germany? There is a gulf between the almost physical and the actually physical: A government issues orders, but it does not touch you except when the police come for a criminal."

For the Schott family, that gulf disappeared during the early hours of November 10, 1938. Francis, now an insurance executive and economist living in Ridgewood, New Jersey, remembers:

A jarring sound jolts us awake in the middle of the night. Glass and wood of the apartment door shatter. My little sister and I sit up in our beds, uncomprehending. The noise gets louder yet, things are breaking and gruff male voices can be heard.

My mother slips in from the adjacent bedroom and stations herself inside our closed door. Heavy steps rush from the living room at the front of the apartment to the dining room at its end. The sound of destruction heightens as china and crystal are thrown into the corridor.

Suddenly, I know. The Nazis have come to get us. They are smashing our things. My mother is trying to protect us. Inexplicably, the cold fear that grips me is not for my own life but for my mother's. The Nazis will kill her. I cower.

Then they are gone. Ghastly silence. We open the bedroom doors. No one is hurt, but the psychic shock is staggering. They knew the apartment layout. While staying away from the bedrooms and the medical area, they reduced the living area to shambles.

My father's Italian cello is nothing but splinters, the Bechstein piano smashed beyond repair. The Emil Nolde watercolors and Paul Klee drawings are on the floor, crushed. The china and crystal, my mother's heirlooms, are in the apartment corridor, in thousands of pieces.

We do not say a word. We clean up so we can walk without getting cut. Kind neighbors from the apartment above come to help. They tell us of the citywide devastation. They make us find our voices again.

Worse is to come, much worse. But a twelve-year-old has absorbed a lesson. The orderly world in which only the police can get you and won't come unless you are a criminal—that world is gone. By fanning prejudice into hate, a government can turn a populace into assault troops. Painful as it is, we must remember.

Cologne, thirty-two kilometers south of Düsseldorf, was originally a Celtic town. It was taken over by the Romans, who built a wall around it and held it for four hundred years—its name literally means colony or outpost. At the peak of the Roman period, Cologne had a population of twenty thousand; by 1938, it was in the region of eight hundred thousand.

An anonymous letter, signed *"Ein Beamter"* ("A Civil Servant"), was sent to the British consul general in Cologne, J. E. Bell, on November 12, giving details of the organization behind the local pogrom. The first orders to the local SA were issued at a quarter to one in the morning— 12:45 A.M. on November 10 over the Cologne police-radio network. The orders were precise and detailed. At 4:00 A.M., the SA were to insure that all Jewish synagogues and chapels were set on fire. Two hours later, at 6:00 A.M., the operation was to be extended to include Jewish shops and houses in the city center. Two hours after that, at 8:00 A.M., when it would be light, the mobs were to move out to the suburbs to continue the good work among the Jewish middle class in places like Lindenthal and Sülz. All action was to cease at 1:00 P.M. on November 10.

The police were also given their instructions. They were to be responsible for supplying the SA men and whatever other riffraff had elected to join the mobs with axes, housebreaking tools, and ladders. These were to be issued by police headquarters—and presumably signed for—along with the names and addresses of suitable Jewish property to be destroyed. This was obviously intended to prevent any unfortunate mistakes resulting in Aryan homes being damaged.

According to the same anonymous civil servant, seventeen Jewish shops in the center of Cologne were looted and destroyed. "At 8 o'clock in the morning," he wrote, "revolting fights among this mob over the booty were still to be witnessed, e.g., one of the robbers was carrying away eight suits of stolen clothing, which he was refusing to share with his dear German comrades." A police commissioner who had attempted to prevent a shop being looted had been suspended from duty.

The consul reported that four hundred Jews had been taken into "preventative arrest" for their own protection—though "I hear, however, that they are unlikely to be set free until they have been financially bled." The local Jewish community was in a desperate plight, and all were eager to emigrate. They overran the consulate, clamoring for visas. One woman "pestered a member of the staff to take her husband into his small flat over the night of the 11th. The man literally arrived at the door with his pyjamas."

Many middle-class Germans disapproved of what had happened, but were too frightened to say anything. One German woman who did so "in a tram which runs past my house, was arrested at the first stop by Nazi guards." But other people he spoke to, local industrialists, for example, insisted that "they had no influence with the Party who have made such a point of racial purity that the Führer must carry his theories to their logical conclusion." Bell's own conclusion about the pogrom was depressing. "I have been more shocked," he wrote, "by the cold blooded and calculated manner in which action was taken than by anything else about recent events. Yet I am inclined to think that the Führer knows his Germans. Amongst the masses of Germans who have nothing to stake there is observable a certain amount of 'Schadenfreude' (joy in mischief). Our German cook, for instance, observed to me a few days ago that it was high time a certain neighbouring Jew was 'washed up.' "

Mainz is a city that is over two thousand years old. It stands on the river Rhine and is the capital of Rhineland-Palatinate. It was also the birthplace of Johannes Gutenberg, the inventor of movable type. Today, the city is famous for its Mardi Gras festival and the September wine market. But, it, too, suffered in 1938.

Lotte Kramer attended the Jewish school that, since 1934, had been housed in the Liberal Synagogue in Mainz. Early in the morning of November 10, she was telephoned by her cousin, who lived opposite the synagogue. "Don't come to school," she was told. "It's on fire. And tell your father to get out. They are taking our men to concentration camps." Herr Kramer left the house at once.

Later, a school friend, Evi, called to see Lotte and her mother. Unaware of what was happening, she had gone to school, only to find the building burning. While the three were talking about the events, they heard a mob outside in the street. Hordes of youths were ransacking Jewish homes and smashing everything they could find. Terrified, Frau Kramer and the two girls went up to the attic and hid behind the trunks and old furniture and bric-a-brac stored there, crouching down below the window level, so that they would not be seen from the street. They heard the mob destroying the home of the Jewish widow who lived opposite them. They were sure they were going to be next. But just then they heard the voice of outraged authority outside on the street. It was the headmaster of the boy's high school who lived nearby. He stopped the mob dead in their tracks. "The führer will not stand for this kind of behavior!" he shouted. Whether they believed that or not, clearly none of the youths— some of whom must have been at his school—were prepared to tackle their headmaster. Sheepishly, they dispersed.

That afternoon Lotte and Evi met one of their own teachers, who had just come from the home of the headmaster of the Jewish school. The teacher had found the bodies of the headmaster and his wife. They were both dead: They had gassed themselves. Gentile pupils from the high school where the Jewish headmaster had once taught science for many years before he was forced to leave had apparently broken into his house and devastated the place. He must have actually taught some of the boys who had destroyed his home.

Herr Kramer returned to the family home after dark, having spent the day hiding in the woods. He and his wife telephoned other members of the family to find out what had happened to them. Some had been arrested. In Herr Kramer's native village, his brother had been beaten badly and then led through the streets on a leash, like a dog.

Frankfurt-am-Main was traditionally a strong Jewish center. Even in November 1938, it still had a Jewish population of some thirty-five thousand—all of whom were expecting trouble. Many had been warned by German friends not to leave their homes the next day—even to go to work—if vom Rath should die.

Acting British consul general A. E. Dowden had an apartment near the headquarters of the local SA troop. At 9:15 A.M. on Thursday, he saw the troop parading there, all wearing civilian clothes. In fact, the pogrom had begun at 5:00 A.M., when the SA set fire to the principal synagogue, and had moved on to the destruction of Jewish homes at about 6:30 A.M. It was all highly organized: SA and SS men heading the various raiding parties, each of which usually consisted of between five and ten men, "were seen consulting lists of names and addresses before proceeding to the next scene of destruction." Dowden also reported that an official of the Post Office Telegraphic Department informed him that he and his colleagues had all had to renew their oaths of secrecy a few days earlier. And three members of the SS told him they had been ordered "to hold themselves in readiness for an impending eventuality."

Dowden and Vice-Consul Sander visited the business sector at midday, to see the extent of the damage for themselves. They found there was not a single Jewish shop that had not been "completely demolished and wrecked inside and out." "The goods were either destroyed or stolen by the rowdies who followed up the organised bands of un-uniformed storm troops and members of the Gestapo," Dowden noted. Several Jewish-owned cafés and a hotel had also been destroyed. Fires that had been started in the city's three synagogues in the early morning had been extinguished by the fire department and police guards posted. But at 5:00 P.M., when factories and offices had closed and the number of rowdies and Hitler Youth increased, the fires were started again, to blaze unchecked until the buildings were completely gutted. Meanwhile, gangs of thugs marched through the streets shouting "Perish the Jews!" and "Beat the Jews to death."

In Frankfurt, it was the sections of the city where the poorest Jews lived that suffered first. "Scenes of indescribable, destructive sadism and brutality were witnessed," said Dowden. "Usually the occupants were locked in the lavatory or told to leave the house and the mob entered and destroyed everything." Later in the evening, the "organised vandals" began to work their way westward, to where the richer Jews lived.

There were clear orders that foreign Jews, businesses that had already been Aryanized, and those that were foreign-owned were not to be touched. Vice-Consul Sander reported, "Disappointment and regret could be heard expressed by some of the demonstrators on their arriving outside premises which still bore a Jewish name, but without their knowledge were shown to have been 'Aryanised' and were therefore sacrosanct." The prohibition did not always work, however. A perfumery business that had been Aryanized only the night before, and that was now 75 percent owned by an American, was attacked. Even though the new owner flourished her American passport in the faces of the SA men, they were so carried away by their enthusiasm that they ignored her and demolished the premises.

On the evening of November 10, the arrests started in Frankfurt. Jewish men were rounded up regardless of age or status, despite the specific instructions from Munich and Berlin, and herded into the exhibition buildings. A large crowd had gathered outside, screaming insults and abuse at each convoy as it arrived. Inside the building, the Jews were stripped of all personal possessions, including money, and held through the night and next day without food or water. The storm troopers forced them to shout "We are Jews!" and to do exercises to keep warm. One man dropped dead from exhaustion, but still they were not allowed to stop. An old man wearing a prayer shawl was dragged around by his beard, while the crowd shouted "Pray, old man!" An SS *Obergruppen-führer* ordered a Jewish opera singer to perform an aria from Mozart's *Magic Flute*.

The arrests stopped on Monday evening, November 14, only to begin again thirty-six hours later. Pairs of SS troopers or Gestapo agents roamed the streets stopping likely pedestrians or entering houses on the pretext of looking for male Jews who might have been hiding. Once inside, they made a thorough search for weapons of any kind, or money, and if either was found, the occupants of the house were arrested on the grounds that weapons were forbidden and that any large sum of money was being hoarded to enable the family to escape from Germany.

During this time, refugees from smaller towns and villages in the region poured into Frankfurt, most of them heading for the British consulate, bringing stories of further violence. In areas where there were only a few Jewish families, they had been made to watch the destruction of their homes and then to flee for their lives. In Heidelberg, students had joined in the raids on Jewish homes. In Karlsruhe, all the male Jews had been collected in the market square and forced to chant "We are murderers," before being led off to the railway station.

Each day, between two hundred and three hundred Jewish women and children invaded the consulate, "eager to clutch at any straw, which will give them the hope of effecting the release of their husbands and sons." The women had no one else to turn to for help or advice, since all their community leaders and rabbis had been taken off to concentration camps, and the Palestine Emigration Office and the Jewish Emigration Advisory Office had been closed down. In many cases, they now had neither homes nor money, and were supposed to be in the care of the NSV, the National Socialist Public Welfare Committee—which, of course, was hardly eager to help them.

In many places, including towns such as Darmstadt, Offenbach, and Frankfurt itself, Jews were not allowed to buy provisions. Many shops refused to supply their old Jewish customers even with milk or bread.

In such circumstances, it was not surprising that many reached the ultimate depths of despair. Dowden said he knew personally of eleven acquaintances who had taken their own lives to avoid being arrested. The corpses of several Jews who had fled on Thursday evening were found hanging from trees in the woods on the outskirts of the city.

Baden-Baden was one of the great international health resorts of the *belle époque*, those golden years before the First World War. Kings and princelings and lesser varieties of aristocrat, industrialists and stockbrokers and *nouveaux riches* of every kind came here to drink the health-giving waters, or to bathe in them or wallow in mud baths. There were many ways of taking advantage of the therapeutic properties of the hot springs. And afterward, feeling virtuous from all that mortification of the flesh, the visitors spent their evenings gambling in the casino. It was all very civilized.

Things had not changed a great deal in the past half century—except, of course, that in 1938 there were fewer crowned heads to patronize the spa. But other visitors came in plenty. A good number were staying there that November, even so late in the season. How would they regard a pogrom? The local authorities wished to avoid offending their foreign visitors as far as possible—the Reich needed all the hard currency it could get. If the pogrom could not be avoided altogether, it could at least be delayed a little, to avoid disturbing the visitors' sleep. And so it was that Baden's spontaneous demonstrations did not begin until 7:00 A.M.

Even then, there was little violence to property, since burning buildings and wrecked businesses could be extremely disturbing. Instead, the Jewish men in the town were quietly rounded up during the morning and held in the courtyard of the local prison, out of sight, until about midday. Then they were marched across to the synagogue. There, they found SS men ominously laying electric cables. These were not the local SS but outsiders, apparently brought in specially to stiffen the resolve of the local SS and SA. As the Jews climbed the steps to the entrance of the synagogue, several older men stumbled and fell. They were immediately pounced upon and beaten until they picked themselves up again. Inside, they were made to walk over prayer shawls while singing the "Horst Wessel Song." As a further humiliation, they were forced to read aloud passages from *Mein Kampf*. One Jew, Dr. Arthur Flehinger, later described the scene, telling how an SS man posted behind him repeatedly hit him on the back of the neck for reading too quietly. After the readings, the men were kept standing for some time; then, according to Flehinger, "those who wanted to relieve themselves were forced to do so against the synagogue walls, not in the toilets, and they were physically abused while doing so," while the guards amused themselves by kicking them from behind.

Eventually, the synagogue was set on fire. "If it had been up to me," one of the SS men told Flehinger, "you would have perished in that fire." As it blazed, the Jews were forced to run the gauntlet through a jeering mob to a waiting bus, which took them to the railway station. There, they were put aboard a train from Freiburg. They had no idea where they were going until, after Karlsruhe, the train branched off toward Stuttgart and Munich. Then they guessed their destination—Dachau, where special stocks of striped blue-and-white drill suits with their Star of David on the left breast had already been made, ready for the influx.

Although it was the home of Naziism, Munich seems to have set an example of comparative moderation in the pogrom, perhaps because it was better controlled than elsewhere. With Hitler himself in the city, together with so many of his Nazi party barons, events could not be left entirely to the lower orders, could not be allowed to get out of hand. And since Goebbels, the instigator of the whole affair, was also on the spot, there was less opportunity for orders to be misinterpreted, either deliberately or by accident. The whole thing, therefore, was done by the book.

The main synagogue in Munich had already been burned to the ground on June 9, 1938, in what could almost have been a rehearsal for the big event. Those that remained were torched efficiently and enthusiastically now. The first burning synagogue, in Herzog-Rudolfstrasse, was reported to the city fire department as early as two minutes after midnight, and five fire engines were sent to the scene, as the fire chief feared "the highest danger of explosion." The fire was spreading to the neighboring Jewish schoolhouse, but when the firefighters tried to stop this, the SA cut off their hoses and fed the fire with gasoline. Over the next two or three hours, the brigade fought four more fires, in two big businesses near the Marienplatz, in the main Jewish community center, and in the villa of a Jewish manufacturer that was burned down to its foundations as SA men drove away neighbors who hurried out to help. Meanwhile, other businesses and homes were being systematically wrecked. The *Münchner Neuesten Nachrichten* of November 11 proudly published an impressive list of stores and businesses—which included Hitler's favorite art and antique dealers, Bernheimer, although the führer is said by one of his adjutants to have ordered special protection for this store.

The first death in Munich was reported to Goebbels shortly before 2:00

A.M. According to evidence given to the party inquiry later, he told his informant "not to get so worked up about the death of a Jew. In the next days, thousands more would kick the bucket." Nevertheless, with telephone calls pouring in to Hitler's private apartment from all over the city from private citizens complaining about fires, destruction, and looting, it was clearly impossible for him or his party hierarchy to distance themselves from what was happening, and something had to be done.

In fact, Hitler could hardly have failed to be aware of what was going on. He must have been able to hear the SA men on the streets outside his window, and the police and fire engines charging around the city, to say nothing of the fires themselves, for major fires are always very noisy. He must, too, have been able to see the glow from the fires lighting up the night sky. And in any case, he had actually been out in the streets at midnight, attending the annual swearing-in ceremony for SS recruits on the Odeonsplatz, accompanied by Himmler. The Munich police chief and commander of all SS in the south of Germany, Obergruppenführer (General) Friedrich Karl von Eberstein, had received news as he was leaving for the Odeonsplatz that the first synagogue was ablaze, as was Schloss Planegg, home of the Jewish Baron Hirsch. By the time Hitler drove back to his apartment after the ceremony, the pogrom was already in full swing.

Nevertheless, soon after 2:00 A.M., Hitler is reported to have sent for Eberstein and to have told him to restore order at once. He also sent out his own adjutant, Julius Schaub, and other members of his personal staff, to see that looting and arson were stopped. At 2:16 A.M., the head office of the Gestapo in Munich ordered plainclothes agents to move around in the demonstrations to prevent looting, and forty minutes later Rudolf Hess's office issued an order forbidding any further arson of business premises.

These precautions appear to have worked. "There was little looting," the British acting consul general, Wolston Weld-Forrester, reported, "and no man-hunting, so far as I can ascertain, while the wrecking of Jewish shops and the attacks on Jewish property had almost entirely ceased by the time people began to go out on their lawful occasions on the morning of 10 November. The populace, in fact, seems to have taken very little part in the manifestations here."

To some party chiefs, the low-key nature of the pogrom in Munich was a grave disappointment. The Munich gauleiter, Interior Minister Adolf Wagner, called twenty mass meetings in the city on the evening of November 11, "to protest against world Jewry." "He doubtless felt," Weld-Forrester remarked, "that the people of Munich had not sufficiently recorded, or had not been afforded an adequate opportunity to record, their reaction to the murder of Herr vom Rath." As an aside, Weld-Forrester noted that "not a few Jewish shops" had been "overlooked" during the action, and a number of Aryan-owned properties were half-wrecked before the mistake was realized. Tongue-in-cheek, he suggested that the fact that the "manifestations" took place in the darkness of the small hours might account for these errors and omissions. Wagner, however, clearly suspected that a lack of popular enthusiasm may have been to blame, and that mass meetings might help to rekindle the fires in Munich's belly. He made a rousing speech to an audience of several thousands in the Circus Krone, which was also broadcast to the other meetings, justifying the pogrom and rejoicing that it had provided the opportunity to get rid of the last synagogues, to close down all Jewish businesses, and to arrest the Jews, "which was promised long ago."

The arrests had not been affected by the orders to cool things down in Munich, and went on over the next few days, with male Jews being held at police headquarters and in the old royal palace of the Wittelsbach monarchy, before making the short journey to Dachau, just outside the city. At the same time, Jews were given up to forty-eight hours to evacuate Munich and Upper Bavaria, and to hand over the keys of their homes, shops, and garages to the local Nazi party leaders.

Those orders were subsequently rescinded, but Wagner continued to satisfy his greed in other ways. On November 10, he told the Bavarian minister president that there would certainly, if spasmodically, be plunder to come, and by no means only from Munich itself. And in his official report on the action, in itself a remarkable piece of whitewashing, he informed the head of the party chancellery, Martin Bormann, that there had been no looting or pilfering from Jewish stores: "Not even a single piece of food was taken, although it was lying out in the open." He then, without any apparent sense of irony, went on to say, "Since it could not be foreseen how far the action against the Jews would continue, both in general and against Jewish residences, I have ordered that works of culture and art found in Jewish property should be safeguarded." The word he used, "*sichergestellt*," also means "confiscated," a double entendre that must have appealed to him. The order was carried out by groups of SS men accompanied by art experts from the state museum who went along to evaluate anything that was found.

In Munich, as elsewhere, most shops obeyed instructions to post notices in their windows saying ENTRANCE FORBIDDEN TO JEWS, making it impossible for Jews to buy food or provisions. But this was soon found to be unworkable, and the notices were taken down, while an announcement in the press stated that arrangements had been made for Jews to buy the necessities of life in special *Verkaufstelle,* sales points, though in fact these were never established.

Nuremberg, principal city of Franconia, the northern half of the state of Bavaria, occupied a special place in Nazi mythology. The city of the Meistersingers and the shoemaker-poet Hans Sachs (who was not an invention of Richard Wagner but a real person), birthplace of Albrecht Dürer, the brass gun lock, and the clarinet, Nuremberg was the setting for the grandiose Nazi rallies. The 1935 laws against the Jews had been formulated and passed there. Its gauleiter, Julius Streicher, was the leading anti-Semite in the whole of the Reich, the publisher of *Der Stürmer,* the most rabid anti-Jewish hate sheet ever printed. If anyone could be expected to revel in the opportunities presented by a pogrom, Streicher could. And yet he slept through most of it.

Although it is known that the Nazi leaders in Nuremberg had been warned on the morning of November 9 "to stand by for action against the Jews," Streicher was asleep in bed late that night when he was woken by the regional SA commander, Hans Günther von Obernitz, who told him orders had come from Munich to start the pogrom. Streicher, still half-asleep, was unmoved by the news. He yawned and said, "If Goebbels wants it, then that's all right by me." Then he rolled over and went back to sleep until morning.

Perhaps Streicher thought he had already done his bit. Thirteen weeks before, on August 10, he had personally driven the crane that had knocked the Star of David from the roof of the main Nuremberg synagogue as a symbolic start to its demolition. This had been decreed by the city council, the first forced sale of a synagogue in Germany, to be followed shortly afterward by similar sales in Munich and Dortmund. Perhaps he felt he could rely on Obernitz to do all that was needed, for Obernitz was his creature, constantly striving to prove his loyalty. During the Night of the Long Knives in 1934, when Hitler had supervised the murder of the entire leadership of the SA, which he saw as posing a threat to his power, Streicher had personally intervened with the führer to save Obernitz's life.

Obernitz was the kind of man Streicher understood, and approved of, a former Freikorps officer as coarse and brutal as himself. If a pogrom was wanted, then he was prepared to insure that Nuremberg's should be the most savage in all Germany. Under his direction, the SA and SS went berserk, smashing everything Jewish in sight, heaping the streets downtown with broken glass from the windows of Jewish stores. Then they turned on the Jews themselves.

The local police were taken by surprise by the events, and made themselves scarce. They did not even answer their telephones. Dr. Benno Martin, the police chief, seems to have had no warning of what was about to happen. He only returned from Munich in the early hours of November 10, found the city in chaos, and spent some time trying to establish whether Hitler had personally ordered the pogrom. As soon as the worst of the wrecking subsided, he sent out his men to arrest as many male Jews as they could find. This was basically for the protection of the Jews themselves. Destruction of property was one thing; but murder in the streets of Nuremberg could do serious damage to a police chief's reputation.

The burgermeister of Nuremberg, Willy Liebel, is alleged to have been most unhappy about the degree of violence involved. Nevertheless, he ordered the city's hospitals to refuse to admit any injured Jews, which left police stations and Jewish hospitals as the only places where Jews could receive treatment.

Nine Jews in all were murdered in twenty-four hours of violence. They included Jacob Spaeth, beaten to death; Nathan Langstadt, found in his bath with his throat cut; Paul Lebrecht, flung from the window of his home, so that his body was found dangling from the railings of a balcony; Paul Astruck, whose half-naked body was found mutilated in a wood; another, unnamed man, flung repeatedly down his own staircase until he was dead. Ten suicides were reported, half of them women.

Old-fashioned, gangster-style extortion was also practiced on a considerable scale. A number of Jews reported that they had been forced to sign over their property at a tenth of its value or less, on pain of death. Once they had signed, they were told that it was a mere formality and they were to be shot. Then, having been held at pistol-point for four hours, they were released. The wives of certain Jewish property owners, too, were summoned to the headquarters of the Deutsche Arbeits Front (National Workers Organization) to make over their property to the party. They were kept waiting for six hours. Every time an Aryan passed through the room where they sat, they were ordered to get to their feet. Every hour, they were made to chant in chorus, "The Jew, Grynzspan, shot an honorable German with a cowardly murderer's hand. We belong to the same rabble."

By November 14, the local party had acquired much of the Jewish property in Nuremberg—569 pieces of land and buildings were recorded as being sold in under a month. These included such items as a synagogue worth in excess of 100,000 Reichsmarks sold for RM100. It was later estimated that the difference between the real value and the sale value of all the property Streicher and his cronies had acquired amounted to a staggering 21 million Reichsmarks ($8.4 million).

Ironically, the pogrom was to be the principal cause of Streicher's fall from power. He had simply become too greedy and had not bothered to use any of this Jewish windfall to buy off his masters in Berlin. He also made the mistake of making a mortal enemy of Göring when he put about the story that the field marshal was impotent and that his daughter, Edda, had been conceived by artificial insemination. Göring retaliated by sending a commission to Franconia to examine Streicher's business activities. As a result, Streicher was dismissed from his party posts in 1940.

It is clear from the police reports that there had been massive damage to property in Nuremberg. Seventy shops were destroyed, including one owned by Aryans, which seems to have been burned down by accident, and 256 homes were damaged or destroyed.

Würzburg, which lies on an axis between Frankfurt-am-Main and Nuremberg, is a great wine center. In 1938, it was an attractive town, full of rococo architecture and with a fine baroque ducal *Residenz* with a famous ceiling painted by Tiepolo and said to contain the finest rococo interior in Europe. In the shops in Würzburg in 1938, one could buy what was described as a "topical and extremely amusing" new board game for two to six players. The game was suitable for grown-ups and children and was played with dice, six little figures (one for each player), and thirty-six hats. What the hats were for is not clear. The game, however, was called *JUDEN RAUS!* ("Jews Out").

The Würzburg pogrom was organized by the kreisleiter (district Nazi party leader) Franz Xaver Knaup, and was a model of its type. Storm troopers and members of the 81st SS Standarte (Regiment) set fire to the synagogue in Domerschulestrasse, while Jewish businesses and stores suffered particularly from the attentions of the mob. Among those helping in the destruction was the rector of Würzburg University.

In reporting the incident, the local newspapers omitted to mention that there had been at least one death and three suicides. Sixty-three-year-old Ernst Lebermann, a Jewish wine merchant, was in bed when the SA burst into his home. His housekeeper, who was Aryan, tried to defend him, but she was thrown downstairs for her pains and called "*Judenschickse*" ("Jew's whore"). Lebermann was beaten up and marched away to the headquarters of the local Nazi party ward for South Würzburg. Later he was taken to the police station in the Schillerschule. They passed him on to the local courthouse jail, where several other Jews were being held in custody. He had a stroke in his cell and was taken to the Jewish hospital, where he died at 4:40 P.M. that day.

He was not the only one to die in Würzburg. In despair at the arrest of their husbands, three Jewish women committed suicide: Frau Friedmann jumped out of the window of her home into the courtyard below, Frau Katzmann drowned herself in the river Main, and Frau Klara Rosenthall took poison.

In some places, the pogrom had a less tragic outcome. Eichstätt is a pretty little town standing amid romantic scenery on the banks of the river Altmühl, roughly midway between Nuremberg and Munich, twenty-four kilometers west of the autobahn linking the two cities. The town is famous for the fossils found in the local limestone quarries, among them the first ever example of *archeopteryx lithographica*, a small, feathered creature, the earliest link between birds and reptiles, discovered in 1861. Very few Jews lived in Eichstätt—never more than ten families, all solidly middle class and well-integrated into the community. After the 1935 Nuremberg Laws, however, which drastically limited Jewish economic activity, they began to leave the town, and by November 1938 there was only one family left.

At 5:00 A.M. on November 10, the Landsrat (county clerk), Dr. Georg Roth, learned that the SA were planning to cleanse the town of the last remaining Jews. Although a member of the Nazi party—curiously, he was one of the few high-ranking civil servants in Bavaria who *were* Nazis—Roth evidently did not welcome the news. A little later, on hearing a commotion in the street, he called on the local police to restore order immediately. The police found a group of twenty men trying to break into the home of the Jewish family, and soon put a stop to it. The recently appointed kreisleiter, a local schoolteacher called Haberl, was called to the scene. He agreed that the Jews, instead of being beaten up, would be placed in police custody.

Clearly, the family could no longer stay in Eichstätt, but where were they to go? It transpired that they had relatives in Augsburg, so Landsrat Roth arranged for them to go there. However, he failed to consult the Eichstätt stationmaster, who refused outright to sell them train tickets. In the end, Landsrat Roth himself was forced to hire a taxi to drive them the 100 kilometers to their relatives' home.

There are many stories of small acts of kindness, even heroism, by ordinary German people who went out of their way to protect their Jewish friends and neighbors. Emil and Charlotte Rotschild, for example, lived in an apartment in the small Thuringian town of Tiefenort. On the night of November 9–10, they were aroused from their beds by the sounds of breaking glass and shouting and the crunch of hobnailed boots in the street below. They guessed that the SA were searching for Jews. Suddenly, there was a loud banging at the front door of the building. Startled, they rushed out of their apartment and peered over the banisters of the central stairway. They could hear more banging at the door and shouts of "Open up there!" At any moment, the mob would break in. Then the door of the apartment above opened, and their neighbor Herr Hüter leaned over the banisters and called them to come up. Still in their bare feet, the Rotschilds ran upstairs. A moment later, the front door was smashed and the mob poured into the building. They broke into the Rotschilds' apartment and began to smash up everything. Frau Hüter ran to the window and shouted to the crowd to be quiet. She recognized someone and yelled, "Ah, I see the mayor's son is taking part."

In the face of Frau Hüter, the crowd soon departed.

Many small German officials also did their best to ease the plight of the Jews. In Düsseldorf, for example, the burgermeister, Dr. Lehr, and the general manager of the local steelworks, Herr Poensgen, are both remembered to this day for their kindness. Police officers, like Herr Kühn of Hamburg, often revealed great courage and humanity. Herr Kühn was responsible for arranging the release of several Jews from concentration camps—even though their emigration papers were not in order.

Some Germans who helped Jews also suffered. The wife and son of Professor Paul Kahle, a noted Arabist who taught at Bonn University, helped their friend Emilie Goldstein to clean up her shop after the mob had wrecked it. They were made the victims of a smear campaign, and ultimately were forced to emigrate to Britain.

Although there were many such acts of courage and kindness shown to Jews by individual Germans, there were also individual acts of betrayal. Fear of the Nazis, fear of the consequences of their generosity, sometimes led people to betray their friends.

In Dresden, a Jew found sanctuary in the home of some Gentile acquaintances. They were a couple he had known for some time, and he thought he would be safe with them, for a little while at least. He and his hosts were very careful and took all possible precautions so that he would not be seen by the neighbors. After a couple of days, the situation in the streets seemed to have eased somewhat, and he decided to take a walk. When he returned to the house, he found two Gestapo men waiting to arrest him. One of the men was a relative of his host's wife. She had betrayed him.

It would be wrong to suggest that the pogrom occurred with equal ferocity in every town and every village in the Reich. In villages, in particular, the action was patchy and frequently nonexistent. There were many reasons for this—one of them obviously being that most Jews lived in urban areas rather than country villages. But there were other factors as well. In some villages there was a serious shortage of keen, card-carrying party and SA members, and without them it was simply not possible to have a successful pogrom.

Peasants, as a rule, do not usually have time for such practices, unless locally organized, and then they might have many reasons for the persecution, none of them ideological. Moreover, pogroms and the like were generally organized by foreigners—which meant, in effect, anyone who came from more than thirty kilometers away from the village—and were therefore suspect. To many Bavarian peasants in the 1930's, for example, when transport was not as easy as it is today, Munich could have been on the dark side of the moon for all the relevance it had in their lives. Not surprisingly, many remote villages remained laws unto themselves, even at the height of Hitler's power.

The village of Warmsried is a good example. Nestling in the foothills of the Alps in the southern corner of Swabia, it has been described as "solidly Catholic and solidly Swabian"—which means its inhabitants did not take kindly to outside interference. From 1930, the village was run by its priest, the formidable Father Andreas Rampp, and its burgermeister, Johann Huber, a devout Catholic and one of the shrewdest of the local peasant landowners. So powerful was the influence of the two men that between 1932 and 1933, when the National Socialist vote rose dramatically throughout the rest of Germany, it actually fell in Warmsried. There were virtually no party members in the village before 1933, and between then and 1945, the local party was able to hold only three or four meetings in twelve years. As for the SA, anyone wanting to join the organization had to go to neighboring villages—because of the priest's opposition, they were not allowed to form a unit in Warmsried itself. The burgermeister saw to it that there were no Nazi women's associations, while Father Rampp forbade the holding of any charity drives or functions intended to aid the party cause. Astonishingly, the swastika was not allowed to be displayed, nor were any of the national holidays sacred to the party—January 20, May 1, or November 9—ever celebrated in the village. And as for organizing a pogrom without Father Rampp's permission, that was totally out of the question.

The village did have a small Jewish population, but on the night of November 9, 1938, they were not harmed. In addition to the fear of Father Rampp and Burgermeister Huber, and the refusal to be told what to do by some foreigner in Munich, there was also a strong practical element in the villagers' decision. The economy of Warmsried depended on the local sawmill, and the engineer there was a Jew, a refugee from persecution in a neighboring town. If he was killed or driven out, the mill would be forced to shut down. In the event, he survived not only the pogrom, but also the entire war in safety.

Warmsried was not the only village to avoid the pogrom because its parish priest and mayor were strongly anti-Nazi. A few others, such as Derching and Laimering in Bavaria, followed the same course. In others, the local SA simply did not have the stomach for the job, and the local party was forced to hire thugs from outside to come in and break Jewish windows.

But most villages were not so squeamish. Hoengen, a small community near Aachen on the Belgian frontier, had only a tiny Jewish population, but they had built their own synagogue on the meadow owned by a butcher, Michael Lucas. Lucas's house was opposite the meadow, and he watched helplessly from a window, restrained by his wife, who clung to him and prevented him rushing out to certain death, as the storm troopers arrived. Lucas's nephew, Eric, later recounted what had happened:

After a while, the stormtroopers were joined by people who were not in uniform; and suddenly, with one loud cry of "Down with the Jews," the gathering outside produced axes and heavy sledgehammers. They advanced towards the little synagogue which stood in Michael's own meadow, opposite his house. They burst the door open, and the whole crowd, by now shouting and laughing, stormed into the little house of God.

Michael, standing behind the tightly drawn curtains, saw how the crowd tore the Holy Ark wide open; and three men who had smashed the Ark threw the Scrolls of the Law of Moses out. He threw them—these Scrolls, which had stood in their quiet dignity, draped in blue or wine-red velvet, with their little crowns of silver covering the tops of the shafts by which the Scroll was held during the service—to the screaming and shouting mass of people which had filled the little synagogue.

The people caught the Scrolls as if they were amusing themselves with a ball-game—tossing them up in the air again, while other people flung them further back until they reached the street outside. Women tore away the red and blue velvet and everybody tried to snatch some of the silver adorning the Scrolls.

Naked and open, the Scrolls lay in the muddy autumn lane; children stepped on them and others tore pieces from the fine parchment on which the Law was written—the same Law which the people who tore it apart had, in vain, tried to absorb for over a thousand years.

When the first Scroll was thrown out of the synagogue, Michael made a dash for the door . . . The stormtroopers, who still stood outside the house watching with stern faces over the tumultuous crowd which obeyed their commands without really knowing it, would have shot the man, quietly, in an almost matter of fact way. Michael's wife, sensing the deadly danger, clung to him, imploring him and begging him not to go outside. Michael tried to fling her aside, but only her tenacious resistance brought him back to his senses. He stood there, in the small hall behind the front door, looking around him for a second, as if he did not know where he was. Suddenly, he leaned against the wall, tears streaming from his eyes, like those of a little child.

After a while, he heard the sound of many heavy hammers outside. With trembling legs he got up from his chair and looked outside once more. Men had climbed on to the roof of the synagogue, and were hurling the tiles down, others were cutting the cross beams as soon as they were bare of cover. It did not take long before the first heavy grey stones came tumbling down, and the children of the village amused themselves flinging stones into the multi-coloured windows.

When the first rays of a cold and pale November sun penetrated the heavy dark clouds, the little synagogue was but a heap of stone, broken glass and smashed-up woodwork. Where the two well-cared-for flower beds had flanked both sides of the gravel path leading to the door of the synagogue, the children had lit a bonfire and the parchment of the Scrolls gave enough food for the flames to eat up the smashed up benches and doors, and the wood which only the day before had been the Holy Ark for the Scrolls of the Law of Moses.

In the newly acquired regions of Greater Germany—Austria and the Sudetenland—the pogrom was particularly savage, as their Nazis sought to affirm their allegiance to Hitler and the Reich. In Danzig, still a free city at that time but coming increasingly under Nazi German control, the pogrom was delayed until the night of November 11–12. The Danzig SA added a refinement of their own to the horrors being inflicted on the Jews: While the synagogues were being torched, they imprisoned local Jews in their homes by nailing planks of wood across their doors.

For the Viennese, however, it was necessary to try harder to make November 9–10 a notable event, for they had had their own pogrom earlier in the year, in the days and weeks immediately following the *Anschluss* of March 13, 1938. Then, according to eyewitnesses such as William L. Shirer, the behavior of the Vienna Nazis had been almost unbelievable, "an orgy of sadism" worse than anything seen until then in Germany itself, as Jewish men and women were beaten up, robbed, made to scrub old political slogans in favor of the deposed chancellor, Schuschnigg, off the pavements, and to clean public toilets and the latrines of the SS and SA barracks. Thousands were imprisoned, their possessions and homes confiscated.

Anti-Jewish activities had continued throughout 1938, with the Nazi coffers being swelled by the savings of thousands of Jews, the cost of freedom paid to the Central Office of Jewish Emigration, under the direction of Adolf Eichmann. A month before the November pogrom, there had been what could almost be regarded as a dry run, in the evening of October 5, when bands of SA men raided houses and apartments occupied by Jews in the eighteenth, nineteenth, and twentieth districts of Vienna. They informed the occupants that they must leave their homes at once and be out of the country within twenty-four hours. There was no time to wait—trains were waiting at the West Railway Station ready to take them away. Not surprisingly, this created a panic among Jews. But when they approached the police, they discovered that the authorities knew nothing about any compulsory evacuation. It was clearly a vicious joke. According to the British consul general in Vienna, D. St. Clair Gainer, a group of Austrian SA men who had just been released after national service had decided to teach Viennese Jews a lesson. They felt that during the *Anschluss* crisis Jews had failed to demonstrate a proper regard for the Third Reich. The upshot of the whole episode was that, as a punishment for their prank, some thirty-five Austrian SA men were sent to Dachau.

On November 9, the pogrom proper was organized by the Austrian SA, who went about their business in full uniform. As in one or two other parts of Germany, the order to wear civilian clothes does not seem to have got through to them.

During the early hours of November 10, synagogues and other Jewish places of worship—the *Völkischer Beobachter* claimed no fewer than nineteen synagogues in all—were set on fire. The synagogue in Leopoldstrasse was blown up, causing considerable damage to surrounding property. At one point, thanks to the efforts of the SA, the situation got so bad and the Viennese Fire Department was under such pressure putting out fires, that there was a real danger of a general conflagration in the city. After the synagogues, Jewish shops and businesses were next on the list. Later, Josef Bürckel, Nazi gauleiter of Austria, officially extended the actions to all houses occupied by Jews, ordering that they should be searched for weapons and illegal literature. This led to thousands of Jews being arrested.

"Vienna presented an extraordinary spectacle," wrote Gainer, "with fires raging all over the city and Jews being hustled along the streets, cursed at and assaulted by crowds of hooligans."

Soon lines of desperate people formed outside the British and U.S. consulates, prepared to wait all night in the hope of getting their applications in first thing the following morning. Four times the police drove them away from the British consulate. The scenes outside the U.S. consulate were even more violent: Gangs of SA men waded in among the crowd wielding ropes' ends—until the U.S. consul demanded that the police put a stop to such brutality.

The Vienna correspondent of *The Times* was arrested twice by the police by mistake. On one of his visits to the police station, he saw terrified Jews cowering in corners and one old Jew with a white beard being savagely kicked by an SA man while the regular police looked on and did nothing.

The anti-Jewish demonstrations in Austria were not confined to Vienna, of course, but spread across the entire country. However, there were more Jews in the capital than in the whole of the rest of Austria, and the worst excesses took place there: Many Jews were attacked with iron bars and suffered broken limbs, and at least eight were actually beaten to death; five thousand Jewish-owned shops were wrecked and closed down, and only one of the city's twenty-one synagogues and prayer houses was not set on fire. That was the central synagogue, next to the Roman Catholic Cathedral of St. Stephen, where records were held of all Viennese Jews that were useful to the authorities in identifying them.

While this was going on, there were some fifty attempted suicides by Jews in Vienna, no fewer than twenty-one of them successful. Among them was Professor Philip Freud, a relative of Sigmund, a chronic invalid in his sixties, who had been beaten up in his bed.

As the violence finally exhausted itself, Goebbels issued a statement to the world through his Ministry of Public Enlightenment and Propaganda. The outrages, he said, were "the justified and understandable indignation of the German people at the cowardly assassination of a German diplomat." He denied that there had been any plundering or looting: "In a few isolated cases, perhaps, old women made off with small trinkets or pieces of wearing apparel, to be used as Christmas presents. There was no robbery, or intention to rob."

Göring added his own touch of fantasy: "No Jew had a hair of his head touched," he claimed. "Thanks to the outstanding discipline of the German people, only a few windows were broken in the riots."

Echoing the cynicism of their chieftains, the rank-and-file Nazis swiftly found a suitable label for their night of vengeance, one that mocked and belittled the terrible events that had taken place. They called it *Kristallnacht*, or Crystal Night—the Night of Broken Glass.

The Camps

Like most young Jews in Vienna, Herbert Finkelstein was unemployed. He managed to earn a little money, however, by giving English lessons to other Jews who were eager to emigrate—everyone wanted to learn English, the open-sesame to a new life in Britain or the United States. The classes usually numbered about twenty students, and were held in a basement in the ninth district of the city, not far from the Finkelstein family's apartment.

On the morning of Thursday, November 10, the class had just started when a group of men in plainclothes burst in and ordered everyone to accompany them to the police station. They were reasonably polite, and it seemed like just another routine inquiry. But after the students had been held for about two hours in the police station, it became clear that the situation was anything but routine. A band of steel-helmeted SS men arrived in one of their notorious "commando" vans, forced the Jews into the van, and drove them off to what appeared to Finkelstein to be the stable to a large barracks. Here, they found hundreds of others, who had been rounded up from various parts of the city.

All through the night, the prisoners were kept standing. No one was allowed to sit or to lie down. It was not until the next evening that they were given their first food—a quarter-loaf of black bread, apparently provided by a Jewish welfare organization. Then they were moved again, this time to the jail attached to the city court, where they were kept in the corridors, as there was no room in the cells. Here, for the first time, their belongings were examined. Finkelstein was taking a course in bookbinding, in order to have a trade when he emigrated, and had his tools with him, rolled up in his overalls. They included a sharp bookbinder's knife. When one of the guards discovered this, he waved it in the young man's face, accusing him of planning to use it on his jailers, then took a pair of scissors and cut a broad furrow through his hair to brand him as a criminal.

Shortly afterward, they were driven to a school in the Kenyongasse, where they were told that they had been arrested as a reprisal against international Jewry for the assassination of Ernst vom Rath. For thirty-six hours, they were held in the school building, while the various shifts of SS guards amused themselves with them. Some they made run the gauntlet between two ranks of SS men who kicked them or hit them with their rifle butts as they passed. Others were taken down into the cellars and beaten up. One guard decided that an elderly Jew needed to be punished, and ordered one of Finkelstein's friends, an amateur boxer called Paul Schneider, to punch him in the face. Schneider slapped the old man, but was himself hit and given a black eye by the guard until he punched the old man with his full weight. When the guards changed at 6:00 A.M., prisoners were made to wash the blood off the walls of the corridors and cellars before the next shift took over.

After another day of this treatment, the prisoners were taken under police guard to the railway station, where they were herded into cattle trucks, locked and bolted in, and hauled off into the night toward an unknown destination. The journey, without food, water, or toilet facilities, lasted a day and a half. Eventually, filthy, starving, and frightened, they were unloaded at a rail siding near Munich, lined up, and marched toward a huge gateway. Above it was inscribed the legend ARBEIT MACHT FREI, "Work Makes Free." They had arrived at Dachau. The second phase of the November pogrom had begun.

Herbert Finkelstein's experience was shared by thousands of other Jewish men across the entire Reich during the week following Kristallnacht, as the Gestapo and the SS quickly achieved their target of arresting thirty thousand Jews. Indeed, they were almost too energetic, even for Heydrich and Himmler, casting their net wider than instructed in their enthusiasm for their task, so that the whole system threatened to collapse under the strain.

On November 11, an urgent message was flashed to all police areas, ordering, "All Jewish women and children arrested in the course of the action are to be released at once, unless specific reasons exist for their continued arrest." The following day, Gestapo headquarters in Berlin was having to send out another urgent teleprint:

TO ALL STATE POLICE HEADQUARTERS AND BRANCH OFFICES
The Buchenwald concentration camp is filled to capacity with current deliveries. Therefore, further transfers to Buchenwald are to be canceled, with the exception of transports already under way. To prevent errors, this HQ will

be informed well in advance of transfers to the Dachau and Sachsenhausen camps.

On the next day, November 13, there were no arrests at all—not because of any weakening of intent, but simply because it was Sunday, a day of rest for German bureaucrats. On Monday, they started up again in earnest, and by the middle of the week, all three of the camps to which the Jews were sent were overflowing. Buchenwald, built on a hill called Ettenberg, near Weimar, reputedly around Goethe's favorite oak tree, had taken 9,845 Jewish men from central Germany; 10,911, mainly from southern Germany and Austria, went to Dachau, on the outskirts of Munich; between 9,000 and 10,000 from Prussia and the Baltic seabord went to Sachsenhausen, near Oranienburg, some 30 kilometers northwest of Berlin.

New building programs had been started at both Buchenwald and Sachsenhausen in September 1938, to extend the accommodation so that they could take more prisoners. At about the same time, in the prison workshops of Dachau, prisoners had been kept busy sewing Stars of David on thousands of blue-and-white striped camp uniforms. By November, preparations in the camps were well advanced. Nevertheless, when the arrests began, the sheer numbers arriving in such a short space of time threatened to overwhelm the organization.

Sachsenhausen normally held some sixty-five hundred prisoners altogether, so the sudden influx increased the camp population by no less than 150 percent within two or three days. Huts designed to hold 40 men had over 150 sleeping on straw. In Buchenwald, the new arrivals were crammed into five "emergency huts," around which an electrified fence was erected to separate them from the other prisoners—Bible students, Jehovah's Witnesses, political prisoners, and common criminals. More than two thousand Jews were packed into each two hundred-foot by eighty-foot hut. In Dachau, it was a similar story.

Soon Dr. Grawitz, chief of the SS Health Department, was asking the Finance Ministry for additional funds to improve sanitary conditions, since, as a result of "the many recent arrests made on the führer's instructions, the concentration camps were so crowded that the situation verged on the intolerable. An epidemic," he said, "might break out at any time."

Heydrich was already alarmed. On November 16, he sent out an order that all Jews who were over sixty years of age, or sick or physically handicapped, were to be released at once. A week later, he followed this up with a distinctly tetchy message: "Numerous reports indicate that

Gestapo offices have not paid sufficient attention to my flash order of November 10, 1938 . . . Jews up to the age of eighty and obviously ill, feebleminded, etc., have been sent to camps. . . ." Clearly, the party leadership realized that the situation was getting out of hand. The intention had been to take rich and well-off Jews and hold them to ransom until they agreed to sign over their possessions and leave the country. By grabbing every male Jew they could lay their hands on, the rank and file of the SS were threatening to spoil the whole plan.

Himmler's orders had also stipulated that those arrested were not to be ill-treated—presumably, he wanted them to be in a reasonable condition when they left the country. Given the nature of the concentration camp regime, however, and the deliberately degraded character of those who operated it at every level, there was never the remotest chance of this order being obeyed. In any case, the accepted form of leaders issuing ambiguous instructions, expecting them to be exceeded, was far too well established for the SS men to believe Himmler or Heydrich could really mean what they said. Orders specifying moderation must surely be for public consumption only, not for real.

The arrests were normally carried out correctly, even politely, in most places—the arresting officers were, after all, members of the SS and Gestapo, always eager to demonstrate their superiority over the undisciplined rabble of the SA. The brutality did not begin until the prisoners were safely out of sight, and was generally regarded as merely a way of alleviating boredom. When the Jews reached the camps, however, the situation changed abruptly.

Twenty-year-old Gerd Treuhaft, the son of a Christian father and a Jewish mother, was already interned in Buchenwald on a charge of treason when the Kristallnacht Jews began to arrive. "We saw motor buses driving up one after the other," he recalled fifty years later, "full of Jews who had been arrested because of the murder [of Ernst vom Rath]. While they were hurried from the buses, the guards tripped them up and rained on them kicks and blows from fists and rifle butts. Lying on the road we saw broken glasses, pocketbooks, watches and rings, and many pools of blood. During the next five or six days, Jews arrived continuously at Buchenwald. Buses drove up day and night."

One of those on the buses, Dr. Georg Wilde, reported, "We had to run . . . to a square not far from the main gate. On our way we had to pass between two rows of SS troopers armed with whips, some of which seemed to be fitted with barbed wire or pieces of lead. One trooper, perched on a platform to one side of the gate, swung a great whip down on the heads of passers-by beneath."

The London *News Chronicle* reported in graphic detail the reception meted out to a group of sixty-two Jews, including two rabbis, at Sachsenhausen. At the gate, they were handed over by their police escort to SS camp guards, who forced them to run the gauntlet of spades, whips and clubs. An eyewitness described how the police, "unable to bear their cries, turned their backs." As the Jews were beaten, they fell. As they fell, they were beaten more. This orgy of violence lasted half an hour. When it was over, "twelve of the sixty-two were dead, their skulls smashed. The others were all unconscious. The eyes of some had been knocked out, their faces flattened and shapeless."

Prisoners who survived the reception committee at the gates were then marched to the *Appelplatz*, the central square of the camp where roll calls were held, and made to stand to attention until they were processed. This could take some time—the guards were in no hurry. In Sachsenhausen, for example, prisoners were kept standing at attention out in the open, in temperatures well below freezing, without food or water, for up to twenty hours, until at last the guards were ready to take down their details. Their heads were then shaved, they were stripped and put through the showers, and eventually given the blue-and-white concentration camp uniform: a cap, a pair of socks, underwear, a shirt, a jacket, trousers, and a towel.

Another survivor, Kurt Hirschberg, told friends of his own experience: "You had to stand in ranks for fifteen hours, in groups of three hundred, lined up like Prussian recruits. Hat in hand. Valuables in your hat. Fifteen hours. Nothing to eat. Nothing to drink. Not a single chance to step out of ranks. Three men died that night, of heart attacks and urine poisoning. It was bad . . . Bad . . . Very, very bad.

"It's bad to sleep in overcrowded barracks, packed together like sardines in a tin. If one man turns over in his sleep, one hundred seventy-five others have to turn with him. The straw bedding rustles. The man next to you groans. One hundred seventy-five men, knee to knee, arm to arm. You aren't asleep, you aren't awake; you lie as if you were stunned. It's bad . . . It's bad, it's awfully bad."

For some, it was even worse. Gerd Treuhaft remembers what happened to them: "On the first night, SS guards entered, picked Jews at random, took them outside to be whipped with steel rods, or battered to death with clubs. Throughout the night we heard shots and cries of mortal terror."

Some did not wait for the guards to kill them. "The following morning I saw the corpses of two suicides," says Georg Wilde. "One of them had thrown himself against the electrified barbed wire; the other had died from a guard's bullet."

Treuhaft confirms such tragedies with his own memories: "Many Jews, driven half-insane and unable to bear the hellish conditions, ran against the electric wire. The guards in the machine-gun tower opened fire. Other Jews broke window panes to cut their arteries; some fell into the latrine in darkness to suffocate.

"We were next to the emergency huts, and evening after evening 'camp seniors'—the inmates placed in charge of the block—came in and ordered us to take buckets of food to our so-called "comrades of race," and to fetch in the dead. Behind one hut was a dirty room known as the 'wash house,' where daily we removed dead Jews. We saw Jews lying on the floor, or on palliasses and blankets; we heard them moaning, we saw their faces and heads clotted with blood from the beatings, their eyes swollen and purple. Many were dead or dying, many others were going mad. They could not get a glass of water, let alone any medicine.

"Each evening, three comrades and I removed one corpse each. He who has looked at such misery cannot be afraid of anything anymore."

The camps to which the November Jews were taken were neither intended nor equipped as "death camps." They were established to provide "protective custody" for opponents of the regime and those who had broken Reich laws, and in the process to supply forced labor for quarries and brickworks turning out materials for Hitler's grand building projects. There were few Jewish prisoners held in the camps simply because they were Jews—Kristallnacht was the turning point in that respect. And there were no gas chambers or crematoria—the policy of extermination had not yet been formulated.

The first camp had been opened in March 1933, following the burning down of the Reichstag, the German Parliament Building in Berlin, on February 27. Using the perpetual German fear of public disorder as a lever, Hitler, who had only been chancellor since January 30, had persuaded the ailing president Hindenburg to sign an emergency decree "For the Protection of the People and the State," which effectively suspended all civil liberties. Göring had promptly rounded up four thousand communists, who were blamed for the fire, though it had in fact been started by Göring's own henchmen, on his instructions. This was followed by a massive campaign of violence by the SA, in which thousands more opponents of the regime were arrested and imprisoned. Being the SA, they did not stop at political opponents, but took advantage of the opportunity to settle old scores. Often regardless of their political persuasion, people were dragged off to SA bunkers—disused warehouses, cellars, barns, whatever was available—where they were held, beaten up, and sometimes murdered. In the big cities, some SA groups simply indulged in plain, old-fashioned gangsterism, holding their prisoners until they had extorted a ransom from them. The police had orders not to interfere—a precedent that was to become a familiar feature of the Nazi regime.

Some of the bunkers later developed into full-fledged concentration camps, such as the SA camp at Oranienburg, near Berlin. But with so many prisoners on their hands in the spring of 1933, the Nazi authorities looked around for somewhere to put them. The solution that Heinrich Himmler, then police chief in Munich, came up with for his region was to take over the grounds and stone buildings of an old gunpowder factory at Dachau, and to concentrate some five thousand of his prisoners there. Turned into a permanent establishment, it became the model for all future concentration camps.

Within twelve weeks of the opening of the Dachau camp, the Munich Public Prosecutor's Office was called in to investigate the deaths of four inmates, and concluded that they had died as a result of torture by the camp guards. Two alleged suicides turned out to have been throttled; the brain hemorrhage that killed another was shown by a post mortem to have been caused by the traditional "blunt instrument." But the culprits were never brought to justice. Although charges were filed by the public prosecutor against the commandant, medical officer, and adjutant of the camp, Himmler succeeded by a variety of legal and political maneuvers in putting a stop to the proceedings, and to any future investigations of crimes committed in concentration camps. Thus, the pattern was set right from the start: The camps were under the control of the SS, whose word was law. Anything that went on in a camp was not the concern of the civilian legal authorities.

The commandant of Dachau, SS Oberführer Hilmar Wäkkerle, was fired, however, for his gross stupidity. He was replaced by Theodor Eicke, a psychopath who took to the job with great enthusiasm. Almost single-handedly, Eicke created the whole concentration camp system, replacing the casual sadism of his predecessor's time with an ordered, murderous brutality. He has been described as having "bureaucratized terror."

The regime in which the Kristallnacht Jews found themselves was laid down by Eicke, who had in 1934 been promoted to SS Gruppenführer (major-general) and appointed inspector of concentration camps and SS Guard Formations (SS Death's Head Formations). The regulations that he had laid down for Dachau had been extended to cover all concentration camps. In 1938 there were six in the Reich: the three major ones at Dachau, Buchenwald, and Sachsenhausen, plus two smaller establishments for about three thousand prisoners each at Mauthausen and Flossenbürg, all of which were for men only, and a women's camp at Lichtenburg.

Eicke's overriding philosophy was laid down in the opening words of his brief introduction to the published regulations. "Tolerance," he wrote, "means weakness. In the light of this conception, punishment will be mercilessly handed out whenever the interests of the Fatherland warrant it." Decent people, he explained, would not be affected by these regulations, but woe betide politicians and agitators who tried to incite troubles within the Reich: "Watch out that you are not caught, for otherwise it will be your neck and you will be dealt with according to your own methods."

The mildest punishment in the camps for any infringement of the regulations was three days' solitary confinement, and that was for such crimes as not immediately getting out of bed at reveille, or taking two helpings of food without permission. A man could get five days' solitary confinement just for sitting or lying on his bed during the day without permission. Eight days plus twenty lashes—"to be administered before and after the serving of the sentence"—could be inflicted on anyone failing to show appropriate respect to any member of the SS, or for similar offenses. For smoking in forbidden areas or leaving any building by any unauthorized entrance, etc., the sentence was two weeks' solitary confinement. Anyone who was found guilty of any kind of political agitation in the camp or who later told tales outside about what went on or who physically attacked any SS guard would be hanged, or in the latter case could be shot on the spot.

Fourteen days of strict arrest and twenty-five lashes at the beginning and end of the penalty period were the punishment of anyone who used letters or other means of communication to make derogatory remarks about National Socialist leaders, the state and the government, its agencies and institutions, or glorified Marxist or liberal leaders.

"Solitary confinement," the regulations declared, "will be in a cell, with a hard bed and with bread and water. The prisoner will receive warm food every four days. Physical work consists of severe physical or particularly dirty work, performed under close supervision. Incidental punishments are: drilling, beatings, withholding of mail and food, hard rest, tying to stakes, reprimands and warnings." Anyone sentenced to any form of confinement or punitive labor had his term of imprisonment automatically extended by at least eight weeks. Anyone who was put into solitary confinement would not be released for a considerable time.

Among the techniques of punishment Eicke tried out at Dachau was what was called "tree-hanging." The victim's hands were tied behind his back. He was then suspended by his wrists from a hook or large nail driven into a tree or post about six feet from the ground. All his weight was on his wrists and shoulders. Gradually, his shoulder bones would be pulled from their sockets. It was excruciatingly painful. Those who fainted were revived with buckets of cold water; those who cried out were whipped. Anyone who survived the torture was left a broken man, mentally and physically.

Eicke's regulations also covered the behavior of the guards:

> Anyone letting a prisoner escape will be arrested and handed over to the Bavarian Political Police for liberating prisoners through negligence.
>
> If a prisoner attempts to escape, he is to be shot without warning. The guard who has shot an escaping prisoner in the line of duty will not be punished.
>
> If a prisoner attacks a guard, the latter is to resist the attack not by physical force but by the use of his weapons. A guard disregarding this regulation must expect his immediate dismissal. In any case anyone who keeps his back covered will seldom have to worry about an attack.
>
> If a unit of prisoners mutinies or revolts, it is to be shot at by all supervising guards. Warning shots are forbidden on principle.

Work had to be carried out during the time allotted, and it was part of a guard's duties to insure that there was no shirking. Any guard who brought his prisoners back too early was guilty of serious dereliction of duty and could be dismissed.

Eicke's official camp notepaper carried the maxim "Only one thing matters: the command given." In other words, obedience was all. According to Rudolf Hoess, later commandant of the Auschwitz concentration camp, who was trained at Dachau under Eicke, it was drummed into them again and again that they must treat all prisoners with maximum, impersonal severity. The purpose of all Eicke's training was "to turn his SS men completely against the prisoners, to stir up their feelings against the prisoners." Any guard who showed any trace of softness would be severely disciplined himself. They had joined the SS and must be prepared to "carry out even the hardest and most difficult of orders without hesitation."

Concentration camp guards were not part of the general SS, but members of the special Death's Head Formations, so named from the insignia on the collar patch of their earth-brown uniforms—the black uniform generally associated with the SS was worn only outside the camp and on special occasions. They were all between the ages of seventeen and twenty-two when recruited, and had to be at least 1.7 meters (five feet seven inches) tall. They tended to be the sort of young men who were too stupid and too lazy to hold down a proper job anywhere but in the SS.

Sometimes they knew their victims from outside the camp. Bernt Engelmann records how a boy once boasted to a friend of his that his brother was with the SS *Totenkopfverbände* at Buchenwald, where one of the Kristallnacht Jews was an old man called Landauer who owned a haberdashery on Maxstrasse in Ludwigshafen, not far from the church. All the youngsters knew the old man—he used to give them sweets when they were sent to his shop to fetch something. "The Jew Landauer has to clean the latrines with a toothbrush," the boy gloated. "And if he misses a spot, up he goes onto the sawhorse!" Engelmann's friend asked what the sawhorse was. The boy explained, "They're strapped on, and then they get twenty-five lashes on their bare backsides with a horsewhip. And then they get a bucket of cold water poured over their heads, and they have to say, 'Thank you, Corporal, sir, I promise to behave better.' My brother even whipped Landauer once!"

Perhaps because they felt more at ease with people of their own age, the young SS guards seemed to reserve their worst cruelties for the old, the fat, and those who were particularly Semitic in appearance. They also seem to have hated any Jew who could boast a distinguished war record. Captain Wolff was a First World War air ace who had flown with Hermann Göring and won Germany's highest decoration for valor, the *Ordre pour le Mérite*, the famous "Blue Max." He was rounded up in the Kristallnacht arrests and taken to Buchenwald. When the guards there discovered who he was, they crucified him on the main gate.

It is clear that the aim and purpose of the camps at this time was not only to debase and dehumanize the prisoners, to terrify the Kristallnacht Jews into getting out of Germany as fast as possible, but also to brutalize the young guards, preparing them for worse horrors to come. After all, once stripped of all human dignity and reduced to little more than stinking scarecrows, Jews seemed less than human, and it therefore no longer mattered how they were treated. In 1938, no one envisaged the possibilities of Xyklon B, or the ovens of Auschwitz and Treblinka. That lay nearly four years in the future. But in the weeks following Kristallnacht, a whole generation of concentration camp guards were given a taste of what was to follow, and were confirmed as suitable instruments for performing the unthinkable. Despite the regulations unifying the whole system, there were slight variations from camp to camp. Ruth Andreas-Friedrich, an active member of the anti-Hitler resistance throughout the entire Nazi period, recounted in her diary what friends returning from the camps had said. "Some of them have one story to tell, others another. At Sachsenhausen you could work, but you froze to death. At Buchenwald, near Weimar, work was prohibited. For hundreds of people there was one privy. The first seven days there were known as Murder Week. Bad food, intestinal grippe, diarrhea. People writhed in spasms. Fall in to fall out; a queue outside the privies. Forward march into the hereafter."

Most prisoners suffered from severe diarrhea as a result of the food—usually whale meat and cabbage soup. The food in Sachsenhausen was said to have been superior to that in the other two camps, particularly when visiting journalists were expected. The problem of hygiene, however, was exacerbated by an acute shortage of water in all camps. "Anyone who wanted to keep clean had to use what was left of the so-called coffee to have some sort of wash," recalls Simon Levi, another victim of the pogrom. "A lot of methods were invented so that one didn't have to sit and sleep in one's own dirt for the rest of one's time in Buchenwald . . . some latrines were provided which were absolutely horrible, and quite a number of people drowned in the dirt of these latrines."

Bruno Bettelheim had the misfortune to spend time in both Buchenwald and Dachau. He also remembers the latrines: "In the camps, defecation was strictly regulated; it was one of the most important daily events, discussed in great detail. During the day, prisoners who wanted to defecate had to obtain the permission of a guard . . . It also seemed to give pleasure to guards to hold the power of granting or withholding the permission to visit the latrines."

Georg Wilde confirms this, recalling that at Buchenwald they rose at about 3:30 A.M. and were lined up in rows of twelve on the parade ground for roll call. Sometimes, instead of standing, the prisoners were made to sit on the gravel. "Anyone who stood up to go to the toilet was given ten, fifteen or twenty lashes. If he yelled, he was strung up on the window grill of the administrative block with hands bound behind his back, in such a way that his toes just reached the ground."

The Kristallnacht Jews were not meant to be permanent or even long-term inmates of the camps. Their arrest and incarceration were intended to persuade them it would be better for them if they left Germany. So, gradually, for those who had survived, the day they had dreamed of came at last, when their names were among those announced over the camp loudspeakers for release that day or the next. Sadly, some were in such a poor state that they could not last those final few hours. When Dr. Georg Wilde was freed, he was one of a group of two hundred men named for that day. But only 194 of them passed through the front gate of Buchenwald—the other six had died since the announcement.

Everyone emerging from the camps had to undergo a medical examination. It soon became clear that this was not to find out if they were fit enough to travel, but rather to insure that their bodies did not bear too obvious signs of the brutal treatment they had received. Anyone who showed serious cuts or sores that were not easily explicable had his release date put back until the wounds had healed. Rabbi Ochs, for example, from Gleiwitz on the Polish border, had been horribly beaten up by the guards on his arrival, and was refused permission to go home—he was even given ultraviolet treatment by the camp medical staff for several days to help his wounds heal faster.

Last of all, just before the main gates swung open to them, came the lecture. In the offices of the camp political section, a Gestapo officer told them Buchenwald, Dachau, and Sachsenhausen were not prisons but institutes of political reeducation set up for enemies of the state like themselves. They were being allowed to go home in order to make the necessary arrangements to emigrate. But if they uttered one word about what went on in the camps, or if they divulged anything that had happened to them there, they would be brought back immediately and would never leave again. Even when they left Germany and went abroad, they would still be under the watchful eyes of German foreign organizations. Any anti-German action on their part would be reported, and they would be punished.

Edward Engelberg remembers his father coming home:

> After three weeks, my father arrived in a taxi. He had been nearly bald but his totally shaved head was a shock. His eyes looked dead. He spoke very little about Dachau. His release was based on a Swiss transit visa and a stipulation that he leave within twenty-four hours. My mother remained behind to salvage some of the household, and the next morning my father and my sister and I boarded the train for Zurich.
>
> It was gray and cold. My father simply put his finger to his lips. We understood. The train trip from Munich to the Swiss border seemed to last forever. I watched my father's face, unmoved and unmoving, and tried to emulate him. . . .
>
> When at last we crossed the frontier, I saw tears roll down my father's pale face onto his stiff white shirt collar. "Now," he said simply. "Now we are safe." And we divided a large chocolate bar.
>
> We were indeed safe. My mother soon joined us and took my sister and

me to America. When his quota number came up, my father joined us, too. But three years to the month of his arrest, he died of head injuries sustained in Dachau, where he was forced to run the gauntlet. Unlucky father, his bald heat met a truncheon.

Sachsenhausen was the first of the camps to begin the release of its Kristallnacht Jews, about a week after their initial arrests, following Heydrich's order that Jews over sixty years of age, plus those who were sick or physically handicapped, were to be set free. Buchenwald and Dachau began doing the same a few days later.

On November 28, Göring, always aware of his status as a war hero, ordered that all Jews who had been front-line soldiers in the First World War were to be released. Two weeks later, on Himmler's orders, the release started of all Jews over fifty. But it was the end of January 1939 before Heydrich instructed that "in principle" prisoners who were in a position to emigrate immediately—those who had a quota number for the United States, or a valid visa for any other country—should be released.

In the meantime, it gradually became clear that anyone who had the means could buy his way out of the camps, by agreeing to sell his business, house, car, or whatever to some Aryan for a ludicrously low sum.

Of course, it all took time, and meanwhile the authorities held on to their hostages, thus keeping the pressure on the German Jewish community to leave the country by whatever means they could find. The last of the Kristallnacht Jews were not released until well into the spring of 1939, by which time it was almost too late for them to go anywhere.

During the weeks and months, the death toll mounted steadily. Besides the constant ill treatment and brutality, the combination of bitter winter weather, unheated barracks, and unsanitary conditions claimed an increasing number of victims. And when the inevitable typhus epidemics swept through Buchenwald and Dachau, the deaths leaped alarmingly. In all, up to twenty-five hundred men, women, and children died as a result of the Night of Broken Glass, most of them during the long, slow aftermath in the camps. Compared with the six million of the subsequent Holocaust, it seems an insignificant number. But for the Nazis, it was a start. And for the rest of the world, it was a clearly visible warning about the nature of the men who ruled Germany, and what they were capable of perpetrating.

VIII

"The Stifling Silence"

Only a minority of the total population of Germany took any active part in Kristallnacht. The majority, as in any violent event in any country at any time, tried to avoid getting involved. Most chose to look away, doing and saying nothing. In the small town of Beckum, in northern Germany, a mainly Catholic community whose prosperity is based on the cement industry, shopkeeper Dorothea Illigens provides a typical reaction:

> I remember the Reichskristallnacht well. My little son was ill with a serious eye infection and I was up and down half the night, caring for him. Then I heard, over and over again, in the street, walking, running, shouting, windows being broken. The SS had broken into the Jewish houses. They had driven the Jews out onto the street. They had beaten them up so badly they needed to go into hospital, but no one dared to do anything about it, or to go outside. One did not quite know what was going on, but one sensed that it was something dreadful. And in the morning, no one spoke about it. Most people stayed in their homes. They were just glad not to have been involved.

Illigens's neighbor Hugo Krick has similar memories:

> My father called me from my bed and showed me, through the window, what was happening on the street. I saw, in the Jews' houses, windows were broken and furniture thrown out onto the street. My father was crying and wanted to stop them, but my mother held him back. He recognized the danger and closed the window.
>
> No one talked about the Reichskristallnacht. Later, I heard the Terhochs died in a concentration camp, as did many other Jewish families from Beckum. Soon, there were no Jews in Beckum, and yet we had lived as part of the community in the Nordstrasse: the Stein family at number 52 sold ladies' and gentlemen's clothing, the Terhoch family at number 34 sold wool, the Lernberg family at number 32 sold furs, the Windmüller family sold horses. And at the bottom of the Nordstrasse was the Jewish synagogue.

It is easy to condemn the Illigens and Kricks, and all the Schmidts and Müllers and millions of others throughout Germany who did nothing and said nothing. But their silence demonstrates the effectiveness of terror as a weapon in subduing and subjugating a population: Violence against any one section always carries the implicit message to the others that it could be their turn next. In this respect, Kristallnacht was doubly valuable to the Nazis—it not only dealt a terrible blow to the Jews, increasing the pressures on them to an intolerable level, it also helped to tighten the regime's grip on the population as a whole. Its success among those who were in a position to do something positive is attested to by Hans Bernd Gisevius, an official in the Abwehr, the military intelligence and counterespionage service, and an active member of the German resistance to Hitler.

"The conclusions that were forced upon every thinking German were grim and depressing indeed," Gisevius wrote in his postwar memoirs. "Not a single general had had the impulse to bring out his troops and see to the clearing of the streets. The army leaders had played deaf and blind. The meaning of this is clear. Everyone had long since given up hope that the Cabinet would ever do anything. From whom could decent Germans now expect protection if these horrible excesses were followed by others—against the Church or the 'reactionaries' or the 'plutocrats'? Everyone quietly determined the category in which he would be included as soon as the Nazi politicians found it necessary to open the exhaust valve again, in order to let off some of their own irritation or ease the pressure of general discontent.

"The spectre of terrorism appeared more threatening than ever; and that was precisely what Hitler, master of dual effects that he was, had wanted . . . the cowed middle class stared at the Nazi monster like a rabbit at a snake. A general psychosis had been created, under which the populace was reduced to absolute submission . . ."

Even those who complained were usually not prepared to do anything. One of Germany's leading playwrights, Gerhart Hauptmann, complained to friends, "This scum will bring war to the whole world. This miserable brown comedian, this Nazi hangman, is rushing us into a world of war, into destruction!" But when asked why, if he felt so strongly, he did not at least emigrate in protest, like other famous writers such as Mann and Zweig, Hauptmann replied with bitter honesty, "Because I'm a coward. Do you understand? I'm a coward."

Such feelings of cowardice and helplessness were deliberately reinforced by the use of the Gestapo to quash any sign of dissidence during the pogrom itself. In Hamburg, for instance, according to the British consul, L. M. Robinson, agents mingled with the crowds who were watching the burning and wrecking and beating, and arrested over three hundred people who were incautious enough to voice their feelings of shame and disgust. About thirty of these, he reported, were detained and sent to a concentration camp. No one arrested the woman in Bremen who was heard to shout to an SA man to kill the elderly Jew he was dragging through the streets, or the shopgirl who proclaimed that the river Weser was deep enough to drown all the Jews in the city, or the young girl traveling on the Berlin Stadtbahn who, seeing the Fasanenstrasse synagogue ablaze, cried out in delight, "Look, Father—beautiful, isn't it?"

All credit, therefore, must be given to those who were prepared to speak out publicly, braving the consequences. On the Sunday following Kristallnacht, Pastor Julius von Jan preached to his Lutheran congregation in Swabia, denouncing the pogrom, "Houses of worship, sacred to others, have been burned down with impunity—men who have loyally served our nation and conscientiously done their duty have been thrown into concentration camps simply because they belong to a different race. Our nation's infamy is bound to bring about divine punishment."

The sermon brought instant and far from divine punishment for Pastor Jan. He was dragged from his Bible class by a Nazi mob, beaten up and thrown on the roof of a shed. Then his house was wrecked, just as so many Jewish homes had been, and he was jailed.

Pastor Jan was one of the few churchmen of any denomination who spoke out. For the most part, the churches all contributed to what Pastor Niemoeller—already imprisoned in Sachsenhausen for his refusal to bend the knee to Hitler—described as the "stifling silence." In fact, there were few Protestant pastors left who had not taken an oath of allegiance to Hitler. The others had all either been imprisoned or forced out of their churches—more than eight hundred had been arrested in 1937 alone, and hundreds more during 1938. They joined thousands of ministers, priests, nuns, monks, and lay leaders of all denominations, Protestant and Catholic, who had been arrested since Hitler's accession.

The Catholic clergy, who had supposedly been guaranteed freedom of worship by a concordat signed by the pope in 1933, were for the most part as silent as the Protestants, many of them concurring with Rome's ambivalent attitude to the "murderers of Christ." They were encouraged in this by certain sections of the Nazi party—Julius Streicher's rabble-rousing journal *Der Stürmer* described the crucifixion of Jesus as the first instance of Jewish ritual murder. Many other Christians saw the terrible events of the pogrom as further proof of God's curse on the Jews.

The pressure on priests often took physical shape—a constant threat epitomized in one of the SA's favorite anthems, which included the refrain "Storm trooper comrades, hang the Jews and put the priests against the wall." A month earlier, when the Austrian cardinal Innitzer had spoken out against Nazi persecution of the Church, his palace opposite St. Stephen's cathedral in Vienna had been totally sacked by a mob. Now, for any waverers, there were sharp reminders of the Nazi threat when most of the windows of Cardinal Faulhaber's palace in Munich were smashed during the night of Friday, November 11. Many priests' houses were also attacked, as were several churches, and piles of paper and cardboard were heaped against the doors of the cathedral, an unspoken but unmistakable threat that they could be set on fire as soon as the word was given.

But some individual Christians did speak. At least one member of the SA, a theological student named Krugel, resigned his membership on the grounds that although he agreed with the Nazi policy of anti-Semitism, he could not condone mob violence. And in Baden-Baden, a citizen who watched helplessly as Jewish men were marched through the streets to the synagogue was moved to make a public denunciation, saying, "What I saw was not one Christ, but a whole column of Christ figures, marching along with heads high and unbowed by any feelings of guilt."

Foreign embassies and consulates were deluged with letters—mainly anonymous—from ordinary Germans, denouncing the pogrom and dissociating the German people from it. Some writers begged the consuls to inform the foreign press, because they themselves were unable to do so. Others pleaded "to be delivered from this reign of tyranny." From Cologne, one correspondent writing to Clement Attlee, leader of the British Labour party, described the burning of the synagogues as "Götterdämmerung," and called for a boycott of all German goods.

From Bremen, Consul Wildman reported, "On all sides and from all classes, even from some of the Nazis, I have heard the severest condemnation of the pogrom. One man said that he was ashamed to be a German. Another said that it would take them a hundred years to live down the shame of it." When the president of the Bremen country club, the Club zur Vahr, stated that he had taken part in the attacks on Jewish shops, one well-known Bremer, a prominent member of the committee, immediately sent in his resignation, saying he "could not sit at the same table as a man who had had a share in such outrageous proceedings and boasts about it."

A letter writer in the *Daily Telegraph* recalled an SS man in Munich saying to him, "For the first time in my life, I am ashamed to be German." He also quoted the buxom wife of a Düsseldorf grocer who observed, "We shall have no peace . . . until that man [Hitler] is under lock and key in Grafenberg [the local lunatic asylum]."

In a Munich street, a holder of the *Blut-Orden*, a high Nazi decoration, met a Jewish friend who had been taken away, stopped him, shook hands, and congratulated him on his release. The Jew suggested that this was indiscreet, and that his friend might lose his *Blut-Orden* if anyone saw them together. The German replied, "I already have. I resigned from the party yesterday." And he produced a copy of his very strongly worded letter of resignation.

Other recorded instances of Germans demonstrating their sympathy included shopkeepers sending to Jewish houses the necessities of life that families were unable to buy because of the ban on Jews entering their shops. Aryan friends of a Jewish woman hid her silver for her to avoid its being confiscated. "We did this," they said, "to show the Jews that the German people had no part in this—it is only Goebbels and his gang."

In Berlin, Ruth Andreas-Friedrich described in her diary how she and many of her left-wing Aryan friends became "apparent capitalists" by taking over Jewish property "in trust," to frustrate the Nazis. "Before the Gestapo gobbles it up," the Jewish owners told them. "And so," Andreas-Friedrich wrote, "apartment houses and businesses, building lots and woodland, change owners overnight. Underneath, everything stays just as it was, only it is no longer the experienced Mr. Abraham who turns up for board meetings of Müller & Co.'s embroidery factory, but Dr. Franz von Hollberg; Miss Schulze collects the rents in the apartment house at No. 12 Köpernickerstrasse, instead of Dr. Cohn. One has only to find some dodge that will make the transfer look credible. Everything else is a gentleman's agreement, in trust, on a simple word of honor." Andreas-Friedrich herself took over a plot of land belonging to a Jewish friend called Schwartz, in Saarow on the Scharmitzelsee, before he left for England laden down with clothes, bed linen, leather suitcases, and trunks crammed with goods bought at the last minute to use up the money he was not allowed to take out of the country with him.

R. T. Smallbones, the British consul general in Frankfurt-am-Main, was a self-confessed Germanophile. He had spent eight happy years in Germany and had developed great admiration and respect for the sterling qualities of the people. "I have known the Germans," he wrote to his superiors in Berlin, ". . . in the hour of their humiliation after the war, and I have been at this post since 1932. I flattered myself that I understood the German character, and I have worked for an Anglo-German understanding to the best of my ability." But what he had seen during the recent events in Frankfurt had "revealed to me a facet of the German character which I had not suspected. They seemed to me to have no cruelty in their make-up. They are habitually kind to animals, to children, to the aged and infirm."

Sounding a little like a missionary who has discovered that, in spite of all his sermons and homilies, the tribe of well-behaved and otherwise charming cannibals he had just converted have not lost their taste for human meat, Smallbones searched for an explanation, an excuse, for what he called "this outbreak of sadistic cruelty." Rather surprisingly, he came up with "sexual perversion, and in particular homo-sexuality," which he said, "are very prevalent in Germany. It seems to me that mass sexual perversity may offer an explanation for this otherwise inexplicable outbreak." Like so many others who knew Germany well, he was persuaded that "if the Government of Germany depended on the suffrage of the people, those in power and responsible for these outrages would be swept away by a storm of indignation if not put up against a wall and shot."

Much of the opposition among the "ordinary" people of Germany did not arise out of sympathy for the Jews. Some were more concerned about the damage to the country's reputation abroad, like the anonymous writer who sent a letter to the Berlin evening paper *Der Angriff*, which was owned by Goebbels himself. "The frightful Paris assassination," he wrote, "gave us the opportunity to gain the general sympathy of the world, but the opposite has resulted from the recent excesses. Even well-disposed foreign nations are disgusted. Our newly begun friendly relations with Britain and France have been destroyed again."

Surprisingly, *Der Angriff* printed the letter. Not so surprisingly, it also printed a column and a half of denunciation, dismissing the unnamed correspondent as part of "the one percent who vote 'no.'" It was also scathing about his reference to those "well-disposed foreign nations." Where were they to be found? it demanded—everyone knew that Germany was surrounded by enemies. Of course, it is possible that the correspondent may have been not merely anonymous but also fictitious, his letter planted by Goebbels as a peg on which to hang the reply. Even so, it did represent a body of opinion, which Goebbels clearly felt needed answering.

What concerned even more Germans was the fear of disorder, and disapproval of the destruction of property. Albert Adler, then a young Jewish boy apprenticed to a Mannheim furniture restorer, Herr Neckenauer, recalls that after Kristallnacht, his employer was inundated with valuable pieces of furniture belonging to Jewish customers, which had been damaged by the mob. Legs had been broken off, SS runes had been carved into highly polished surfaces, doors had been ripped off cabinets. Herr Neckenauer was deeply shocked. "Barbarians!" he cried. "How could anyone treat furniture like that?" About the treatment of the furniture's owners, he said not a word.

Hitler's favorite architect, Albert Speer, then in the process of completing the great new Reichschancellery, drove to his office on the morning of November 10 past the still-smoldering ruins of the Berlin synagogues. After the war, while serving his sentence in the Spandau prison as a war criminal, he described the memory as

> one of the most doleful of my life—chiefly because what really disturbed me at the time was the aspect of disorder that I saw on Fasanenstrasse: charred beams, collapsed facades, burned-out walls—anticipations of a scene that during the war would dominate much of Europe. Most of all, I was troubled by the political revival of the "gutter." The smashed panes of shop windows offended my sense of middle-class order.
>
> I did not see that more was being smashed than glass, that on that night Hitler had crossed a Rubicon for the fourth time in his life, had taken a step that irrevocably sealed the fate of his country. Did I sense, at least for a moment, that something was beginning that would end with the annihilation of one whole group of our nation? Did I sense that this outburst of hoodlumism was changing my moral substance? I do not know. I accepted what had happened rather indifferently . . .
>
> It is true that I did not know what was really beginning on November 9, 1938, and what ended in Auschwitz and Maidanek. But in the final analysis, I myself determined the degree of my isolation, the extremity of my evasions, and the extent of my ignorance.

This selective blindness, this ability to switch off one's sensibilities, was a common factor in many of the less extreme rank-and-file members of the party. Melita Maschmann, for example, was a young party stalwart, the kind of person for whom Hitler and National Socialism represented something new and exciting in German life. What drew her to Naziism, she says, was not hatred of anybody or anything, neither Jews nor communists, but love of Germany. Melita lived on the outskirts of Berlin, and had slept well on the night of November 9–10. She had not been woken by any disturbances. In the morning, she went into Berlin very early, to go to the Reich Youth Leadership Office.

"I noticed nothing unusual on the way," she continued. "I alighted at the Alexanderplatz. In order to get to the Lotheringerstrasse I had to go down a rather gloomy alley containing many small shops and inns. To my surprise, almost all the shop windows here were smashed in. The pavement was covered by pieces of glass and fragments of broken furniture. I asked a patrolling policeman what on earth had been going on there. He replied: 'In this street they're almost all Jews.'

" 'Well?'

" 'You don't read the papers? Last night the National Soul boiled over.'

"I can remember only the sense but not the actual wording of this remark, which had an undertone of hidden anger. I went on my way shaking my head. For the space of a second I was clearly aware that something terrible had happened there. Something frighteningly brutal. But almost at once I switched over to accepting what had happened as over and done with, and avoiding critical reflection. I said to myself: the Jews are the enemies of the New Germany. Last night they had a taste of what this means. Let us hope that world Jewry, which has resolved to hinder Germany's 'new steps towards greatness,' will take the events of last night as a warning. If the Jews sow hatred against us all over the world, they must learn that we have hostages for them in our hands.

"With these or similar thoughts, I constructed for myself a justification of the pogrom. But in any case, I forced the memory of it out of my consciousness as quickly as possible. As the years went by, I grew better and better at switching off quickly in this manner on similar occasions. It was the only way, whatever the circumstances, to prevent the onset of doubts about the rightness of what had happened."

The picture of Melita picking her way through all the broken glass in the alley while en route to her work in the Youth Leadership Office seems a perfect symbol for the attitude of so many young Germans during the Hitler period. Certainly it was the attitude of many toward the events of Kristallnacht: They were like sleepwalkers, mysteriously protected from reality in the midst of chaos. They were, as Melita describes herself on another occasion, "armed with moral blinkers that prevented me from noticing anything likely to worry me or arouse my sympathy."

The evident lack of enthusiasm among party members, and the positive hostility and resentment of the greater part of the general population toward the pogrom, created a certain amount of alarm in the party leadership. Old rivalries and divisions were exacerbated. A great deal of anger was directed at Goebbels—but this was not the result of any moral indignation, simply the feeling that the pogrom had been ill-judged and unnecessary, and the wanton destruction that had taken place had interfered with economic plans.

The minister of economics, Walther Funk, called Goebbels in the middle of the action, cursing him roundly on the telephone. "Are you crazy, Goebbels?" Frau Funk heard her husband scream. "To make such a mess of things? It makes one ashamed to be a German. We are losing our whole prestige abroad. Night and day I'm trying to conserve the national wealth, and you toss it out the window regardless. If this thing does not stop at once you can take the whole filthy mess!"

Ribbentrop, who had not been consulted—as a Johnny-come-lately to the party he did not qualify for attendance at the old fighters' dinner—was angry at the effect the pogrom would have on "his" foreign policy. Himmler, who most certainly had known all about it, now purported to be angry at the way Goebbels was supposed to have made free with the SS and the Gestapo. This did not, of course, prevent his taking over the whole of the second phase of the pogrom and thus finally confirming the ascendency of the SS in its internal power struggle against the roughnecks of the SA.

Goebbels's greatest opponent among the Nazi leadership, Herman Göring, was particularly furious. Göring, who in addition to his positions as commander in chief of the Luftwaffe and president of the Reichstag was economic supremo of Germany as head of the Four-Year Plan, had only discovered about the pogrom after traveling back to Berlin overnight in his special train. Although he always attended the annual Feldherrnhalle march, he did not usually bother with the old comrades' dinner in the Rathaus, preferring to make use of his time in Munich to deal with other business. On the evening of November 9, 1938, therefore, he had been unaware of Goebbels's speech, or of the teleprint messages flashing across the country as he boarded his train. By the time the first incidents happened, he was already well on his way, settled down in his sleeping car for the night.

As the train drew into the Anhalter station in Berlin the following morning, the conductor told Göring he had seen fires blazing in Halle, some 130 kilometers southeast of the capital, when they had passed through. Half an hour later, when he was dressed, Göring called his adjutant, who reported that there had apparently been riots during the night, that Jewish stores had been broken into and plundered, and that synagogues had been set on fire. Driving through the streets to Göring's apartment, the extent of the damage quickly became clear, and the field marshal's temper began to flare. As soon as he arrived, he had a call put through to Gestapo Headquarters and demanded a full report.

By the time Hitler arrived back in Berlin late that morning, having flown up from Munich, Göring was steaming. He had established Goebbels's part in the affair, and complained bitterly that the propaganda minister was sabotaging his efforts to prepare the economy for war. It was impossible, he told the führer, for him to have such events taking place at such a time, when he was reaching the peak of effort for the Four-Year Plan. "I have been making speeches asking the nation to save every old toothpaste tube, every rusty nail, every bit of scrap material so that it can be collected and used," he raged. "It is intolerable that a man who is not responsible for these things should upset my difficult task by destroying so many things of economic value on the one hand, and by causing so much disturbance in economic life on the other."

Hitler, Göring later testified, "made some excuses for Goebbels, but on the whole he agreed that such events were not to take place and must not be allowed to take place. I also pointed out to him that such a short time after the Munich agreement, such matters would also have an unfavorable effect on foreign policy."

Having unburdened himself to Hitler, Göring then went home again and phoned Goebbels, to give him a piece of his mind. He told him, he said, "in unmistakable terms and in very sharp words, my view of the matter. I told him, with emphasis, that I was not inclined to suffer the consequences of his uncontrolled utterances, as far as economic matters were concerned."

It is doubtful if Göring's outburst had much effect on either Hitler or Goebbels. Although Hitler was still pretending to distance himself from the whole business, his protests had a hollow ring. "It is terrible," he told Frau Gerdy Troost, widow of a leading architect whom he had much admired. "They had destroyed everything for me, like elephants in a china shop . . . and much worse. I had the great expectation that I was about to come to an understanding with France. And now that!" But on the morning of November 10, before leaving for Berlin, he had addressed some four hundred Nazi newspaper editors and journalists in Munich, and had completely ignored the events of the previous night.

Although he was speaking mainly about the Munich agreement, convulsing his audience with laughter at his wicked impersonations of Chamberlain and Daladier, some of his words to the editors on psychological warfare were equally applicable to the pogrom. It had been necessary, he said, to reeducate the German people psychologically, to make it clear that there were things that must be achieved by force if peaceful means failed. It was essential for the press, he concluded, "to acknowledge blindly the following maxim: the leadership is always right!"

Later in the day, after a session with Hitler, Goebbels issued a statement to the press, the first official acknowledgment from the leadership that anything untoward had taken place:

> The justifiable and understandable indignation of the German people at the cowardly murder of a German diplomat in Paris manifested itself in a wide degree last night. In numerous towns and villages of the Reich, reprisals were carried out against Jewish buildings and places of business.
>
> The whole population is now strictly enjoined to abstain from all further action of whatsoever nature against the Jews. The final reply to the Jewish outrage in Paris will be given to the Jews by legal means, i.e., by decree.

The ominous closing words of Goebbels's statement arose from a further meeting that Göring had had with Hitler in the late afternoon. The field marshal had been surprised to find that Hitler appeared to have changed his approach since he had agreed earlier that such things should not happen. In the meantime, it seemed, he had talked over lunch with Goebbels, who had been totally unabashed by criticism, insisting that the pogrom had shown international Jewry that the Reich was not to be trifled with. When Göring attempted to continue with his protests, Hitler, perhaps only half joking, told him, "You had better be careful. People might get to know of your sympathy for the Jews!"

Goebbels then entered the room and joined the discussion, starting what Göring described as "his usual talk: that such things could not be tolerated; that this was the second or third murder of a National Socialist committed abroad by a Jew." It was at this point that the subject of delivering a final reply by "legal means" was raised for the first time.

According to Göring, it was Goebbels who suggested imposing a fine—not on the rioters or the SA, but on the Jews. He wanted this to be collected by each *Gau*, the Nazi party's main administrative districts, and named "an almost incredibly high sum." There was then an argument between the two henchmen—not about whether it was right to impose such a fine, but about who should collect it. Goebbels, who was himself gauleiter of Berlin, with more Jews in his district than any other, obviously stood to gain enormously from local collections. Göring, being responsible for the national economy as a whole, insisted that only the sovereign state had the right to take such measures.

The squabble was finally resolved by Hitler. He decided Göring was right, such a fine was a matter for the national government. As for the amount, they settled on a nice round sum: one billion marks—at that time worth some $400 million; the equivalent, fifty years later, of about $3.7 billion. This massive payment, which became known as the Jewish

Atonement Fine, represented one fifth of all Jewish holdings. The government knew the exact value of these, since a decree issued by Göring on April 27, 1938, had ordered the registration of all Jewish bank balances, savings accounts, bonds, stocks, real estate, and other property.

But the führer was still not finished with the Jews. It was time, he told Göring, for what he described as "the economic solution" to be carried through—in other words, for the Jews to be finally eliminated from the economic life of Germany. For a start, all businesses "known to be Jewish and obviously Jewish" were to be Aryanized—a step that would insure there were no more Kristallnachts. This applied particularly to department stores, he said, which were often a source of friction, since officials and employees from government offices who could only shop between the hours of 6:00 and 7:00 P.M. often went to these stores and had difficulties. After outlining what he wanted done, he ordered that a committee should be set up at once to deal with the matter. To Göring's dismay, he insisted that Goebbels should be a member, though he had nothing to do with economic affairs. Presumably, he was afraid that Göring might be too soft on the Jews if left to his own devices.

Hitler need not have worried about Göring's ruthlessness—even though he was less rabid in his attitude to the Jews than Goebbels, Himmler, or Heydrich, or for that matter than Hitler himself. Certainly, there are many instances of his deliberately and openly falsifying documents and blood certificates, particularly for Luftwaffe officers of mixed parentage who were valuable to him, or whom he simply liked. "In these cases," he is known to have declared, "I decide who is Jewish!" Throughout the war, Jewish members of the Luftwaffe arrested by the Gestapo were regularly freed on Göring's orders, as he continued to assert his independence and personal authority.

As late as 1943, he obtained the release of a former member of the First World War Richthofen Squadron—which Göring had commanded after the death of the Red Baron himself. The man, who had the decidedly un-Jewish name of Luther, had been arrested after being caught in a hotel with an Aryan woman. Such an "offense against decency" automatically carried the death penalty, but Luther was handed over without any fuss and spent the rest of the war under the personal protection of Göring. And when Göring heard that two elderly Jewish couples named Ballin, who had taken him into their home and helped him after he had been wounded outside the Feldherrnhalle in the 1923 Munich putsch, were being taken to a concentration camp, he ordered his aides to see that they were rescued and taken to safety in a foreign country.

When it came to economics, however, Göring could be relied upon to do the right thing. While the more radical Nazi leaders were fired by racial hatred in their actions against the Jews, Göring was motivated primarily by greed. To Göring, the Jews represented money—and where money was concerned, either for himself or for the state, he had the morals of an Al Capone. No Mafia godfather was ever more adept than Hermann Göring at extracting wealth from others and diverting it to his own purposes, and the Jews were a convenient soft target. In this, he can be seen as representing another factor in the equation that made the persecution of the Jews in Germany possible: the large sector of the community who did not necessarily approve of the violence, but who were delighted to cash in on the results. Fueled by avarice and jealousy, they shook their heads and tut-tutted with distaste, but seized every opportunity to take advantage of the situation and enrich themselves.

From the time of his appointment as head of the Four-Year Plan on September 4, 1936, Göring had seen the elimination of the Jews from the economic life of Germany as an essential goal. There were two main reasons for this, one economic, the other political. The whole purpose of the plan was to prepare the nation for a major war within five years, against the Soviet Union. The vast rearmament program that this entailed was enormously expensive, and since the national coffers were almost empty, any source of capital was welcome. At the same time, Nazi philosophy equated bolshevism with the Jews; the Soviet government was therefore seen as being essentially Jewish, and German Jews as sympathetic to it. They could not be trusted, this warped reasoning continued, to control large, vital industries, including armaments factories.

At first, Göring claimed at his trial in Nuremberg after the war, he had not been bothered about small businesses, individual stores, and such. They only entered into his calculations when he needed to restrict retail trade in order to divert resources away from consumer goods—squeezing out Jewish stores was a simple way of achieving this. Until then, although the rest of the Nazis were constantly attacking Jewish shops and those who bought from them, Göring was more interested in the richer pickings offered by larger concerns.

Right from the beginning of the Four-Year Plan, he had taken steps to prevent Jewish capital leaving Germany and so escaping from his grasp, by issuing a decree making it an offense punishable by the death penalty to transfer property abroad. No German was allowed to have an account in any foreign country without government permission. Anyone found guilty would forfeit all property to the state. In April 1938, he signaled his intention of taking over Jewish property by making it an offense for anyone to veil the true ownership of a Jewish business—no doubt a response to the activities of people like Ruth Andreas-Friedrich taking over businesses from their Jewish friends on trust—and then followed this with decrees requiring all Jewish-owned property to be registered and forbidding its disposal without the permission of the authorities.

While individual Nazis made hay, blackmailing and beating Jews into signing over their homes and businesses, the state had so far been missing out. Although the ground had been thoroughly prepared, there had not yet been any large-scale move. It was as though Göring had been waiting for the right moment. Now, with the assassination of vom Rath and the explosion of Kristallnacht, it had arrived—and not a day too soon, for the economy of the Reich was in a parlous condition. Germany was about to go bankrupt. Without a rapid injection of funds, all Hitler's grandiose plans would end in a heap of broken dreams. There would be no war of conquest in the east, no great empire, no master race purified and strengthened for one thousand years.

As economic supremo, Göring had the responsibility of dealing with the problem, and he moved swiftly and surely. The solution, by a terrible irony, lay with the despised Jews. As the minutes of the working committee of the Reich Defense Council—which Göring also chaired—recorded a week later:

> Very critical situation of the Reich Exchequer. Relief initially through the milliard imposed on the Jews and through profits accruing to the Reich from the Aryanization of Jewish enterprises.

This, then, was the purpose of the committee that Hitler ordered Göring to set up. It was to settle the fate of Germany's remaining Jews, and organize the ways in which they were to be stripped of everything they owned, in order to finance the continuation of the Nazi regime and the fulfillment of Hitler's vision.

IX

"Atonement"

The committee met at 10:00 A.M. on Saturday, November 12, in the Air Ministry Building, the *Haus der Flieger*, with Göring in the chair. Goebbels brought along several subordinates from the Propaganda Ministry. Heydrich and SS general Kurt Daluege represented the Gestapo and the Security Police, respectively. The Foreign Office was represented by Ernst Woermann, head of its political department. Others present included the minister of the interior, Dr. Wilhelm Frick, the economics minister, Walther Funk, the finance minister, Count Schwerin von Krosigk, the Austrian finance minister, Dr. Hans Fishböck, and several other senior officials. As with all Göring's meetings, a stenographer took down every word for the record, much of which survived the war to be used as evidence at the Nuremberg trials. From this, it is clear that however much the party tried to dissociate itself from the events of Kristallnacht, it was determined to take complete control of the aftermath.

Göring opened the proceedings with an inordinately long speech outlining exactly what was to be decided. "Gentlemen," he began, "today's meeting is of crucial importance. I have received a letter, written on the führer's instructions by the chief of staff of the führer's deputy, Bormann, asking that the Jewish question should now be coordinated and settled once and for all, one way or another. Yesterday, in a telephone call, the führer reiterated that I was to coordinate the decisive steps."

Since the problem was mainly an economic one, he told the meeting, that was how it had to be tackled, but there would naturally be legal measures involved that would fall into the spheres of the Interior and Justice Ministries. There were also, he said with a nod in Goebbels's direction, propaganda implications, which would be his responsibility. Warming to his theme, Göring spoke of how the party had already taken steps toward Aryanizing the economy: The Jews would be taken out of it and "put in the debit ledger."

"But dear God," he went on, "all we've done so far is make very beautiful plans. We've been too slow in carrying them out. We had a demonstration right here in Berlin. As a result, the people were told: now, there will be a settlement. But still nothing happened. Now we have this affair in Paris. Again demonstrations followed, and now something will have to happen. Because, gentlemen, I have had enough of these demonstrations. They don't harm the Jews—they harm me, since I am the final authority for holding the economy together. If a Jewish shop is destroyed today, if the goods are thrown into the street, then the insurance makes good the damage to the Jew—he doesn't suffer at all. And furthermore, the goods that are destroyed are consumer goods, the people's goods!

"In the future, if we consider it necessary for demonstrations to take place, I beg you to see to it that they are directed so as not to wound us, ourselves. Because it is insane to clear out and burn a Jewish warehouse and then have a German insurance company cover the damage—and the goods which I desperately need—whole bales of clothing and I don't know what else—are burned, while I need them everywhere. I might as well burn the raw materials before they arrive. Of course, the people don't understand that, so we must now make laws, to show clearly that something is being done.

"I am not going to tolerate a situation in which German insurance companies are the ones to suffer. To prevent this, I will use my authority and issue a decree. In this, of course, I am going to ask for the support of the competent government agencies, so that everything will be settled properly and the insurance companies will not be the ones to suffer.

"But another problem immediately emerges: it may be that these insurance companies have reinsured in foreign countries. In those cases, I would not want to lose the foreign exchange they bring in. The matter must be looked into. For this reason, I have asked Herr Hilgard from the insurance companies to attend, to give us the best advice on the extent to which the companies are covered against such damages by reinsurance. I would not like to give this up under any circumstances."

Stressing once again that the purpose of the meeting was not just to talk but to make decisions, Göring turned to the mechanics of grabbing Jewish businesses, which he explained at some length. Basically, what was to happen was that Jews would turn their businesses over to the state, at a valuation fixed by the state trustee. In return, they would receive government bonds paying 3 percent interest, on which they would be expected to live. Naturally, the price would be fixed as low as possible. The state would then sell the business to an Aryan German, with a preference being given to party members, particularly those who could prove they had suffered in the past because of their membership. However, any party member who tried to make a profit out of such a transaction—presumably by selling the business to another German for its proper price—would be dealt with "ruthlessly" by Göring. He cited past examples of such "underhand dealings," where "little chauffeurs of gauleiters have profited so much by the transactions that they have raked in half a million." If any prominent person should be involved in such things this time, he warned, "I shall go straight to the führer and report these dirty tricks without fear or favor." Only the party, it seemed, was entitled to profit by such swindles.

When it came to factories, Göring was even more ruthless. The larger plants would be dealt with in exactly the same way as other businesses and stores, that is, by the issue of 3 percent bonds to the Jewish owners and the sale of the plant to Aryans. But with the smaller factories, only those that Göring felt he needed would be handed over. The others would simply be shut down, and those that could not be converted to another use would be demolished. In all cases, the Foreign Office claimed the right to represent foreign Jews with German holdings—Ribbentrop, who had actually been a very successful businessman himself, clearly did not intend to miss an opportunity to enrich either himself or his ministry, while at the same time being aware of the difficulties of handling owners who, although Jewish, were often British or American citizens.

For a while, those concerned with the economy discussed the finer details of the confiscation. Walther Funk, the minister of economics, even argued that the Jews should be allowed to keep their shareholdings, but he was soon put in his place. By his own estimate, the government stood to gain some half-billion shares of capital stock, and there was no way in which Göring was going to pass up such an opportunity.

Characteristically, Göring also had his eye on works of art, jewelry, real estate, and stocks held by Jews. The question of exactly how their owners could be relieved of these desirable goodies should, he decided, be examined immediately by a small subcommittee under the chairmanship of Funk. Another, more sinister question that was also referred to a subcommittee was the subject of using the dispossessed Jews as a source of forced labor.

Goebbels seemed to be more interested in what was going to be done with the sites of the burned-down synagogues. Some towns would want to turn the sites into parking lots. Others might wish to erect other buildings. In any case, it was time for all synagogues to be dissolved. The Jews themselves, he proposed, should be made to pay for leveling and clearing the sites.

Warming to his theme, Goebbels threatened to take over the conference. "I consider it necessary," he announced, "to issue a decree forbidding Jews from going to German theaters, cinemas and circuses. I have already prepared such a decree, by the authority of the Reich Chamber of Culture. I believe we can achieve this in the present state of the theater—our theaters are crowded, we have hardly any room. I am of the opinion that it is not possible for Jews to sit next to Germans in music halls, theaters and cinemas. I think we could possibly consider, later on, setting aside one or two cinemas where Jewish films may be shown, but we cannot afford to lose a German theater.

"Furthermore," he continued, "I advocate that Jews be banned from all public places where they might cause provocation. It is still possible for a Jew to share a sleeping car with a German. Therefore, the Reich Ministry of Transport must issue a decree ordering that there shall be separate compartments for Jews. If this compartment is full, then the Jews cannot claim a seat. They can only be given separate compartments after all Germans have seats. They must not mix with the Germans: If there is no more room, they will have to stand in the corridor."

"I think it would be more sensible to give them separate compartments," interposed Göring, who was irritated by Goebbels's shifting the subject away from the economy.

"Not if the train is overcrowded," Goebbels replied.

"Just a moment!" snapped Göring. "There will be only one Jewish coach. If that is filled up, the other Jews will have to stay at home."

"But supposing there are not many Jews going, let us say, on the long-distance express train to Munich. Suppose there are two Jews on the train, and the other compartments are overcrowded? These two Jews would have a compartment to themselves. Therefore, the decree must state that Jews may claim a seat only after all Germans have secured theirs."

"I would give the Jews one coach or compartment," Göring repeated, "and if a case such as the one you mentioned should arise, and the train is overcrowded, then believe me, we won't need a law! He will be kicked out and he'll have to sit on his own in the toilet all the way."

In front of all the assembled ministers, the two Nazi leaders went on squabbling like a couple of spoiled schoolchildren. Rarely in history can the fate of an entire people have been dealt with in such a grotesque fashion.

"The Jews should stand in the corridor!" Goebbels shouted.

"They should sit in the toilet!"

Goebbels kept harping on, still not satisfied. Summoning his authority as chairman, Göring thundered, "I don't need a law. He can either sit in the toilet, or leave the train!"

"I don't agree," Goebbels grumbled. "I don't believe in this. There ought to be a law! There ought to be a law banning Jews from beaches and resorts, too. Last summer . . ."

"Above all, here in the Admiralspalast, there were really revolting things," Göring interposed enthusiastically.

"And in Wannseebad," Goebbels continued. "A law—that Jews are absolutely banned from all German places of recreation."

"We could give them their own," Göring suggested.

"We will have to consider whether we should give them their own resorts, or place some German bathing places at their disposal—but not the best, or people might say 'You are allowing the Jews to get fit by using our bathing resorts.' " There was no stopping Goebbels, now. He had the bit well and truly between his teeth, and for the moment all thoughts of economic matters were set aside as he ranted on. "The question must also be considered whether it is necessary to ban the Jews from German forests. Herds of Jews are today running around in the Grünewald. That is a constant provocation—we shall have constant incidents. What the Jews do is so provocative that it constantly comes to blows."

"Well, then," Göring responded with heavy sarcasm, "we shall have to give the Jews a certain part of the forest, and rangers will see to it that the various animals which are damnably like the Jews—the elk has a hooked nose, too—go into the Jewish enclosure and settle down among them."

Stung by Göring's tone, Goebbels snapped back at him, saying he found his attitude provocative. "What is more," he went on, "the Jews must not sit in German public parks. I am starting a whispering campaign about Jewish women in the gardens at Fehbelliner Platz. There are Jews who don't look so Jewish. They sit down alongside German mothers with children and start to moan and grouse." Jews would have to be banned from most parks, he insisted, but could have certain parks and gardens— "not the prettiest, of course"—set aside for them. In others, there would be special benches where they were allowed to sit.

Finally, Goebbels turned to the question of schools. It was, of course, intolerable to him that Jewish children should be allowed to attend German schools and sit next to German children. He proposed putting an end to this situation by ejecting all Jewish children, and decreeing that they should only attend their own, special Jewish schools. Segregation could never be too complete for Goebbels, but it is appalling to note how many of the measures he introduced have been maintained over the years since then, right down to the present day, in countries that continue to practice racial discrimination. The segregated park bench is still with us.

Göring finally put an end to Goebbels's diatribe by calling in Herr Hilgard, who had been waiting outside all this time, to discuss the question of insurance. But anyone who thought this would mark the end of the lunatic black farce that had so far dominated the conference was in for a disappointment.

Having established that many of the Jews who had suffered during the pogrom were insured against damage caused by public disorder, and that the damage would have to be paid for by the German insurance companies, Göring put the matter bluntly to Hilgard: "The thing is simple enough. I have only to issue a decree to the effect that losses resulting from these riots shall not have to be paid by the insurance companies."

Unfortunately, Hilgard pointed out, it was not as simple as the field marshal thought. For a start, there were basically three types of insurance involved: for riot damage, fire, and theft. And while the damage to synagogues was certainly suffered by the Jews, most of the other buildings were actually owned by Aryans and only rented to Jews. Therefore, any damage to the buildings, including broken windows, fell on Germans.

To Goebbels, there was still no problem: "The Jews must pay for the damage."

"It's no use," Göring snarled. "We have no raw material. It's all foreign glass. That will need foreign currency. You might as well ask for the moon!"

Hilgard supported Göring. "May I draw your attention to the following facts?" he asked. "Plate glass is not manufactured by the Bohemian glass industry, but is entirely in the hands of the Belgians. In my estimation, the damage amounts to six million marks. That is to say, under the terms of the insurance policies, we shall have to pay the owners—who for the most part are Aryans—about six millions' compensation for the glass. Incidentally, the amount of damage equals about half a year's production of the whole of the Belgian glass industry. We believe the manufacturers will take six months to deliver the glass."

"We must make a national declaration," Göring said.

"We can't do that at the moment," Goebbels quickly replied.

"Then we can't go any further. There's nothing more we can do. It's impossible!" Göring turned back to Hilgard for confirmation. "In your view, the Aryans carry the burden?"

"Yes, for the most part, for the glass insurance."

Turning to the question of looted homes and shops, Göring tried hopefully to draw distinctions between theft and losses incurred during riots or civil disturbances. But Hilgard had little comfort for him in this area, either. "Let me give you an example," he said. 'The biggest incident is the case of Margraf, on the Unter den Linden. The jewelry store of Margraf is insured with us under what is known as a comprehensive policy. This covers practically any damage that may occur. The damage reported to us amounts to 1.7 million, because the store was completely ransacked."

Göring turned furiously to the Gestapo chiefs. "Daluege and Heydrich," he shouted, "you must get me that jewelry back. Stage large-scale raids!"

"The order has already been given," Daluege assured him. "People are being searched and places raided all the time. According to my reports, one hundred fifty people were arrested yesterday afternoon."

Heydrich added that there had been around eight hundred reported cases of looting throughout the Reich, but already over a hundred culprits had been arrested. "We are trying to get the loot back," he said.

"And the jewels?" Göring demanded greedily.

"That's hard to say," Heydrich replied. "Some of the articles were thrown into the street and picked up. The same thing happened with the furriers. In the Friedrichstrasse, for instance, in police district C, the crowd naturally rushed to pick up mink and skunk furs, and so on. It will be very difficult to recover them. Even children filled their pockets just for the fun of the thing. One must suggest that the Hitler Youth should not be employed on such actions without the party's consent. Such things are very easily destroyed."

"The party should issue an order," Daluege added, "to the effect that the police must immediately be notified if a neighbor's wife—everybody knows his neighbor very well—has a fur coat remodeled or if somebody is seen wearing a new ring or bracelet. We should like the party to assist in this matter."

At this point, Hilgard came back into the discussion, risking Göring's wrath by daring to argue with him. Although the loot picked up in the Friedrichstrasse and elsewhere was not covered, he said, the companies set great value on being allowed to fullfil their obligations by paying out on their policies. When Göring, predictably, exploded and said he forbade it, Hilgard bravely went on to explain his reasons.

"It simply has to do with the fact," he said, "that we do a large foreign business. Our business has a sound international basis, and in the interests of the foreign-exchange position in Germany we have to make sure that confidence in the German insurance business is not shaken. If we were now to refuse to honor commitments entered into through legal contracts, it would be a blot on the escutcheon of the German insurance business."

"But it wouldn't be, the moment I issue a decree. A law sanctioned by the state!" Göring responded.

"I was coming to exactly that," Hilgard continued patiently.

"By all means let them pay the claims," Heydrich interjected. "But as soon as payment is made, it will be confiscated. That way, we will save face."

"I'm inclined to agree with what Obergruppenführer Heydrich has just suggested," Hilgard said. "First, use the apparatus of the insurance companies to check on the damage, to regulate it and even to pay it, but give the insurance companies a chance to—"

Göring interrupted him sharply: "Just a minute! *You'll* have to pay in any case, when it's the Germans who have suffered the damage. But there'll be a legal decree forbidding you from making any direct payment to Jews. You will have to make payment for the damage the Jews suffered, but not to the Jews—to the Ministry of Finance. What they do with it is their business."

An official of the Finance Ministry, Herr Schmer, spoke up at this. "Herr Field Marshal," he said, "I have a proposal to make. From all the registered Jewish wealth—and a billion of it is already to be collected— a certain fixed percentage, say fifteen, should be raised, so that all Jews pay equally. And from the money raised in this way, the insurance companies could be refunded."

"No," Göring responded flatly. "I have no intention of refunding the insurance companies. The companies are liable. No, the money belongs to the state. That is quite clear. It would be making a present to the insurance companies. They will fulfil their obligations. Leave it at that."

In vain, Hilgard tried his best to persuade Göring that the result of paying for the glass alone would be "a great catastrophe" for the German insurance industry. At an estimated 14 million marks including administrative costs, it was more than double the entire outlay for a normal year. The whole of the profits of the insurance companies would be wiped out. Many smaller companies would go bankrupt.

Göring was unmoved by their predicament, but when Heydrich told him the state stood to lose more than 100 million marks in taxes on the materials and goods damaged in the pogrom, his temper began to rise again. And when Daluege pointed out that most of the goods that had been destroyed were not the property of the Jewish shopkeepers but of

Aryan suppliers, on consignment, and Hilgard said the insurers would have to pay for these, too, he blew up.

"I wish you'd killed two hundred Jews instead of destroying such valuables!" he cried.

"Well, there were thirty-five killed," Heydrich responded, as though this were a defense.

The prospect of being able to hold on to the payments, however, was clearly enough to pacify Göring. The process was completed for him, after a brief discussion on the question of foreign exchange, by yet another bright thought: Any of the jewels stolen from Margraf's and other stores that were recovered by the police would not be returned, but handed over to the state. Not even Hilgard's insistent return to the profits that were to be lost by the insurance companies could ruffle his good humor now.

"The Jew must report the damage," he told him. "He will get the insurance money, but it will be confiscated. The final result will be that the insurance companies will gain something, since not all the damage will have to be made good. Hilgard, you can afford to smile to yourself."

"I have no reason to," Hilgard replied, understandably bitter, "if you describe the fact that we shall not have to pay for all the damage as making money."

"Wait a minute," Göring told him, clearly enjoying himself. "If you are legally bound to pay five million, and suddenly an angel in my somewhat corpulent form appears before you and tells you you can keep one million, by thunder, isn't that making money? I wouldn't mind making a straight split with you, or whatever you call it. I have only to look at you—your whole body is smiling. You are getting a big rake-off!"

But Hilgard was far from smiling. "All the insurance companies are the losers," he complained. "That is so, and it stays so. Nobody can tell me different."

"Then you should see to it that fewer windows get smashed." Göring had obviously had enough of this man with his tiresome questions, and now dismissed him. "Send your representatives out—they should clear it up in no time. If you have any particular questions to ask, then speak to Herr Lange."

With the troublesome insurance man out of the way, it was the turn of Ernst Woermann to raise the Foreign Office's worry about foreign Jews in Germany. This was a difficult question, particularly when the Jews concerned claimed American or British citizenship. But at least there were relatively few of them, and the occasional diplomatic complaint could be passed off quite easily. When there were larger numbers, the problem was much greater.

"As the führer says," Göring stated, "we must find a way to talk over this question first with those countries who are also doing something about their Jews. That every dirty Polish Jew has a legal position here, and we have to put up with it—that has to stop. The führer was not very happy about the agreement he made with the Poles. [In 1934, Germany and Poland signed a treaty of friendship requiring each to give equal treatment to citizens of the other.] He thinks we should take a few chances and say to Poland, 'If you please, we are not going to do that. Let's talk over together what's going to happen. You are doing things against your Jews in Poland, but the minute a Yid leaves Poland and arrives here, we have to treat him like a Pole. I'd like to have this reversed a little.' "

Woermann, however, was still worried about America. "We must weigh over whether we should take steps against American property in Germany," he said.

This brought a violent tirade from Göring against the United States, "that country of scoundrels . . . that robber state." But he conceded that there were risks involved in upsetting the Americans, and that this needed to be considered. Where possible, the involvement of foreign Jews was to be avoided.

Walther Funk, the economics minister, was still concerned whether or not Jewish shops and stores were to be allowed to reopen. Fishböck, the Austrian finance minister, was quick to report that in Austria they already had a very complete plan. In Vienna, he said, there were twelve thousand Jewish workshops and five thousand Jewish retail shops. Even before the *Anschluss*, the Austrian Nazis had drawn up a plan to close down ten thousand of the workshops and four thousand of the retail stores, leaving some three thousand businesses, which would be Aryanized. All they were waiting for, he said, was a law empowering them to withdraw business licenses from whomever they chose, irrespective of the Jewish question. They had asked for this in September.

"I shall have this decree issued today," Göring promised.

"I do not believe there will be one hundred stores left," Fishböck told him, "probably fewer. And thus, by the end of the year we will have liquidated all the recognized Jewish-owned businesses."

"I must say, that proposition is wonderful," Göring responded. "This way, the whole affair in Vienna, one of the Jewish capitals so to speak, would be wound up by Christmas or the end of the year."

"We can do the same thing here," Funk said, eager not to be left out of the self-congratulations. "I have already prepared a law elaborating it. Effective January 1, 1939, Jews will be prohibited from running retail stores and wholesale establishments, as well as independent workshops. They will be further prohibited from keeping employees, or offering any ready-made products on the market, and from advertising or receiving orders. Where a Jewish store is open, the police shall close it down.

"From January 1, 1939, a Jew can no longer be head of any enterprise, as stipulated in the law for the organization of national labor of January 20, 1934. If a Jew holds a leading position in an establishment without being the head of the business, his contract may be declared void within six weeks by the head of the business. With the expiration of this period, all claims of the employee, including all claims to maintenance, become invalid. That is always unpleasant and a great danger. A Jew cannot be a member of a corporation. Jewish members of corporations will have to be retired by December 31, 1938. Special authorization is not necessary. The competent ministers of the Reich are being authorized to issue the necessary provision for execution of this law."

"I believe we can agree with this law," Göring announced. There was a general shout of "yes, indeed!" from everyone else.

After considerable discussion of the detailed technicalities of Aryanization and the issuing of bonds to Jews whose businesses had been seized, the meeting turned to the continuing problem of forcing the remaining Jews out of the country. Heydrich proudly stated that by setting up a central organization for Jewish emigration—the office that was headed by Adolf Eichmann—he had been able to get at least fifty thousand Jews out of Austria, while at the same time in the old Reich, only nineteen thousand had been got out. This had worked through a successful collaboration with the Economics Ministry and the foreign aid organizations.

Göring was worried that there should be no repetition of the situation when thousands of Polish Jews had been stuck in no-man's-land on the green frontier, giving the foreign press a field day. But Heydrich reassured him that at least forty-five thousand Jews had been made to leave the country by legal means. "Through the Jewish societies we extracted a certain amount of money from the rich Jews who wanted to emigrate," he explained. "By paying this amount plus an additional sum in foreign currency, this made it possible for a number of poor Jews to leave. The problem was not making the rich Jews leave, but getting rid of the Jewish mob."

Even with these pressures and devices, however, Heydrich pointed out, this level of emigration could not be maintained. He estimated that it would take eight to ten years to get rid of those remaining. The problem would be compounded by the fact that because of Aryanization and all the other restrictions, they would be creating a vast number of unemployed Jews. He believed, therefore, that they would have to take measures to isolate the Jews, so that they would no longer take part in the normal life of Germany, but that they should be allowed to work with a restricted clientele in certain specified professions, as doctors, lawyers, hairdressers, and so on.

"As far as isolating them is concerned," he continued, "I would like to make a few proposals regarding police measures, which are also important because of their psychological effect on public opinion. For example, anyone who is Jewish according to the Nuremberg Laws will have to wear a certain badge."

"A uniform!" Göring exclaimed enthusiastically.

"A badge. In this way, we would put an end to foreign Jews being molested because they do not look any different from our own."

"But my dear Heydrich," Göring replied, "you will not be able to avoid the creation of ghettos on a very large scale in all the cities. They will have to be created."

The idea of ghettos aroused the interest of the entire meeting, sparking off a general discussion of the finer points of how they should be organized and run, how they should be policed, how they should be supplied.

"Once we have a ghetto," Göring said, "we could determine what stores ought to be there, and we would be able to say, 'You, Jew So-and-so, together with So-and-so, shall take care of the delivery of goods.' Then a German wholesale firm will be ordered to deliver the goods for this Jewish store. The store would then not be a retail shop but a cooperative store, a cooperative society for Jews."

"All these measures will eventually lead to the establishment of a ghetto," Heydrich pointed out. "I must say, one should not want to set up a ghetto nowadays, but if these measures are carried through, they will automatically drive the Jews into a ghetto."

For the time being, the prospect of physically creating ghettos was shelved—though it was agreed that the Jews would inevitably have to congregate together, if only for their own protection, and because of new housing laws that Goebbels wanted to introduce, removing Jews from Aryan apartment blocks and forcing them to sublet their own houses and apartments to other Jews. Jews were also to be forbidden to own cars and banned from certain streets and whole areas of cities, and from health spas and general hospitals.

Finally, Göring came to the question of the Jewish Atonement Fine. "How would you feel, gentlemen," he asked, "if I were to announce today that a fine of one billion is to be imposed on the Jews, as their contribution?"

Inevitably, the idea was received with enormous enthusiasm. Gratified, Göring announced, "I shall decide on the wording—that German Jewry as a whole shall, as a punishment for the abominable crimes, etc., etc., make a contribution of one billion marks. That will do the trick! The swine won't be in such a hurry to commit a second murder. For the rest, I must say, I would not like to be a Jew in Germany right now."

For several minutes, the meeting was taken up with eager discussion of possible methods of collection, and making sure no Jew was allowed to escape payment. To insure that they did not rock the economy by selling government stocks and bonds to raise the money, Göring said he would simply suspend all dealing in them for three days. And on that happy note, the meeting ended, at 2:30 P.M., in a mood of great satisfaction. The same day, Göring issued the first three decrees: imposing the billion-mark fine, eliminating all Jews from the German economy by January 1, 1939, and laying down that Jewish property owners and tenants would have to make good the damage to their businesses and homes immediately and pay the costs themselves.

In order to avoid any possible complications, Göring had one other decree up his sleeve, which he instructed the Justice Ministry to issue: All Jews of German nationality were barred from starting any legal proceedings in German courts over any matters arising from the events of the pogrom.

Goebbels followed with his decree banning Jews from theaters, concert halls, motion-picture houses, and exhibitions throughout Germany. And to round off the day's work, the meeting of ministers promised "further decisive measures to exclude Jewry from German economic life and to prevent provocative activities," in the near future.

X

"Humanity Stands Aghast"

International reaction to Kristallnacht and the events that followed was predictably outraged. Throughout most of the nonfascist world, press headlines were uniformly anti-German—though oddly enough, in the Soviet Union there was not a single direct mention of what had occurred until nearly a week later, apart from a brief story in the German-language newspaper *Deutsche Zeitung* and even briefer quotes from foreign papers.

In London, the Liberal *News Chronicle* called it "a pogrom hardly surpassed in fury since the Dark Ages" and declared, "Not on the basis of such savagery can there be any hope of understanding between the leaders of Germany and the people of this country. Britain will be revolted to a man by this sadistic outbreak." *The Times* thundered magisterially, "No foreign propagandist bent upon blaspheming Germany before the world could outdo the tale of burnings and beatings, of blackguardly assaults upon defenceless and innocent people, which disgraced that country yesterday."

But many papers in many countries, while expressing revulsion at the pogrom, swallowed at least in part Goebbels's assertion that it represented a spontaneous outburst of anger by the people at the Paris murder. The *Daily Telegraph*, a Conservative daily that supported Chamberlain, declared, "Germany has delivered herself over to an orgy of savagery which will send a thrill of horror throughout the civilised world. . . . Nazi revenge is one of the most terrible things of the present century."

During the Armistice Day service held at Westminster Abbey on Friday, November 11, the dean offered up a special prayer for the Jews: "Let us remember in silence and in sympathy the Jewish people and their troubles." The archbishop of Canterbury, Cosmo Gordon Lang, hitherto a keen advocate of friendship with Germany and a supporter of appeasement, wrote a letter to *The Times* that same day to express his horror. "There are times when the mere instincts of humanity make silence

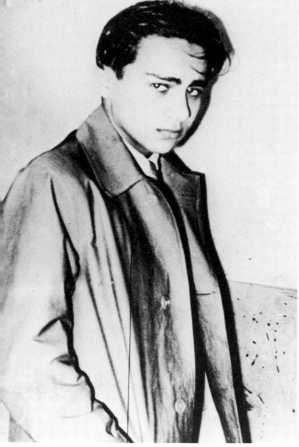

Herschel Grynszpan, the young Jewish assassin whose five shots provided the Nazis with their excuse for a pogrom.

The victim, Ernst vom Rath. On receiving news of the shooting, Hitler promoted him instantly from third secretary to counselor.

Herschel Grynszpan is led away for interrogation.

Ernst vom Rath lies in state in the Rheinlandhalle in Düsseldorf.

At the memorial service, Hitler, seated between Ernst vom Rath's parents, presented a picture of grief. The burial was also conducted with full military and party honors.

e they were all
ed on Kristallnacht,
shop windows were
d with graffiti such
.

On June 21, 1938, Austrian Jews were forbidden to
wear traditional Tyrolean costume. This cartoon was
published in the Swiss-German newspaper the *Basler
Nachrichten* that day, and in the SS journal *Das
Schwarze Korps* the following week. The caption is
a pun on the word *Tracht*, translating as "The only
traditional costume (*Tracht*) such types have a right
to is a good thrashing (*Tracht Prügel*)!"

setting in motion monstrous at-
n the Jews, Joseph Goebbels
ed to remain a devoted father.
May 1, 1945, Goebbels had his
dren given lethal injections, then
his wife committed suicide.

A synagogue blazes in the Sudetenland . . .

. . . and in Bamberg, where an SA ma
pervises the fire department's efforts to pr
the flames spreading elsewhere.

In Berlin, too, fire engines stood by to protect
the nearby main post office while the Oran-
ienburgstrasse synagogue burned.

In Baden-Baden, Jewish men were marched
through the streets to the synagogue. The leading
figures carry a Star of David bearing the
inscription "God will not fail us."

Inside the synagogue, Dr. Arthur Flehinger is made to read aloud from *Mein
Kampf* before the building is set on fire.

Inside the main Munich synagogue, the Ark and Torah scrolls were vandalized before the building was torched and gutted by fire.

In other places, synagogue furnishings were dragged out and piled up for public burning. The notice here reads "Revenge for the murder of vom Rath! Death to international Jewry and Freemasonry!"

The charred remains of the interior of a synagogue in Czechoslovakia.

Private homes suffered, too, throughout t Reich, as seen in this wrecked interior of apartment in Vienna.

morning after in Berlin: Jewish shop-
ers clear up the broken glass . . .

. . . while German citizens
pass by, unconcerned.

In cases of doubt, Jewishness was sometin established by such "scientific" methods measuring the size of a man's nose.

Thirty thousand Jewish men were arrested and marched off to concentration camps in an orderly manner, as shown here in Oldenberg.

Throughout the Reich, shuttered stores bore testimony to the fate of their owners with messages such as this.

Hard labor, at right, and below, roll call at Sachsenhausen concentration camp. The motto painted on the huts in the background reads "Truthfulness, Sacrifice and Love."

Jews in Vienna were forced to scrub walls and pavements after the *Anschluss* to remove pro-Schuschnigg slogans. As an added indignity, many were forced to scrub streets under the supervision of mere children of the Hitler Youth. Some discovered their buckets contained acid paint stripper, which severely burned their hands.

On October 28, 1938, the Nazis expelled some fifteen thousand Polish-born Jews from Germany, including the Grynszpan family. Seen here are some of the seven thousand who were stranded in the border village of Zbaszyn.

Despite the horrors of the pogrom, the French made a pact of friendship with Germany on December 6, 1938, signed in Paris by the two foreign ministers, Joachim von Ribbentrop (left) and Georges Bonnet.

Goebbels, and Görach took advantage of nacht in his own way.

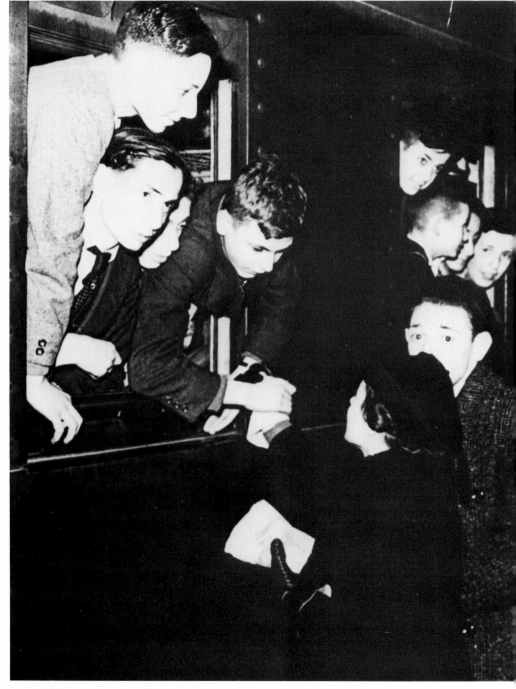

In 1939, Britain accepted ten thousand Jewish children from Germany, some of whom are seen here leaving Berlin.

of the refugee children were initially housed in holiday camps, such as this, Dovercourt, Harwich.

"Why don't they go?" As always, cartoonist David Low captured the situation in a single image.

impossible," he wrote. "Would that the rulers of the Reich could realise that such excesses of hatred and malice put upon the friendship which we are ready to offer them an almost intolerable strain."

At a mass meeting in the Royal Albert Hall, two of the most senior archbishops of the Anglican and Catholic hierarchies, Dr. Temple of York and Cardinal Hinsley of Westminster, both condemned the events of Kristallnacht. Temple warned that in the face of such horrors there was a real danger that the world would sink into moral numbness and lethargy. "We must try and keep alive," he said, "our capacity for feeling and for moral judgement." The moderator of the Federal Council of Evangelical Free Churches of England, Dr. Robert Bond, and the chief rabbi, Dr. J. H. Hertzl, as well as an assorted collection of the great and the good—including Herbert Morrison MP, L. S. Amery MP, and Lady Violet Bonham-Carter—also spoke.

Across the Atlantic, America, too, was flooded by a torrent of righteous indignation. *The New York Times* wrote, "No man can look on the scenes witnessed yesterday without shame for the degradation of his species." The *Herald Tribune*: "One cannot understand how even the present masters of Germany can imagine that in permitting this sort of thing they are inviting for their great creation anything but the disgust of all civilized men." The *New York Sun*: "The outside world, which has fully appraised the iron discipline of National Socialism, can draw but one conclusion—that the outrages committed by those mobs were winked at if not actually approved, by the governing authorities." Echoing the London *New Chronicle*, Thomas E. Dewey wrote, piously but inaccurately, "Not since the days of medieval barbarism has the world been forced to look upon a spectacle such as this."

It would be natural to expect condemnation in New York City, with the largest Jewish population in the United States. But elsewhere the American press was equally vehement: "Humanity stands aghast and ashamed at the indecency and brutality that is permitted in Germany" (*Syracuse Post-Standard*); "Reprisal against a whole people for the crime of an overwrought youth is a throwback to barbarity" (*St. Paul Dispatch*); "The people outside Germany who still value tolerance, understanding and humanity, can no more keep silent in the face of what has just taken place than they would in the face of any other barbarity" (*Hartford Courant*). Columnist Anne O'Hare McCormick described the pogrom as "a threat to the civilization of the world." And in a similar vein, former president Herbert Hoover weighed in with a statement to the Associated

Press agency saying, "It is the duty of men everywhere to express our indignation, not alone of the suffering these men are imposing on an innocent people, but at the blow they are striking at civilization."

The headline in the *Washington Post*, however, seemed to demonstrate a greater interest in more parochial concerns. NAZIS PILLAGE JEWS AS NATION RIOTS; SEIZE 2 U.S. CAMERAMEN, it trumpeted. Only toward the end of the story did the reader learn that the two photographers who had been arrested in Berlin while taking pictures had been released unharmed after questioning.

Most American papers, and indeed most of the papers in every country, resorted to overblown rhetoric, which often seems repetitious and threadbare in retrospect. One of the pities of events such as Kristallnacht is that all too often they expose the inadequacies of the world's leader writers and copy editors. Great disasters tend to sit on the chests of journalists with the weight of rhinoceroses, reducing their sparkling or hard-hitting prose to mere squeaks of indignation. On occasions that demand the descriptive powers of a Milton or a Dante, they often end up sounding either pompous or hysterical. There was, however, an unmistakable and genuine sense of outrage everywhere. And some American papers did manage to provide a clear verbal perspective. Dismissing the overused medieval allusions, the *Atlanta Journal* pointed out that to compare Nazi Germany to the Middle Ages was "slandering the Middle Ages," while the *Springfield Republican* described Kristallnacht laconically as "a lynching party at its worst."

The great American public responded to the press and radio reports with rallies and demonstrations, at some of which swastika flags were burned. On November 15, many prominent figures took part in a coast-to-coast radio broadcast protesting against the outrages. Secretary of the Interior Harold L. Ickes was one of them, saying, "There can be no peace if national policy adopts as a deliberate instrument the dispersion all over the world of millions of helpless and persecuted wanderers." The next day, a gala concert by more than four hundred stars of stage, screen, radio, and opera was held at Madison Square Garden on behalf of a Palestine appeal.

New York Mayor Fiorello La Guardia played his part with a typically flamboyant gesture, creating a special "Nazi Guardian Squad" under the command of fifty-one-year-old Captain Max Finkelstein, president of the Shamrin Society, the New York Police Department's Jewish benevolent organization. His two assistants were Lieutenant Jacob Licker of the Simpson Street station and Sergeant Isaac Goldstein of the White Plains station, both in the Bronx. The new squad had twelve patrolmen, every single one of them Jewish. Its job was to guard the German consulate and "to perform general police duty on all occasions requiring protection for Nazi sympathizers."

The plan appealed enormously to New Yorkers as characteristic of their much-loved mayor. But in fact it was not original—Teddy Roosevelt had pulled the same stunt some forty years before when he was police commissioner of New York. Faced with a hell-fire anti-Semite German preacher, Pastor Ahlwardt, who was determined to speak out against "the murderers of Christ," Roosevelt had been unable to ban the man from speaking. To register his disapproval of the pastor's message, therefore, he had organized an all-Jewish unit consisting of a sergeant and forty patrolmen to "protect" him. Whenever Ahlwardt rose to deliver one of his diatribes against the Jews, he had been forced to do so from behind a solid phalanx of blue-uniformed Jewish cops. His campaign had collapsed in mocking laughter.

When questioned about his new squad, Mayor La Guardia was straight-facedly noncommittal. "Purely routine," he told reporters. "Purely routine."

In a more sober vein, Cardinal William O'Connell, archbishop of Boston and doyen of the Catholic hierarchy in the United States, blamed the pogrom on "intellectualism gone mad." In a speech on Sunday, November 20, to a meeting in Boston of the Federation of College Catholic Clubs, O'Connell declared Germany was the most intellectual nation on earth. It used, he said, to be considered a great place to go to school. "But today, they are under the heel of a little group who are trying to cast out not only the Jews but God himself and bring the nation back to paganism."

As public opinion in America mobilized on behalf of the Jews, the German ambassador in Washington, Hans Heinrich Dieckhoff, reported anxiously back to Berlin:

At the moment, a hurricane is raging here that renders steady work impossible. The fact that a great section of the American press has long been attacking Germany in the most spiteful and bitter manner, and that this campaign has embraced comparatively wide circles, is well known to you. Until November 10, however, large and powerful sections of the American people had still remained aloof from this campaign . . . partly out of sympathy for the Third Reich, in which they saw a stronghold of order and a bulwark against riots and against unlawful encroachments against private property. Today, this is no longer the case. . . . The fact that Jewish newspapers write still more excitedly than before and that the Catholic bishops' campaign against Germany is still waged more bitterly than before is not surprising; but, that men like Dewey, Hoover, Hearst, and many others who have hitherto maintained a comparative reserve and had even, to some extent, expressed sympathy toward Germany, are now publicly adopting so violent and bitter an attitude against her is a serious matter. One central theme runs through all these utterances, and a trusted American friend characterized it as follows: "It is generally felt, even among well-wishers of Germany, that the recent events are the best thing that could have happened to the Jews because they arouse universal sympathy, and the worst thing that could have happened to Germany. It jeopardizes the appeasement that was to follow Munich."

Three days later, Dieckhoff wrote a letter to Ernst Weizsäcker, state secretary at the Foreign Office, reiterating much of what he had said, bemoaning that "the good prospects for a gradual spread of anti-Semitism had suffered a serious setback." He cited one extremely telling incident as an example of the strength of feeling in the United States: "Yesterday in an old Protestant church in Massachusetts they went so far as to have a rabbi preach for the first time, departing from a 300-year-old tradition, in order to show that in a situation like the present they stand by the Jews."

North of the border, the Canadians were also expressing shock at the reports from Germany. Packed meetings of protest were held in practically every large town in Canada. In Montreal, the meeting was presided over by the chief justice of the Quebec Superior Court, while Sir William Mulock, former chief justice and chancellor of the University of Toronto and other well-known figures occupied the platform at a similar demonstration in the Ontario capital. "Not since the dark years of the war," the *Montreal Daily Star* claimed, "has Canadian opinion so unanimously and so articulately expressed itself on any world issue."

Naturally, the ways in which this opinion was expressed varied widely. Sometimes they were distinctly bizarre. In the small town of Goderich in Ontario, for example, the Huron County Council unanimously adopted a resolution on November 15 authorizing the courthouse officer, Sergeant Major George James, to arrest anyone found wearing a Hitler mustache.

But much North American reaction was neither eccentric nor angry. Some of it was not even particularly concerned, for there was still a strong and instinctive distaste for getting involved in what many perceived to be Europe's problems. The *Philadelphia Inquirer*, for example, pointed out in its editorial on Wednesday, November 16, that while there had no doubt been worse pogroms in czarist Russia, or China, or even in

Spain during the civil war that was still raging, "the furies loosed in Hitler's Reich have implications more terrible, perhaps, than any that have scourged the world in two thousand years of blood and death." It then went on to point an accusing finger at Chamberlain and Daladier.

"Britain and France," it said, "were forced, at the Munich showdown, to agree to a peaceable solution of the Czechoslovak issue. They could do nothing else. But why, before the Munich crisis, didn't they at least strive to drive a sharper bargain with Hitler? Why didn't they try to exact pledges that he would curb racial persecution, that he would stop condoning, if not directing, lawlessness against race and religion? This was not an extraneous subject. It had a proper place in the councils which culminated at Munich."

The *Inquirer* concluded by washing its hands of the whole distasteful business. "The present horror in Germany holds the potentialities of an international crisis scarcely less menacing than that of Czechoslovakia," it warned. " . . . It may be that hatred and brute force will overflow the Reich's borders and strike at other Powers. That is Europe's problem. It isn't ours. Let Europe take care of Munich's homing chickens. They aren't ours."

French reaction to the events of Kristallnacht tended on the whole to be careful and cautious. Not for them the grand rhetorical gesture, the wallowing in public indignation. France felt threatened by what had happened—after all, the assassination of vom Rath had occurred on French soil, and on their border was the German Army, ready to do the bidding of a violent madman. And then there was the possibility of divisions within France itself. The wounds of the Dreyfus Affair, the celebrated case when a Jewish officer was falsely convicted of passing secrets to a foreign power in 1894, had never completely healed, and there were many on the French right who were fiercely anti-Semitic and eager to enflame them once again.

La Lumière, a left-wing weekly, did not see it that way. WHAT BARBARITY! THE WORLD IS OUTRAGED! FRANCE IS SILENT! screamed the headline of an article by Albert Bayet. "In the past, when we protested against massacres in Ethiopia, China, Spain, we were told, 'Silence! You are warmongering.' When we protested against the mutilation of Czechoslovakia, we were told, 'Keep quiet! You are a war party.' Today, when we protest against the contemptible persecution of defenseless Jews and their wives and their children, we are told, 'Be silent! France is afraid.' "

In an article in the same magazine, Nicolas Paillot complained that while even Neville Chamberlain had spoken out against the Nazi atrocities in the House of Commons, Edouard Daladier and Georges Bonnet had remained silent: The subject had not even been debated in the National Assembly. Paillot accused the French press of indifference to the Nazi terror. It was perfectly true that on the first day most of the moderate press had confined itself to purely factual reporting, and after that there had been silence, or at best the most discreet condemnation. *Le Matin*, Paillot complained, had tried to sit on the fence from the first, making only the vaguest protest against all the violence. At the same time, it had tried to please its Jewish readers: "One looks vainly in the headline of M. Lauzanne for the name of Germany, of Hitler, or even of any mention of the Jews." *Le Journal* devoted much space to Goebbels's justifications of the pogrom and said very little on the other side. *Le Temps*, noted for its formidable editorials, failed to fire off one of these against Nazi Germany, limiting its coverage to a foreign report.

The Jewish Chronicle, the British Jewish newspaper, however, did not share Paillot's view of *Le Temps*. Instead, it praised FRANCE'S SHARP REBUKES. "The horror felt at the pogroms seems to have completely overcast that aroused by Grynzspan's crime," it claimed, and praised the paper for speaking out against the "monstrous attempt" to force Jews in Germany to expiate the crime of a single individual. It quoted *Le Temps* approvingly: "No persecution has ever succeeded in extinguishing hatred and renewing confidence. On the contrary, it is to be feared that the international effect of the treatment meted out to the Jews in Germany will be to increase the mistrust felt in many countries for German policy."

An additional concern for the French was the fact that the trial of Herschel Grynszpan would take place in Paris under well-nigh intolerable pressures. After the first day of the pogrom, the right-wing newspaper *L'Ordre* published a piece by Emile Bure entitled "In the Midst of Barbarism," which voiced the fears and opinions of many Frenchmen:

> The court itself will hardly be able to prevent witness after witness from declaring that violence leads to violence and that persecution leads to revolt. They will be reminded of the spectacle of Polish Jews domiciled in Germany being driven to the frontier and herded there like animals waiting for slaughter. Germany has returned to the Middle Ages, and the führer, drunk with his unexpected and menacing victories, is burning to renew the exploits of those days.
>
> The world will one day rise up against the führer and force him to respect a civilization of which Germany in her better moments only a short time ago was justly proud. I am not suggesting an ideological crusade, but is it possible to believe that France and Great Britain run no risk of bringing upon themselves the same evils that, as a result of their indifference and complacency,

have befallen so many peoples and individuals who invoke democratic principles?

This danger exists if we willfully ignore the sufferings of the minorities subject to Nazi laws and basely encourage those who decree and enforce those laws, often with all the refinements of sadism."

As in France, press and public reactions in most other countries of Europe failed to follow a clear moral line of outright condemnation, but reflected national and sectarian attitudes toward the Germans, the Nazis, and the Jews. In Belgium, for example, where memories were still vivid of the German invasion of the First World War, the general opinion was expressed by *Nation Belge*, a Catholic newspaper that normally followed a far-right line on most issues. In an article entitled "Furore Teutonico," it declared that however fatuous and provocative the murder of vom Rath might have been, no nation that considered itself civilized should stoop to inflict such unheard-of brutalities upon people who had nothing to do with the crime in question. But it refused to lay all the blame on the Nazi regime, believing it sprang rather from what it saw as the natural brutality of the German character. As proof, it compared the pogrom with the brutal repression of the Spartacists, a group of the far left led by Rosa Luxemburg and Karl Liebknecht in 1919, at the beginning of the Weimar Republic.

While *Het Laatste Nieuws*, a Flemish paper, was bitterly critical of the German government, the Catholic *Standard* quoted Vatican opinion, which blamed the persecution of the Jews on atheism.

From the British legation in Berne, the minister, Sir George Warner, reported that the outcry in Switzerland was not particularly loud, apart from the extreme-left newspapers. There was, he said, a fair amount of anti-Semitism in Switzerland, and the Swiss were not anxious that the Jewish population, especially in Zurich, should be increased.

In Poland, official press reaction was guarded, partly because violent criticism of Germany was banned under an agreement made between the two countries. In any case, although not as strictly controlled as in Germany, the Polish press was kept on a tight rein by the ruling military junta. The National Democrat paper, *Dziennik Narodowy*, which was near-fascist, had little sympathy for the German Jews. In its opinion, they fully deserved their fate. The *Gazeta Polska* and the *Kurjer Poranny* took the slightly softer official line: Poland was overpopulated and was now becoming the focus for Jewish immigration. Instead of leaving Poland, as they had done in the past, Jews were now pouring back into the country, fleeing ill-treatment elsewhere. In 1937, for example, only nine thousand Jews left Poland, compared with a normal average of nearer one hundred thousand a year. Obviously, the papers said, this could not continue.

According to the British ambassador in Warsaw, Sir Howard Kennard, nearly all the Poles he spoke to expressed "horror and disgust that human beings should be treated so outrageously." But this did not stop them from supporting their government in its efforts to reduce Poland's own Jewish population. Unlike the German Nazis, the Poles did not expect their Jewish problem to be solved overnight—with 3.25 million Jews to be resettled, it could only be achieved in stages, over a period of time. It was felt in Warsaw that if, as a result of the German excesses, the international community ever did succeed in putting together some humanitarian package to assist the emigration of Jews, then it should not be confined to German Jews—Poland was just as deserving of help in that respect as was Germany.

One official of the Polish Foreign Ministry remarked to an English journalist that failure to include Poland in any such package would be "an incitement to pogroms." Ambassador Kennard agreed. "Local excesses," as he called them, were "of not infrequent occurrence" in Poland, and though it was difficult to get much information about them, because of press censorship, he did not believe they were nationally organized, as they were in Germany. But, he said, most Poles "generally regard it as inevitable that in order to induce a state of mind favorable to migration among the Jews, their position here must be made less comfortable."

There was certainly little comfort for the Jews in the Soviet Union's response to Kristallnacht. *Pravda* finally got around to mentioning it in a short article on November 16—no doubt it had taken that long for Stalin, still preoccupied with his purges, to decide what line the party should take. Predictably, it compared the German pogrom with czarist pogroms in Russia, and then in a classic example of Marxist logic concluded that Kristallnacht had essentially been a kind of Roman circus, intended to divert the downtrodden proletariat. "The economic difficulties and the discontent of the masses have forced fascist leaders to resort to a pogrom against the Jews," it stated, "to distract the attention of the masses from grave problems within the country."

The next day, *Pravda* returned to the attack with a prominently printed leading article. The anti-Jewish atrocities, it declared, not only branded German fascism as an enemy of civilization but also proved that the end of Hitler's rule was near. As the last efforts of a dying regime, it told its readers, the pogrom would not help Hitler any more than the czarist pogroms helped Nicholas II. But after lengthy quotes from the works of Stalin, intended to show the dictator's abhorrence of anti-Semitism, the article concluded with a prophetic warning that Western leaders would have been wise to heed. Although "bourgeois circles" in the United States and Great Britain had shown themselves horrified by the treatment accorded to the Jews in Germany, it said, they nevertheless did not sufficiently realize that such savagery constituted an integral part of fascist policy, and that the treatment accorded to her own Jews was what Germany was reserving for the world at large.

Apart from issuing such admonishments, the Soviets did not seem inclined to offer any practical help. Eleven days later, *Trud*, the organ of the Central Council of Soviet Trade Unions, was chosen as the mouthpiece for the next public statement. "German and Austrian Jews must be saved," it said, but then went on to argue that emigration was "no solution, only a subterfuge." German Jews had a right to live as free persons in their own country—"The fascist regime must be compelled to stop its crimes." It failed to suggest how this could be achieved, but blamed Chamberlain and French capitalists for what had happened, accusing them of knowing that the Munich agreement would result in the persecution of Jews in Germany, and of now shedding crocodile tears over something for which they themselves were partly responsible.

When it came to the question of offering asylum to German Jews, *Trud* was less positive, warning that under the Soviet constitution this might prove to be impossible. The constitution granted the right of asylum only to specific categories of persons: "foreign citizens persecuted for defending the interests of the workers, or for their scientific activity, or for their struggle for national liberation." Since the bulk of the Jewish victims of Nazi oppression were shopkeepers, bankers, businessmen, intellectuals, and so on, they could hardly be said to fit into any of the approved categories.

The general hostility of foreign press and public reaction can hardly have been a surprise to Goebbels. From the start, he fought back as well as he could, even though for the most part it was inevitably an exercise in damage control. He began by banning some seventy-seven foreign newspapers, including, according to the *New York Herald Tribune*, the November 6 and 7 issues of *The New York Times* and most recent issues of the leading Swiss, Danish, Yugoslav, Czechoslovak, Polish, and Vatican

City dailies, which contained descriptions of anti-Jewish activities in Germany. The *Herald Tribune* headline summed up the situation rather neatly: NAZIS BAN 77 PAPERS FOR TELLING ON THEM.

The Nazi newspapers counterattacked boldly, concentrating their fire particularly against the American press, bravely trading cliché for cliché and arguably getting the better of the exchanges in some cases. The *Berlin Nachtausgabe* charged that "whenever there is an opportunity," the United States government made use of "the Jewish newspapers" in its attacks on Germany. Anti-Nazi agitation in the United States, it alleged, was "manifestly hypocritical." The same theme was taken up by the party's own paper, the *Völkischer Beobachter*, which proclaimed, "The Americans who continue to treat their Negroes as second-class citizens and in whose country lynch justice is, so to speak, good manners, are the last people who should take upon themselves the role of judges of morality."

In a similar vein of what a British diplomat called "this stone-and-glass-house method" of justifying Nazi actions, the German press launched into a violent attack on British policy in Palestine against the Arab population. If the question of the pogrom was raised in the British Parliament, it was said, then Hitler would retaliate by calling a special session of the Reichstag to discuss Palestine.

Berlin cinemas began showing carefully edited newsreel film showing the blowing up of Arab houses, British military patrols in action, and police pushing back groups of weeping women and children. The *Völkischer Beobachter* carried an aggressive leading article that ended with the bitter comment, "British sympathy with the Jews in Germany would still be out of place even if the bloody wounds which British force and severity has caused in Palestine were healed."

At 2:30 P.M. on Friday, November 11, Goebbels called a press conference for all foreign correspondents in Berlin, "to remove certain misunderstandings that appear to have found their way into reports sent abroad of yesterday's anti-Jewish demonstration." He did not doubt their honesty, he told them, but he hoped that, following his statement, they would be able to pass on to their editors an explanation for the events of November 9–10.

The correspondents were decidedly frosty, appalled by what they had witnessed, and resentful both of Goebbels's criticisms and his attempts to tell them what to say. For once, he was nervous and ill at ease, and according to Ribbentrop "betrayed a complete lack of inner conviction." Nevertheless, he ploughed on hopefully, playing down the worse excesses and plugging the party line on Jewish provocation.

First and foremost, he began, the correspondents must understand the psychological and historical background to what had happened. To do this, they must go back to February 1936, when David Frankfurter, a young Jewish medical student, the son of a Yugoslav rabbi, had shot and killed Wilhelm Gustloff, the Swiss Nazi leader, in Davos, Switzerland. "That shot," declared Goebbels, "should have been a warning to the world. Frankfurter had not killed a man because he had a grudge against him, he had killed him in order to kill a representative of National Socialism." At the time, German reactions had been confined to grief, to giving Wilhelm Gustloff a grand state funeral. But now it had happened again, and it must be stopped. With a breathtaking lack of any sense of irony, he warned that if Jews were allowed to kill anyone who belonged to a regime they disliked, then world politics would rapidly descend to mere gangsterism.

The previous day's demonstrations, he insisted, had been a spontaneous reaction by the German people to a repetition of the Gustloff assassination. The circumstances were identical—a German National Socialist had been gunned down in a foreign country by a Jew. But this time, he said, "the wrath of the German people was too great to be curbed." He would have found it difficult, if not impossible, to order the police to open fire on crowds with whom he inwardly sympathized, and in any case there simply had not been enough police to control the demonstrations that had occurred—spontaneously, he repeated—all over Germany at the same time. And even if he had wished to intervene, it would have been impossible, since the entire government had been in Munich at the time.

Under hostile questioning, Goebbels's nerve began to give, and his answers became more and more querulous. When pressed on the spontaneity of the demonstrations, he replied that the Jews of Germany should be grateful that they had been spontaneous, because if they had been organized properly, if he himself had organized them, there would not have been a mere seven thousand demonstrators on the streets of Berlin but seven hundred thousand—and just imagine what the results of that would have been!

He did not deny that shop windows and synagogues had been smashed, but he did deny most emphatically that there had been any looting, or that any Jews had been hurt or killed. Blundering into bathos as his powers of invention ran away with him, he conjured up the image of a little old woman wandering through streets where all the shop windows had been broken. If she had "here and there picked up and taken an overcoat for her daughter as a Christmas present," he felt sure the correspondents would sympathize and understand. That, he said, was not looting—looting was the smashing of premises with the deliberate intention of stealing, and that had nowhere been the case.

As for the police and fire department, they had done everything they could. If the fire department had in some cases appeared not to have been doing very much, that was because the synagogues had been burned out when they arrived, and there had been nothing left for them to save. In his view, the demonstrations had done as little harm as could have been expected under the circumstances, he said.

The correspondents, of course, were hardly satisfied with any of this, and went on hurling awkward questions. Badly rattled, Goebbels snapped back that if Jews continued to spread "exaggerations of yesterday's happening, of the kind contained in the accounts and leading articles of the American press, then they would defeat their own ends, and they would be digging the graves of the Jews in Germany." They must realize now that the German government would not give way under outside pressure. The treatment of German Jews, therefore, "depended entirely upon their behavior and upon the behavior of Jews living outside Germany." From now on, he promised, the government would take matters into their own hands, as representatives of the German people. "The wishes of the people would, as always, be considered. And what those wishes were," he concluded ominously, "everyone has seen for himself." And with that, he brought the press conference to a premature end and marched out of the room.

XI

"A Wasps' Nest"

With so much public outcry, there can be no doubt that both press and people throughout most of the world, and certainly in the Western democracies, had received the message of Kristallnacht loud and clear: The Nazi regime was a beast that could not be reasoned with. It did not conform to any normal standards of decency or humanity, and could never again be trusted. Its brutality, mendacity, and evil intentions had been exposed for all the world to see, and in retrospect it is difficult to understand how any civilized nation could continue to maintain normal relations with such a monster.

Hindsight, of course, is a notoriously selective guide to history, highlighting those events that help to prove a thesis and ignoring the mass of others that obscured their true significance at the time. It is all too easy, more than fifty years later, to assume that it was obvious in 1938 that acquiescence, however tacit, in the horrors of Kristallnacht and its aftermath would open the doors to the greater horrors of the Holocaust. In truth, no one's imagination in 1938 could possibly have been black enough to envisage the creation of the machinery for mass murder on such a vast scale. Few of us have the powers of a Dante or a William Blake—and even if such a prophet had emerged in 1938, he would have been treated as a dangerous lunatic for daring to suggest such unthinkable nightmares.

In fact, it is immaterial whether or not anyone knew or even suspected what Hitler was planning. Kristallnacht was surely a powerful enough signal that the Nazis were unhindered by conscience or any moral concern, were capable of committing such atrocities, and would undoubtedly go on doing so unless they were stopped by some drastic action. As it happened, their intentions were not even that secret. One British official reported to London a long conversation he had had immediately following the pogrom with a Herr von Pfeffer, described as number two to Rudolf Hess, the deputy führer of Germany, in which he was told that "Germany intended to get rid of her Jews, either by emigration or if necessary by starving or killing them, since she would not risk having such a hostile minority in the country in the event of war. He also said that Germany intended to expel or kill off the Jews in Poland, Hungary and the Ukraine when she took control of those countries." Far from being hidden, this was a deliberate message from the German government to the British government, setting out what was to happen to the Jews of Central Europe and inviting Britain to relieve Germany of the "problem" by providing a home for them. It was also, coincidentally, a true statement about German intentions regarding Eastern Europe.

In spite of all the noise, however, foreign governments for the most part stayed silent. There were, it is true, over one hundred diplomatic protests in the days following Kristallnacht, but they were restricted to damage or injury suffered by Jews who were nationals of the countries concerned. All messages to and from foreign missions in Berlin were regularly intercepted and deciphered by the *Forschungsamt*, the "Research Department," of Göring's Luftwaffe. As it became increasingly clear from these that there was to be no drastic action from any quarter, Goebbels's confidence was restored. He must have been particularly heartened by the advice telephoned to London by Sir George Ogilvie Forbes, the British chargé d'affaires.

On the afternoon of November 9, before the pogrom had actually exploded, Dr. Chaim Weizmann, president of the World Zionist Organization, had telephoned the British foreign secretary, Lord Halifax, "in considerable distress." German Jews, he told him, believed the situation was deteriorating so rapidly that the only chance of averting a catastrophe was "for some prominent non-Jewish Englishman to go over to Berlin immediately." While Goebbels was fanning the flames in Munich, Halifax was blowing cold over Weizmann's suggestion in London. He cabled Ogilvie Forbes to ask his opinion, adding, "Prima facie, it seems to be fraught with difficulties." On November 10, while the SA mobs were still rampaging through German cities and towns, Ogilvie Forbes replied.

"I can see no advantage and indeed every objection to the proposal," he said. "Not only is public feeling profoundly roused by the recent murder of a German diplomat, but also the treatment of German Jews is fiercely and jealously regarded as a purely internal matter. As you are aware from his recent speeches, the Chancellor is at present in an aggressive and anti-British mood and it will be difficult enough to protect British Jewish interests.

"The visit of a prominent Englishman, far from being a deterrent, would have exactly the opposite effect. He would receive a crushing snub and the British name at the moment of deep indignation at a brutal murder, would still more be associated with what had been the championing of the cause of the Jews who after the bolsheviks are regarded as public enemy number two . . . In short, it is a wasps' nest in which we would be ill-advised in our own interests and that of the Jews themselves, gratuitously to poke our fingers."

Halifax took the chargé's advice. Even after the full extent of the pogrom was known, the only official British protest was over an article in *Der Angriff* linking various anti-Nazi British politicians—Churchill, Eden, First Lord of the Admiralty Duff-Cooper and others—with the supposed conspiracy of "international Jewry and Freemasons" behind Herschel Grynszpan's act.

Within twenty-four hours of his disastrous press conference, Goebbels was back in action, as though nothing untoward had happened. Knowing he had got away with Kristallnacht, he could attend Göring's conference with complete self-assurance. The Nazi machine could stay in top gear against the Jews, secure in the knowledge that there would be no reprisals. That day, Hitler opened a special public exhibition in the Reichstag Building, called "The Eternal Jew." The next day, Goebbels, reveling in his role as party spokesman, addressed a meeting of five hundred members of the winter relief organization, which extracted money from the German public ostensibly to help the poor during the harsh winter weather, but in reality simply to swell party funds. Released from the need to restrain his language, and with no danger of awkward questions from his audience this time, he tore into the Jews with full force. Justifying his own decree, he said, "It is equivalent to degradation of German art to expect a German to sit next to a Jew in a theater or cinema."

"If the parasites had not been treated too well in the past," he declaimed, "it would not have been necessary to make short work of them now. The very fact that such legislation [as the new decrees] has been possible at all proves to the world that the Jews have been having much too good a time in Germany!"

The new decrees were published in full in the *Reichesgesetzblatt* on Monday morning, November 14. The *Völkischer Beobachter* welcomed them with the comment that the German people were filled with satisfaction and gratitude that the National Socialist government had identified its will with their own. They had hoped, it said, that the Nuremberg Laws would have taught the Jews to keep at a respectful distance from them. But since the Jews had not done so, but had instead started to look

down upon Germans with greater contempt than ever from their mountains of gold, they had only themselves to blame that the need to respect
the Germans had now been dramatically brought home to them. If they
did not tell their racial comrades outside to stop their dirty games with
Germany, the paper concluded threateningly, then every Jew in Germany
would from then on be treated with merciless severity.

Keeping up the pressure, on November 15 the education minister, Dr.
Bernhard Rust, joined in with an order banning all Jewish children from
German schools. "After the ruthless murder in Paris," he said in a statement to the press, "no German teacher can any longer be asked to give
lessons to Jewish schoolchildren. It goes without saying that it is intolerable for German pupils to sit in the same classroom with Jews. The
separation of the races in schools has in general been carried through
during the past few years, but a remnant of Jewish children has remained,
and this remnant can no longer be allowed to go to school with German
boys and girls."

Any remaining children who were Jewish as defined by the Reich
Citizenship Law were to be dismissed at once. This was another vital
step in insuring the total separation of the races that was essential to the
success of the Nazi program. The use of violence, indeed, was in some
respects only a component in this form of psychological warfare. In
addition to strengthening the rule of terror, and trying to force the Jews
to emigrate, violence was intended to demoralize and depersonalize the
Jews and to increase the divide between them and the rest of the population, turning them into outcasts whom the people would not wish to
help. Such an outcast becomes a nonperson, somehow less than human,
and therefore unworthy of sympathy or consideration.

Goebbels was at pains to stress the separation of the Jews in an interview
he gave to Reuters's correspondent, Gordon Young, on November 15—
no doubt hoping that in a one-to-one situation he could avoid having to
answer the sort of hostile questioning of a full press conference. "The
events of the last few days in Berlin," he began, "are nothing but symp-
toms of an infection which has sought to creep into the body of the
German people—indeed, in my opinion, into the body of all the nations
of Europe and beyond. We Germans have come to grips with the symp-
toms of this infection, and must continue to do so." The attacks on the
Jews were not, as some foreign newspapers had suggested, a form of civil
war in Germany, "but a separation of a people from its parasites."

Perhaps as some sort of cynical sop to foreign critics, Goebbels made
some grotesque amendments to the apartheid regulations that he himself
had introduced so recently. "We do not want to destroy the Jews cul-

turally," he explained, "they must cultivate their own culture for themselves. There exists in Germany a Jewish cultural association which has its own theater, music halls, concerts and its own orchestra in Berlin. Three days ago it was closed down, but I have today opened it again. In other words, what we want is a clear division between Germans and Jews."

What Goebbels did not explain was that on his direct orders one of the first Jews to be released from Sachsenhausen concentration camp was the well-known theatrical impresario Fritz Wisten. Wisten was told, as if he were living in a Hollywood musical of the thirties, that he had five days to put on a show. And not just any show, either. It was to be a production of a comedy based on Shakespeare's *Twelfth Night* called *Rain and Wind*. It was to be put on at the Jewish Theater in Berlin.

Wisten protested that the Jewish community was hardly in a mood for comedy. Moreover, in purely practical terms, since all Jewish newspapers were banned, how could they advertise the production, even supposing they could mount it in time? Incredibly, Goebbels ordered the *Judische Rundschau*, a Jewish newspaper, to resume publication on Tuesday, November 22. But it was to carry no news and no advertisements—only general announcements of interest to the Jewish community. Among these, of course, would be the announcement of the opening of *Rain and Wind* at the Jewish Theater. Goebbels also ordered a Jewish vaudeville troupe to begin work on Saturday, November 26. They were to perform a popular farce entitled *Stewed Fruit*.

At the same time in Munich, the Nazis started seizing radio sets belonging to Jews, going from one house to another requisitioning them. No Jewish home was to be allowed a set: "Radio is a matter of German culture and is nothing to do with Jews."

It was not until Monday, November 14, that the first public statement was made by any world leader, and then only in the mildest terms. British prime minister Neville Chamberlain's first reaction on reading the reports of the pogrom had been characteristic: "Oh, what tedious people these Germans can be!" he told Air Minister Sir Kingsley Wood. "Just when we were beginning to make a little progress." On November 14, he was given the opportunity to condemn the pogrom, when Philip Noel-Baker, a prominent Labour MP, put a Private Notice Question in the House of Commons: "Would the Prime Minister make a statement concerning the actions taken against the Jews in Germany since the attack on Ernst vom Rath?"

Chamberlain's reply was not one of his most scintillating performances at the dispatch box. At a moment when even the strongest language would have been an understatement, he chose to be at his most non-committal, determined to cause no offense to his newfound friend Herr Hitler. He "regretted to have to say" that the press reports appeared to be "substantially correct," and had indeed been corroborated to some extent by Dr. Goebbels himself when speaking to foreign correspondents.

"No one in this country," he went on lamely, "would for a moment seek to defend the senseless crime committed in Paris. At the same time, there will be a deep and widespread sympathy here for those who are being made to suffer so severely for it." He assured the House that the British chargé d'affaires in Berlin had taken immediate steps to safeguard British subjects, and that he had been instructed to present any claims for damages by British subjects to the competent authorities. He also announced that the British government was protesting about the recent articles in the German press that had associated former British ministers and members of the House with the murder in Paris. But still he made no condemnation.

Philip Noel-Baker tried again. "Will the Prime Minister endeavour to find some means," he demanded, "either alone or in co-operation with other powers, by which he can make known to the German government the deep feeling of horror aroused in this country among all sections of the people by the action which has been taken against the Jews?"

Other members joined in the attack. If Chamberlain was determined not to say anything to Hitler, couldn't the government at least show the feelings of the country by doing something for the victims? they demanded. Could they not be allowed into Britain, or Palestine, or to some part of Britain's "vast colonial empire?" Had the prime minister considered taking joint action with the United States? Or with the Dominions of the British Commonwealth? In response, Chamberlain simply stonewalled. One point he could not answer without notice, others were not a matter for the British government, or were "under consideration" by someone else. Still there was not a word of censure against the Nazis.

It was several days before Chamberlain found a safe way of expressing his personal disapproval of the pogrom. He had been asked to become president of the German Shakespeare Society, and he now took the opportunity to decline the honor. He could not, however, abandon his fear of offending Hitler: He wrote that he could not accept because of "lack of time," and only had it whispered around privately that he had really refused "because they have banned Jewish members."

In France, the subject was not even raised in the National Assembly, so Prime Minister Daladier was spared the embarrassment of evading the issue. He and his foreign minister, Georges Bonnet, were enthusiastic advocates of appeasement, and were still sighing with relief at the successful conclusion of the Munich agreement. But there was one part of the whole business of Munich that had stuck in their throats: Chamberlain's famous piece of paper, on which he had persuaded Hitler to sign a declaration that Germany and Great Britain would never go to war with each other again, and that the question of Anglo-German relations was of the first importance not only for their two countries, but also for Europe. The French leaders thought Chamberlain had gone behind their backs to steal a march on France. Honor demanded that something should be done to restore French prestige, and fortunately there was something on hand that would do the job perfectly. For some time, they had been talking of the possibility of a new treaty of friendship between Germany and France, and after Munich Bonnet had been pressing forward with all haste to have Ribbentrop come to Paris to sign it. Herschel Grynszpan's assassination of Ernst vom Rath had placed the pact in jeopardy, despite Bonnet's fulsome apologies that such a thing should have happened on French soil. Any untimely outbursts about German reactions could sink the pact altogether.

But there was another factor, too, which weighed in the political balance against any government statements—the strength of French anti-Semitism. Sir Eric Phipps, the British ambassador in Paris, reported that descriptions of the pogrom had been received with "undisguised horror and disgust," and that this had done much to head off, "for the present at any rate, the explosion of anti-Semitic feeling in France, which has recently been predicted in some well-informed quarters as a result of the influx of Jewish refugees." The fact that the assassin of the Rue de Lille was "a foreign Jew against whom an expulsion order had been issued" had exacerbated the situation.

On the afternoon of November 11, Sir Eric went to the Quai d'Orsay to see Bonnet. The foreign minister, too, was worried at the growing anti-Semitic feeling in the country. He blamed this on the French public's belief that prominent Jews had wanted war at the time of Munich—in other words, that they had been against the capitulation to Hitler over the Sudetenland, a heinous crime in Bonnet's eyes. Bonnet also claimed that funds raised for the relief of refugees in France had been used to bribe "certain bellicose organs of the press." He spoke bitterly about the numbers of undesirable foreign immigrants in France. All the recent political assassinations had been committed by such foreigners, he said, adding that the French government intended to take stringent measures against them, expelling many of them and throwing others into concentration camps. France, he declared, could no longer serve as a dumping ground for them.

The next day, he summoned Baron de Rothschild, as one of the leaders of the Jewish community, and warned him that "the impression must not be allowed to grow that the French Jews want war in order to avenge their luckless brethren in Germany."

At noon, Bonnet had another appointment—to attend the memorial service for Ernst vom Rath in the German Lutheran church at 5 Rue Blanche. He had also persuaded the president of the Republic, Albert Lebrun, to attend. On the German side, in addition to Ambassador Count von Welczek and the embassy staff, Goebbels had sent a representative of his Propaganda Ministry, Professor Friedrich Grimm, while Hitler and the Foreign Office were represented by the state secretary, Baron Ernst vom Weizsäcker.

Weizsäcker, a highly respected professional civil servant, gave a short address that was diplomatic and noncontroversial, sticking to the dead man's character and career, and avoiding political rhetoric. After the service, Bonnet was relieved to be told by Weizsäcker that France "would not be blamed for this dastardly crime," and that it would not be allowed to stand in the way of the proposed pact.

With Britain and France staying silent, the Nazi hierarchy must have felt reasonably sure there would be no major repercussions from the United States, either. Less than a month before, on October 13, their ambassador in London, Herbert von Dirksen, had reported on a significant conversation he had had with U.S. ambassador Joseph P. Kennedy, in which Kennedy had stressed his "understanding and sympathy" for Germany, and his intention of telling Roosevelt this. After assuring Dirksen that his friend Neville Chamberlain "was convinced, above all things, that the führer was sincere and well-intentioned and that he would always honor the obligations he had undertaken," Kennedy had turned to the subject of German-American relations.

"He repeatedly emphasized the sympathy that the average American felt for the German," Dirksen reports, "and which is greater than his liking for the average Englishman. Today, too, as during former conversations, Kennedy mentioned that very strong anti-Semitic tendencies existed in the United States, and that a large proportion of the population had an understanding of the German attitude toward the Jews."

It must have come as something of a shock, therefore, when at his five-hundredth regular press conference in the White House on November 15, President Roosevelt launched into a public rebuke of the Nazi government for its persecution of the Jews. "The news of the last few days from Germany has deeply shocked public opinion in the United States," he said. "Such news from any part of the world would inevitably produce a similar profound reaction among American people in every part of the nation. I myself could scarcely believe that such things could occur in a twentieth-century civilization."

At last, five days after the event, someone in a position of power and influence had spoken out against Kristallnacht. And more than that, Roosevelt announced that he was actually taking action—though he still wrapped it up in conventional diplomatic language. "With a view to gaining a firsthand picture of the current situation in Germany," he continued, "I asked the Secretary of State to order our ambassador in Berlin to return at once for report and consultation."

These were strong words for a president whose foreign policy regarding the Third Reich had hitherto been cautious in the extreme. Indeed, when briefing his first ambassador to Berlin, William E. Dodd, as far back as June 1933, the president had told him, "The German authorities are treating the Jews shamefully and the Jews in this country are greatly excited. But this is not a governmental affair. We can do nothing except for American citizens who happen to be made victims. We must protect them, and whatever we can do to moderate the general persecution by unofficial and personal influence ought to be done."

A professor of history at the University of Chicago and an old alumnus of Leipzig University, Dodd had been born in North Carolina and was a classic southern liberal. Strongly anti-Nazi, he had been a popular choice in American Jewish circles, which may have been the reason why Roosevelt chose to replace him as ambassador in December 1937. It had taken Roosevelt a long time to decide how to react toward fascism. While it was against his principles as a good democrat, circumstances at home were such that he felt constrained to be cautious and pragmatic. Principles were fine, and he was not averse to a small demonstration of U.S. anger. But with America just emerging from the Great Depression, with 13.7 million unemployed, he could not afford to take any action that might interfere with international trade or business at home. That was why as the new ambassador he chose a career diplomat, Hugh R. Wilson. Wilson had been assistant secretary of state, and as U.S. minister in Switzerland he had acted as unofficial observer at the League of Nations.

Withdrawing Wilson from Berlin now was a dramatic move that could not be misread by the German government. It was the first time since the First World War that an American ambassador to a major power had been summoned home under circumstances akin to an official recall. It was one step from breaking off relations with Germany. In a tit-for-tat gesture, the German government on November 18 recalled their ambassador, Hans Dieckhoff, from Washington.

Ironically, Wilson himself was unhappy with his president's action. He feared that any hardening of American attitudes toward Germany could prove to be counterproductive. He was also concerned about the effect that the stories of Nazi atrocities might have on the American public, feeling it was becoming more and more difficult for friends of Germany to speak up on their behalf. "Even those most inclined to think that Germany . . . had a cause now find the ground cut from under them," he complained. By this time, he was the target for a considerable quantity of anonymous mail. This divided evenly, he told a colleague, into those calling on him to resign so that he could tell the world the horrors that he had witnessed in Nazi Germany, and those eager for him to prevent relations between the two countries from deteriorating into war. The latter correspondents kept insisting that the United States must not go to war on behalf of the Jews.

At first, on his return to Washington, he did his best to play down the significance of his recall. In order to minimize the effect of the president's gesture, he had left his wife behind in Berlin, thus suggesting that his absence was purely temporary. But his persistent requests to his superiors in the State Department for permission to rejoin his wife were ignored. Mrs. Wilson was forced to remain in Berlin for some time.

It would be a mistake to imagine that Wilson was not utterly appalled by the barbarities of Kristallnacht, which he had witnessed. As "the full tale of these attacks on Jews becomes known," he wrote, "one experiences a sensation akin to nausea. The blatancy of the evil that is going on is as revolting as any part of it." He was, however, a realist. He did not share the general and sentimental belief that the Nazis had somehow hijacked Germany by force and were a temporary aberration within the body politic. Unlike many diplomats, he quickly recognized that Hitler had considerable—though by no means total—support within the country. He was also painfully aware that there were many Americans, particularly among the military, who admired the spirit and dynamism of the new Germany.

Lieutenant Colonel Truman Smith, U.S. military attaché in Berlin, was probably the best known of these. He had known Hitler, Göring, and Company since the 1920's. In 1935, for example, he wrote an admiring report on the Nuremberg Rally of that year, which he attended. In his view, it demonstrated many of the classic military virtues—"love of country, democratic indifference to caste, fanatical hatred of Jews and bolshevists and everyone else who differed from [the Nazis], and above all the pride in Germany's armed forces." As a military man, the colonel no doubt found the last particularly inspiring.

In later reports, Truman Smith favorably compared Hitler to Napoleon—that was after the *Anschluss*. After Munich, he expressed his admiration for the Axis, which he regarded as the most vital new alliance in international politics. In particular, he admired Mussolini and Hitler because in his view they had "found a better solution of the capital-labor problem than any other nation in the world." He was also of the opinion that the West had nothing to fear from German expansion, since Hitler's eyes were fixed firmly on the East, on the USSR. One day Hitler would lead a "European Crusade to extend the boundaries of Europe and push back Asia into the steppes." As for Nazi anti-Semitism, the colonel declared himself surprised at its relative mildness. In a report in January 1939, he ascribed the horrors of Kristallnacht to the Nazi belief "in the existence of a Jewish war plot during the summer of 1938," and concluded—correctly enough—that "the determination of Germany to expel the Jews finally and completely cannot be doubted."

As for Hugh Wilson, it was not until after the German occupation of Czechoslovakia in March 1939 that he finally accepted that he would not be allowed to return to his post in Berlin. He therefore brought his wife home. He resigned from the State Department on September 1, 1939.

Undeterred by foreign criticism, the Nazis pressed on with the beatification of Ernst vom Rath. The theatrical opportunities offered by a grand state funeral were simply too good for Hitler to pass up. At one and the same time, it would be a gesture of defiance to the rest of the world, and a potent reminder to the German population of the murderous intentions of the Jews, justifying violence against them.

At 10:15 P.M. on Tuesday night, November 15, the coffin was taken from the vault of the Lutheran church to Paris's Gare de l'Est. There, it was put on a train for Aachen, the border town known to the French as Aix-la-Chapelle, accompanied by the same group of German notables who had attended the funeral service. At the border, both coffin and notables transferred to a specially chartered German train.

At dawn on Wednesday, after a speech by the local kreisleiter, a man called Grohe, the train set off at a stately twelve miles per hour on the fifty-mile trip to Düsseldorf, where the vom Rath family vault was located. All the stations along the route were decorated. Flags flew at half-mast. Uniformed SA and SS men stood at attention as the train passed through.

In spite of the miserable, foggy weather, thousands of ordinary Germans crowded into the stations or lined the track itself to pay their last respects to the fallen hero.

At the Düsseldorf station, the coffin was loaded onto a waiting gun carriage, which was drawn slowly through the silent crowds to the Rheinlandhalle, a large hall on the banks of the Rhine. There, Ernst vom Rath's mortal remains were to lie in state. All that day the bells of Düsseldorf tolled, and thousands of people, two abreast, filed silently past the coffin.

The Rheinlandhalle had been decorated like a stage set, draped in black, with Nazi swastikas everywhere. The area where the coffin lay was brilliantly lit, leaving the rest of the hall in semidarkness. The coffin, covered in a large German flag, lay on a bier draped in black velvet and surrounded by wreaths made of white chrysanthemums. All the Nazi leaders had sent wreaths, as had Georges Bonnet and Count Ciano, the Italian foreign minister.

Above the coffin, dominating everything, hung a huge symbolic German eagle gripping a Nazi swastika in its claws. On the floor, in front of the bier, lay a black velvet cushion on which were pinned vom Rath's decorations. At each corner of the bier stood a uniformed figure—an SS man, a storm trooper, a member of the Hitler Youth, and a soldier from one of the motorized regiments, all standing stiffly to attention. Four silver lamp standards, each over seven feet tall and carrying two flambeaux, completed the picture. When evening came, the flambeaux were lit, adding a touch of barbaric splendor to the scene.

The next day, Thursday, November 17, just before noon, Hitler himself arrived in Düsseldorf by train. There was no special ceremony for him, no large-scale organized reception. He was driven straight to the Rheinlandhalle. The crowds that lined his route were silent: There were no cries of "Heil Hitler." He entered the hall and took a seat between vom Rath's mother and Ribbentrop. For a few minutes, he sat in silence—every inch the simple German paying homage to this son of the Fatherland who had fallen in a foreign country. At last he rose to his feet and, stern-faced, stood in salute before the coffin. He did not rant or rave: He made no speech.

A band played Beethoven's Heroic March. Then State Secretary Ernst Wilhelm Bohle, head of the *Auslandsorganization*, the Organization for Germans Living Abroad, rose to speak before the fifteen hundred mourners. Ernst vom Rath's murder, he said, was merely the most recent in a series of political murders of loyal Nazis working abroad during the past few years. He was referring to the shooting of six Germans in Barcelona during the Spanish civil war, and in particular to the assassination of Wilhelm Gustloff, head of the National Socialist organization of Germans resident in Switzerland, by David Frankfurter, on February 4, 1936. "Vom Rath," said Bohle, "was the eighth victim abroad of the Jewish-bolshevik lust for murder. The shots fired at Davos, Barcelona and Paris had but one aim—Germany, the Third Reich. Germans living abroad are everywhere attending to their callings, and work as loyal guests of the states in which they live. Yet they are today targets for hatred, persecution and the calumnies of international subhumanity that concentrates all its strength upon the destruction of the resurrected Reich. The Jew, Grynszpan, by his own admission, wanted to strike at Germany in shooting vom Rath. We were hard hit. But such persons always forget the Nazi movement grows but stronger through its martyrs."

After Bohle, Ribbentrop rose to deliver the funeral oration. He began, "The entire German nation is in mourning . . . Lies and calumnies, persecution and murder, are the means employed by international Jewry and other destructive powers that would like to block Germany's road into the future. German and French medical skill, the comradeship of a French war veteran [the extraordinary M. Thomas] have proved to be in vain. On November 9 Comrade vom Rath closed his eyes in eternal sleep. Party comrade, now you can sleep in peace!" He went on, "If now a new wave of hate strikes out at us in the world, if an attempt is made to desecrate the sacrifice of our dead party comrade by new lies and calumnies, a storm of indignation will sweep across Germany. As a result, the determination of our people to sacrifice everything for the führer and the Reich will become all the stronger." He concluded by quoting Hitler's words at the memorial service in honor of Wilhelm Gustloff at Schwerin on February 12, 1936: "We understand the challenge and will know how to answer it."

The ceremony closed with the playing of the German and French national anthems. Afterward, Hitler, still silent, saluted the crowd. He spoke briefly and quietly to the vom Raths, and then left the Rheinlandhalle.

The coffin was removed from the hall and placed on the gun carriage again. Then, followed by the vom Rath family and various Foreign Office officials, it was drawn through the streets to the treelined old cemetery, where many of the graves bore the names of Frenchmen killed in the First World War. Flags fluttered at half-mast as a minister read the burial service at the family vault. As the coffin, still draped with the Nazi swastika, was lowered into the ground, the mourners tossed flowers into the grave and a military guard of honor fired a volley of shots.

The ceremonies in Düsseldorf were broadcast and reported throughout the Reich, and in schools and factories everywhere work was stopped while memorial services were held. Hitler and Goebbels were making quite sure that every ounce of capital was extracted from this most potent emotional occasion—in death, Ernst vom Rath had proved infinitely more valuable to the Nazi party than he could ever have hoped to be in life.

As the weeks passed and nothing more menacing than hot air came out of the Western democracies, it became clear that Roosevelt's recall of Ambassador Wilson was the strongest action any of them were prepared to take. There was even comfort for the Nazis from their friends in countries such as Romania, Hungary, and, of course, Italy, all of which supported the German actions.

Mussolini did not have any deep feelings against the Jews, but periodically, wishing to show solidarity with Naziism or to prove he was just as tough as Hitler, he flourished the banner of racism. In July 1938, he had published a "Charter of Race," which he always claimed was largely his own work, in which he identified Jews along with Arabs and Ethiopians as inferior beings. After Kristallnacht, as a result of Mussolini's interest, the Italian press devoted a considerable amount of space to the question of the Jews in Germany. Italian correspondents in Berlin followed the Goebbels line religiously, describing what had happened as the natural reaction of a people exasperated beyond measure by numerous provocations in the past.

Editorially, the Italian papers tended to be more cautious, probably because they were given no clear line from above. But they most certainly did not condemn Germany in any way. It was left to *Tevere* and *Regime Fascista*, neither of them important or with large circulations, to promote the anti-Semitic cause. *Tevere*, in an article on Göring's levy on Jewish property, idly wondered—"out of mere curiosity"—what the value of Jewish property in Italy might be.

The one Italian voice that really counted, not only in Italy but in Germany, France, and the rest of the world, was silent. Pope Pius XI, Achille Ratti, was a staunch opponent of racism, and in July had publicly condemned Mussolini's "Charter of Race" and the fascist government's "disgraceful imitation" of Germany's racist laws—another reason why the editorials in the Italian press were so muted on the subject.

The pope had already provided Hitler's most serious prewar challenge in 1937, with an encyclical, *Mit Brennender Sorge*—"With Burning Sorrow"—which had been smuggled into Germany and read out in every

Catholic church in the country. Although the encyclical had been mainly concerned with Catholic grievances and with violations of the 1933 concordat, it had also condemned "the idolatrous cult of race and nation." With some 40 percent of the population Catholics, and most of the rest practicing Christians likely to follow the pope's lead, such a challenge could present a serious threat. The Nazi press had naturally mounted a furious attack, but, significantly, had then stopped all criticism of the pope, on Hitler's orders.

In the autumn of 1938, however, Pius XI was a sick man, laid low by a serious heart condition and likely to die at any moment. He had, in fact, commissioned the drafting of a powerful new encyclical during the summer, condemning racism and anti-Semitism, with particular reference to Nazi Germany. At a time when much of the Catholic clergy was anti-Semitic, Pius XI had carefully chosen an American Jesuit, Father John La Farge, to prepare the draft for him. Father La Farge was well known for his strongly antiracist writings. He was helped in his work by an anti-Nazi German Jesuit, Father Gustav Gundlach, so there can have been little doubt of the line the encyclical would take. They completed their draft, and delivered it to the general of their order, Vladimir Ledochowski, who was to pass it on to the pope himself for approval. Ledochowski held on to it, perhaps because of the pope's condition—he suffered another massive heart attack on November 22 and was not expected to live—perhaps for other reasons. No one can be certain.

What is certain is that although Pius XI did not die in November, he never regained his strength, and in fact did die after his next coronary on February 10, 1939, never having seen the draft encyclical that might, just possibly, have stopped Hitler's plans for the extermination of the Jews. Pius XI's successor, Eugenio Cardinal Pacelli, who took the title Pius XII, was the papal secretary of state and had been papal nuncio in Munich and then in Berlin for twelve years. He was known to be strongly pro-German, and it was suggested by many that he was also pro-Nazi— he had been largely responsible for the 1933 concordat and had in fact signed it on behalf of the Holy See.

Whether Pius XII was actually pro-Nazi is a matter of debate. But he declined to issue the encyclical prepared for his predecessor, and during his entire tenure of the papacy until 1958, he never spoke out against racism or anti-Semitism. The Catholic Church had failed to take the opportunity of actively opposing one of the greatest evils of the time, and of providing the rest of the world with a clear moral lead.

XII

"We Do Not Wish to Export Anti-Semitism"

With no positive opposition, the Nazis pressed on through the rest of November and early December, implementing all the proposals made at Göring's November 12 conference, plus a few additional refinements. On November 16, Hitler signed an order depriving Austrian Jews who had belonged to either the old or the new Wehrmacht, the Austrian Federal Army, or the Austro-Hungarian Army, of the right to wear uniforms.

It is difficult for those who live in less formalized cultures to appreciate the psychological blow that this represented to Jews who had always considered themselves patriotic citizens of Austria, a nation where any uniform traditionally commanded respect. Already, on June 21, 1938, the Austrian Interior Ministry had banned Jews from wearing Tyrolean costume—*Lederhosen*, dirndl skirts and dresses, knee-length stockings, and feathered hats.

On November 28, more detailed regulations were announced for the winding up and dissolving of all Jewish enterprises. Only in special cases would permission be given for Aryanization. Realization of their existing stock-in-trade either by auction or by sales direct to the public was forbidden.

That same day, regulations restricting the movement of Jews in public places were also announced, to come into force on December 6. Under these regulations, German and stateless Jews were forbidden to walk or drive in certain places. Those who were unfortunate enough to live within a forbidden area needed a police permit to cross the boundary—and were given warning that such permits would no longer be issued after July 1, 1939. If a Jew was called to appear at a public office within a forbidden area, he could obtain a twelve-hour permit from police headquarters.

In Berlin, the ban covered all theaters, cinemas, cabarets, public concert and lecture halls, museums, fairgrounds, exhibition halls, the Sportpalast, the Reich Sports Field, all recreation grounds including ice rinks, and all swimming pools, both public and private, open air and covered. Jews were forbidden to walk in the Wilhelmstrasse from the Leipziger-strasse to Unter den Linden, including the Wilhelmplatz; Voss-strasse from the Hermann-Göring-Strasse to the Wilhelmstrasse; the Reich War Memorial and the north pavement in Unter den Linden from the university to the Custom House. Any Jew caught in a forbidden area was liable to a fine of 150 marks or six weeks in prison.

The police chief of Berlin warned that this first, limited list of streets and places would soon be extended to a much greater number, including in particular the main and luxury streets such as Kürfurstendamm, Fried-richstrasse, Tauenzienstrasse, the whole of Unter den Linden, Kaiser-damm, Bismarckstrasse, and so on. Jews living in these areas were advised to start looking for accommodation somewhere else—preferably in those streets in the center and north of the city "in which for years already the Jewish element has been predominant." They could perhaps exchange residence with German citizens living in those areas. Keepers of public houses and hotels were said to have asked for a decree banning Jews from their premises, and as a consequence, "Jews must expect in the future to be limited to purely Jewish establishments of this nature."

Similar regulations were introduced in other towns and cities throughout Germany. The first steps were being taken toward the creation of ghettos.

On December 3, abortion ceased to be a crime where Jews were concerned, when a Jewish offender was acquitted on the grounds that it was "not permissible to protect the offspring of a race opposed to the German race." And two days later, Himmler, as chief of the German police, issued a decree withdrawing all driving licenses and permits to own motor vehicles from Jews.

The way in which these moves in the process of separating the Jews from the rest of the population were sold to the German public was crystallized by the report on this latest measure in the financial daily, the *Börsen Zeitung:*

> With this measure of defense against Jewish arrogance, the National-Socialist state has given new expression to the feeling of justice of the German people. The German man has long felt it as a provocation and as an impediment to public life that Jews can sit at the steering wheel of a motor car in the traffic of German streets, or should profit by the roads of Adolf Hitler that German labor has created. This situation, until now tolerated by the German people with incredible patience, has now reached its end. Jews in Germany can no longer sit at the wheel of a car. Instead, the working German man will have more opportunity than hitherto by means of the motor car, the work of

German intelligence and German hands, of learning to know the beauties of his homeland and of acquiring new strength for his labor."

While the screws were being tightened inexorably on the Jews, their tormentors received much better treatment. On Göring's orders, the party supreme court was investigating "excesses" committed by SA men during the pogrom. Six members of the SA were found guilty of serious offenses: Heinrich Frey, of Rheinhausen, was expelled from the party for sexual and race violation on a thirteen-year-old Jewish schoolgirl, Ruth Kaltner; Gustav Gerstner, of Niederwerrn, near Würzburg, was expelled from the party and the SA for theft, and was turned over to the criminal court "on suspicion of race violation"; Friedrich Schmidinger and Hans Hintersteine, of Linz, were expelled from the party and held in protective custody for sexual assault on a Jewish woman called Unger; Franz Norgall, of Heilsberg, East Prussia, was reprimanded and declared unfit to hold office for three years for a disciplinary offense—killing a Jewish couple named Selig contrary to orders; and Rudolf Rudnik, of Dessau, was reprimanded and declared unfit to hold office for three years for shooting a sixteen-year-old Jew, Herbert Stein, after the action had ended, and against orders.

A further twenty-four storm troopers were charged with the lesser offense of simply killing Jews. They were either reprimanded or had proceedings suspended—and the court asked the führer to quash any criminal proceedings against them. Clearly, the only offenses considered serious enough to warrant a criminal trial were those that were sexual—and in those cases it was not the actual rape that counted but the fact that the rapists had had sexual intercourse with a Jewish female. While murdering a Jew was worth, at the most, a reprimand, "race violation" carried a statutory penalty of ten years' imprisonment. In many cases, the courts arbitrarily substituted the death penalty—not that this made much difference in the long run, since offenders were usually transferred from jail to a concentration camp at the end of their sentences.

All the new measures against the Jews were taken in full view of the outside world. None of them was kept secret—indeed, the Nazis went to great lengths to insure that everyone knew exactly what they were doing. There was no sense whatever that their actions were in any way wrong, only a defiant insistence that what was happening was an internal affair, and strictly Germany's own business. Neither was there any attempt to hide the purpose of the measures: to force the Jews to leave, and to blackmail the "soft" democracies into finding them new homes.

In a speech at Reichenberg in the Sudetenland, on Sunday, November 20, during the election campaign in the newly annexed territory, Goebbels mocked the West: "We do not wish to export anti-Semitism. On the contrary, we want to export the Semites! If the whole world were anti-Semitic, how should we get rid of the Jews? We would like the whole world to become so friendly to the Jews that it would absorb all our German Jews."

In an effort to stop any foreign governments from taking action against Germany, or even voicing outright condemnation, there was a constant threat of reprisals against the Jews still in the country. The Jews, therefore, were being used as hostages—a ploy that has since become all too familiar in international politics. In 1938, it was notably successful—perhaps because it provided a very convenient excuse for inaction by governments that did not want to see either their trade or their policies upset.

On the political front, action was inhibited for two reasons. The United States was still overwhelmingly isolationist—whatever Roosevelt may have felt personally, well over 80 percent of the population wanted no part in Europe's problems or quarrels. As for Britain and France, both Chamberlain and Daladier were still wedded to the policy of appeasement, which they were determined to pursue at any cost.

From the beginning, there had been many voices calling vociferously for an end to appeasement after the pogrom, particularly in Britain. "How can British electors," asked the *News Chronicle* of November 14, "be expected to wax enthusiastic for friendship with a regime that seems to rejoice in cruelty for its own sake?" "It is impossible to understand how anyone," declared the *Yorkshire Post* as early as November 11, "can talk seriously of producing European appeasement in confident collaboration with the convinced exponents of Nazi methods." The *Spectator* put it more bluntly: It said that the word "appeasement" had now been "obliterated from the political vocabulary."

Even newspapers that had been among the most ardent supporters of an Anglo-German rapprochement, like Lord Astor's Sunday *Observer*, found it hard to stay with Chamberlain's policies. After Kristallnacht, it complained that Hitler "has by one fell stroke brought even his friends to the verge of despair."

On November 16, Ambassador Joseph P. Kennedy called at the Foreign Office in London to warn the British government of what he described as "the dangerous reactions on American public opinion of the recent German policy toward the Jews." The American public, he said, was beginning to think the policy of appeasement was mistaken, and consequently was becoming less sympathetic to Britain. The response from

Sir Alexander Cadogan, the permanent undersecretary, was measured and decidedly cool. Why should American opinion blame the British government for what the Germans were doing to the Jews—"especially as the United States did not show much desire to do anything substantial themselves?"

Cadogan continued to defend his government's efforts at appeasement, which he said deserved support. The fact that these efforts "were now encountering difficulty" was no fault of theirs, he claimed, clearly blind to the fact that Hitler viewed such an approach as weakness, which he could exploit without scruples and which encouraged him into further excesses. Cadogan asked Kennedy to try to persuade American opinion to "take a more sensible line," since "after this recent exhibition of German methods it was more important than ever that lovers of liberty should stand together."

Kennedy promised to do what he could, but he could have had little hope of success. American press reports confirmed the way opinion in the country was moving. The *Baltimore Sun*, for example, felt that Berlin must have been fully aware of the effects of "such spectacles" on the rest of the world. A revulsion of feeling had swept over the nations, it said, prejudicing the whole case that had been built up in England and France for friendship with Germany. The *Richmond Times Dispatch* agreed; the only bright spot in the whole miserable business, it suggested, lay in the hostile reaction of Britain to the Nazi brutalities. Surely, now, the policy of appeasement was dead?

Sadly, appeasement was still very much alive. Sir Samuel Hoare, the home secretary, confirmed the government's determination not to budge from its existing position in a speech at the Cambridge University Conservative Association dinner on the evening of Thursday, November 24. His subject was the future of the British Empire. "We intend to show the world," he said, "that so far from drifting into our decline and fall, we are entering on a new and inspiring chapter of Imperial greatness." As for defense, it was true that Britain had its defense deficiencies. But for all its incompleteness, rearmament had reached a stage at which Britain would prove "unshakable in the early days of a war and irresistible as the war progressed." Nevertheless, he continued, Britain must still cling to the aim of Anglo-German peace despite the "setback" caused by Germany's treatment of the Jews, which was proving an obstacle to the prime minister's post-Munich appeasement policy.

"The plight of Jewish refugees has deeply stirred every British heart," he said. "It has made much more difficult the discussion of many questions that we wish to see settled between Germany and ourselves." But

Sir Samuel went on to declare that the British must not give up hope. "On no account must we fall from the height of exultation to which the world was lifted by the Munich peace to the slough of despond in which there is no hope."

It did not seem to occur to Hoare that already there was no hope for hundreds of thousands of Jews in Germany and Austria, now joined not only by those in the Sudetenland but also by the Jewish populations of the free cities of Danzig and Memel, where the pogrom had taken place on November 19 in imitation of the Reich that both cities wished to rejoin. To these could be added the tens of thousands in Slovakia, the semiautonomous province of the truncated Czechoslovakia, where open season had been declared for violent attacks on Jews.

It may be that Hoare could not bring himself to believe that things could really be as bad as they were painted, even though it had only been the day before his speech that the *News Chronicle* had carried its horrifying eyewitness account of the entry of sixty-two Jews into the Sachsenhausen concentration camp. If that is so, he was not alone, for there were many others who could not accept that such terrible things could really happen. Hilaire Belloc, historian, poet, and essayist, and since the death of his great friend G. K. Chesterton undoubtedly the most distinguished Roman Catholic writer in Britain, took exception to the *News Chronicle* story. On December 1, 1938, in the pages of the *The Weekly Review*, Belloc questioned its veracity.

"The account," he wrote, "is precise, simple and bearing all the marks that usually accompany a reliable piece of news and give it the stamp of reality. When some exceptional statement appears, reasonable men first ask themselves the degree of its probability . . . Is it true or false?" In the course of his next three articles for *The Weekly Review*, he continued to wrangle with the question, seeking a truth that he could accept.

Belloc, like his friend Chesterton, like so many of the English middle class, was prejudiced against Jews. He did not like them: They were foreigners. He equated them with bolshevism and moneylending, two things he abhorred. Nevertheless, he was not anti-Semitic—certainly not in the Nazi sense and the idea of employing physical brutality against a single Jew would have appalled him. He was an honorable man, uneasily aware that there was something going on in Germany of which, in conscience, he could not approve. He therefore desperately needed to know if the Sachsenhausen story was true. But whose evidence could he trust?

On the one hand, he admitted, "the *News Chronicle* cannot, obviously, hand over its informant to vengeance by giving his or her name." But he complained that none of the journals that, as he put it, usually "make it their special business in this country to defend the Jews [has] said anything. Neither the *New Statesman* nor the *Manchester Guardian* [has] said a word. On the other hand, the accused seemed equally silent." What did this signify? Did it signify anything? Surely if Goebbels were innocent of what had happened at Sachsenhausen, then he would indignantly and immediately have denied the reports. But he had not done so. Was one entitled to conclude from this that the incident had really occurred and that the Germans were guilty of barbaric and uncivilized conduct? If that were so, then British relations with Berlin clearly became impossible—and that had far-reaching political consequences.

Belloc's predicament was shared by many of his generation, both in Britain and in the United States, who had convinced themselves that the stories of Nazi brutality were exaggerated, if not actually Jewish fantasies. But younger men, too, found it hard to swallow what they read—and continued to do so for some time. Sir John Colville, then a twenty-four-year-old diplomat seconded from the Foreign Office to 10 Downing Street as assistant private secretary to Neville Chamberlain, could write in his diary as late as October 31, 1939, two months after the declaration of war:

> The Government White Paper on German concentration camps is a sordid document calculated to appeal to people's lowest instincts, and reminiscent of the "Corpse Factory" propaganda in the last war. It does shed a lurid glow on the bestial sadism of the Germans at their worst; but after all most of the evidence is produced from prejudiced sources, and it is in any case undesirable to arouse passions before the war has begun in earnest. Lord Halifax, of all people, is said to have pressed for its publication, but I understand that the fanatically anti-German Kirkpatrick is the man behind it all. Alec Dunglass, Cecil, Arthur and I all agree in condemning its publication.

Cecil and Arthur were Cecil Syers and Arthur Rucker, Chamberlain's two principal private secretaries, and therefore men of some knowledge and influence. Alec Dunglass was Lord Dunglass, Chamberlain's parliamentary private secretary, later to become foreign secretary as Lord Home, and prime minister as Sir Alec Douglas-Home in 1963–64. If such well-informed men could, after the war had begun, dismiss reports of Nazi atrocities as being "from prejudiced sources," and declare loftily that it was "undesirable to arouse passions," what hope could there be of any government action against Hitler in 1938?

The Sachsenhausen incident was by no means the only one of its type reported in the Western press, proving quite clearly to those who were prepared to believe what they read in reliable newspapers that the appeasers were guilty of handing over their fellow Europeans to thugs and sadists—and that they were apparently prepared to go on dealing with and even trusting such people. Already, there were signs that the general public, in Britain as well as America, were beginning to have their doubts.

At the time of the Sachsenhausen report, the *News Chronicle* commissioned an independent poll from the British Institute of Public Opinion, which was affiliated with Dr. Gallup's American Institute. One of the questions asked was, "Do you think that the persecution of the Jews in Germany is an obstacle to good understanding between Britain and Germany?" The result, published on November 28, showed that four out of five persons polled said they were disgusted by the persecution. But, as one person put it, no matter what anyone said, "Nothing will prevent the collaboration of Chamberlain and Hitler."

According to the interviewers who conducted the poll, they encountered remarkably little anti-Semitism. And where they did find people with strong feelings against Jews, these were confined mostly to London.

Whether the correspondent to *The Weekly Review* who signed himself by the initials "M.W." came from London is not clear. But on December 1, in the same issue of the magazine as the first of Hilaire Belloc's articles, M.W.'s letter was published. The subject was the $3 million that was said to have been collected from American Jews and given to the Jewish International Alliance for the purpose of making propaganda in France. The writer alleged that the object of this propaganda was "to make the French favourable to action against Germany on behalf of the Jews." With all the money being collected for Republican Spain, the Chinese, the Czechs, the Jews, "how about the English unemployed?" he asked. The writer added a slightly paranoid postscript to his letter: "I regret that I can only sign this letter with my initials since the head of the firm by which I am employed is a Jew."

If the Jewish International Alliance was really spending $3 million on propaganda in France, it was singularly ineffective. Daladier and Bonnet insisted on pursuing an agreement with Germany, come what may, and on November 19, Bonnet renewed his invitation to Ribbentrop to come to Paris to sign the joint declaration they had been discussing for several weeks. The German foreign minister accepted two days later, and said he would come during the week of November 28 to December 3.

On November 23, the French Cabinet was told of the negotiations for the first time—until then, Bonnet and Daladier had kept everything strictly to themselves. There was a fair amount of grumbling among the ministers at being presented with what was virtually a fait accompli, but no one objected to the idea of a pact, or made any suggestion that they should not seek a closer relationship with Germany. What they were worried about was the timing. According to Education Minister Jean Zay, "several ministers regretted the untimeliness of this declaration, in view of Germany's isolation after the anti-Semitic demonstrations."

Bonnet, ever the archappeaser, continued to fight for Ribbentrop's visit to take place during the next few days, despite the arguments from other ministers that this would have a bad effect in Britain and America. It was suggested that perhaps it would be better if the agreement were signed by the German ambassador, or if Ribbentrop were received in Strasbourg rather than in Paris. But Bonnet was undeterred, and told German ambassador von Welczeck later that same day that the French government would like Ribbentrop to come to Paris to sign the agreement on November 29.

Anxious to secure American approval, Bonnet sent details of the agreement to Washington, and asked that when it was made public, the United States government should make at least a press statement supporting the French action. He had been made uncomfortably aware during the summer that in the event of war in Europe, the 1935 Neutrality Act would prevent the United States giving France men, money, or equipment— even military aircraft already on order might not be delivered. "The American government cannot at one and the same time deny us any support in a conflict, and not approve our attempt at European understanding," he concluded.

The American government's response, however, was that it could, and would, do precisely that. "This government does not feel itself able to make any public statement with regard to the signing of a Franco-German agreement," Sumner Welles, then acting secretary of state, told French ambassador René Doynel de Saint-Quentin. "In view of the strained relationships existing between the United States and Germany it would be very difficult for this government . . . to express approbation of an official act on the part of the German government." At least one of the Western powers, it seemed, was prepared to stand up and say it did not wish to be friends with the Nazis.

While Roosevelt had recalled his ambassador, the French had not even taken advantage of the fact that they were in the process of changing theirs to delay making a new appointment. Their new ambassador, Robert Coulondre, paid his first visit to Ribbentrop on November 20, when he went out of his way to apologize for the fact that the murder of vom Rath had taken place in Paris, and to assure the Germans that the many expressions of sympathy sent to the embassy in Paris were a true reflection of French feeling.

Chamberlain had a ready-made excuse for doing nothing—the British ambassador, Sir Nevile Henderson, was already back in London for an operation for cancer of the tongue, and could not therefore be recalled. But there is no indication that the British prime minister would have considered doing so, in any case. In the event, Ribbentrop's Paris visit was postponed for a week, but this was not because of any consideration for the persecuted Jews of Germany, or even of the disapproval of Britain or the United States. The problem was a threatened general strike in France over deflationary measures introduced by the newly appointed finance minister, Paul Reynaud. When the strike collapsed, the visit went ahead.

Ribbentrop arrived in Paris on December 6, having demanded a reception "at least equal to that shown when the King and Queen of England came to Paris [on July 19–22, 1938]." Since France was still a democracy, however, the size and nature of the popular reception could not be prearranged, as it would have been in Berlin or Rome. There were no hostile demonstrations, to be sure, but the Parisians made their attitude clear by staying away in droves. Ribbentrop drove through empty streets, and any other contact with the public was prevented by elaborate police precautions.

In the afternoon, the Franco-German declaration was signed at the Quai d'Orsay by Ribbentrop and Bonnet, following a luncheon hosted by Daladier at the Hotel Matignon. It was a brief document, hardly longer than Chamberlain's piece of paper, which had inspired it. It consisted of three clauses. The first affirmed that "peaceful and good neighborly relations between France and Germany" were "one of the essential elements" necessary for general peace. The second clause dealt with the recognition that the frontier between the two nations "as it stands at present" was fixed and final. The third stated that the two countries resolved, "subject to their special relationships with other powers," to maintain contact and to consult on all questions affecting their two countries "should the subsequent development of these questions run the risk of leading to international difficulties."

Clearly, Germany's treatment of the Jews, even though it meant thousands of them fleeing across the frontier to seek refuge in France, did not count as such a question. In fact, Bonnet did not raise the subject at all on the first day. According to one version of Bonnet's memoirs, Ribbentrop had refused to discuss it during their official talk at the Quai d'Orsay on December 6. In another version, Bonnet claims that he had "expressed our indignation at the persecutions." But he told American ambassador William C. Bullitt that he had not mentioned it on December 6 because the ambassadors were there, and "he was certain Ribbentrop would refuse to discuss it in their presence."

Bonnet's main concern seems to have been the financial aspect, the cost to France of supporting thousands of Jews who had left Germany with nothing. He did raise this question during the afternoon of December 7, in a private meeting in Ribbentrop's room in the Hotel Crillon. Ribbentrop refused to speak about it officially, and insisted there should be no mention of Jews or refugees in the press statements. Off the record, however, he had no hesitation in speaking his mind. The Jews in Germany without exception, he said, were pickpockets, murderers, and thieves. The property they possessed had all been acquired illegally. The German government had therefore decided to assimilate them with the criminal elements of the population. The property that they had gained illegally would be taken from them. They would be forced to live in districts frequented by the criminal classes, where they would be kept under police observation like other criminals. They would be forced to report to the police, as other criminals had to. The German government could not help it if some of these criminals escaped to other countries, which seemed so anxious to have them. It was not, however, willing to allow them to take with them the property that had resulted from their illegal operations. There was, in fact, nothing it could or would do about this.

Bonnet does not appear to have pressed the matter. Nor did he manage to disabuse Ribbentrop of the notion that France, after Munich, was prepared to allow Hitler a free hand to expand eastward, in return for the assurance contained somewhat ambiguously in the joint declaration that he had no westward ambitions. The clear signal that Ribbentrop received from his Paris visit was therefore that France had no intention of interfering with the Nazis' plans in either area. Perhaps symbolically, the menu for the dinner hosted by the German Foreign Minister at his embassy that evening included *jambon de Prague*.

While political appeasement was facing a certain amount of opposition—several French Cabinet ministers, including the presidents of both Senate and Chamber, Jules Jeanneney and Edouard Herriot, and the chief of the general staff, General Maurice Gamelin, had carefully arranged to be out of Paris during Ribbentrop's visit—economic appeasement was flourishing. Although there were large-scale cancelations of German contracts from individual customers in France, Britain, the United States,

Canada, and even anti-Semitic Yugoslavia, with many German companies losing 20 percent to 30 percent of their export business, no country officially stopped trading with the Reich, or made any moves to impose sanctions.

In fact, this was one area where the Nazis were particularly vulnerable, and could have been badly hurt by concerted action. Germany's precarious financial situation was well known, and could have been used as a powerful weapon against her. It is even conceivable that a collapse might have toppled Hitler from power by destroying the German people's belief in him—though it could also have provoked a siege mentality that he could have used to strengthen his position. At the very least, however, Germany's desperate needs could have provided a bargaining counter. But it is difficult to find a place on a balance sheet for moral rights and wrongs, and the habitual reluctance of the international business community and financial institutions to do anything that might lose them money was reinforced by the vivid memory of what had happened the last time the German economy collapsed. And so, another opportunity of bringing pressure to bear on Hitler was lost.

There was, in fact, a considerable element of competition between Britain and France in economic as well as political relations with Germany. In both, the British were the pacemakers—which meant inevitably that French pride was challenged. In mid-October 1938, the British had held informal talks with a German delegation in London on the possibility of increasing German exports to British colonies. In December, economic talks formed part of Ribbentrop's visit to Paris, and from then until March 1939, there were more or less continuous talks on Franco-German trade prospects, and on projects for collaboration in South America, the Balkans, and French colonies. In January, there was an Anglo-German coal agreement, and in February a British Foreign Office official was sent to Berlin to size up the opportunities for economic cooperation, while preparations were made for an official visit to Berlin by Oliver Stanley, president of the Board of Trade. By February 21, Robert Coulondre, the French ambassador in Berlin, was complaining to Bonnet that France was lagging behind Britain in making economic approaches to Germany. On March 1, Coulondre was pleased to be able to hand over to Hitler a personal message from Daladier, saying France was ready "to pursue and to develop with the Reich the policy of collaboration affirmed in the declaration of December 6." And so it continued. Hitler's invasion of Czechoslovakia only created a temporary hiccup. By mid-July, Chamberlain was offering him a world partnership and £1 billion, nearly $5 billion at that time, in loans and credits.

On January 30, 1939, Hitler made an important speech to the Reichstag to mark the sixth anniversary of his coming to power. The speech centered on two main themes: Germany's need of international trade, for which he coined the slogan "export or die"; and a declaration of war against the Jews. "If international Jewish finance inside and outside Europe should succeed once more in plunging the nations into a world war," he thundered, "the outcome will be not the bolshevization of the world and thus the victory of Jewry, but the annihilation of the Jewish race throughout Europe!"

The appeasers failed to make any connection between the two parts of Hitler's speech. While they shook their heads in impotent disapproval of his bloodthirsty threats against the Jews, they fell over each other in their eagerness to aid his survival by economic cooperation that could only serve to finance his deadly designs.

XIII

"The Jewish Munich"

In November 1936, Chaim Weizmann spoke in Jerusalem of "six million Jews in Europe for whom the world is divided into two parts: places where they cannot live and places which they cannot enter." Two years later, that chronic problem had become not just acute but critical. Having failed to do anything to alleviate the first part of Weizmann's diagnosis, the world's statesmen were left to face up to the second. All anyone could now do for the Jews of Germany, Austria, and the other anti-Semitic states of Central Europe was to provide them with a refuge. At its simplest, this was a test of common humanity—unfortunately, it was also a question of political will.

The problem of refugees was by no means a new one for Europe. Revolutions, wars, religious persecutions, plagues, famines, had for centuries driven people to flee their homes and seek safety elsewhere. But without doubt the largest migration of human beings since the Thirty Years' War had occurred during and immediately after the First World War. The problems caused by the devastation of parts of France, Belgium, Eastern Europe, and the Balkans, not to mention the Middle East and Russia, were compounded by the politicians at the Paris Peace Conference in 1919 redrawing national boundaries like demented children. Whole countries vanished overnight, and new ones, such as Czechoslovakia and Yugoslavia, sprang into being. It is ironic that men of such obvious goodwill as David Lloyd George, Georges Clemenceau, and Woodrow Wilson should unwittingly have caused as much suffering as the Mongols.

During the 1920's, the League of Nations, that curiously ineffectual creation of Wilson's, acquired responsibility for the postwar refugee crisis. The man charged with looking after the hundreds of thousands of lost and desperate souls as high commissioner for refugees was the remarkable Norwegian arctic explorer and oceanographer turned diplomat Dr. Fridtjof Nansen. Looking like an aging Viking warrior—tall, gaunt, white-haired, with piercing blue eyes and a drooping mustache—Nansen had been given the job of organizing relief work in Russia in 1919 and at the same time had been appointed League high commissioner for the repatriation of prisoners of war.

Nansen set about his new task with vigor, and no little success. Most refugees had no nationality, no valid papers, and therefore faced serious problems in traveling across frontiers. Nansen gave his name to a new document, the Nansen passport, which was recognized by thirty-one of the states who were members of the League. This provided stateless people with official identity papers enabling them to move from one country to another.

Nansen's achievements can be judged from the fact that when he died, in 1930, the refugee problem seemed to be within sight of solution—certainly within seven or eight years. The League planned to close down the Nansen Office for Refugees in Geneva at the end of 1938, little realizing what that year would bring. When the problem erupted again with the new wave of refugees from Nazi Germany—fifty thousand in the first year of Hitler's rule alone—the machinery should therefore have been in place for coordinating and directing relief efforts.

Sadly, this was not the case. The League decided to appoint a new high commissioner for refugees, to replace Nansen, and after much bickering settled on an American academic, James Grover McDonald, a product of Indiana University and Harvard who had for fifteen years served as chairman of the American Foreign Policy Association. The United States was not a member of the League—although the organization had been largely Woodrow Wilson's brainchild, the U.S. Congress had rejected the proposal—and the Secretariat was always looking for ways of involving America in its affairs. No doubt it also hoped that McDonald's appointment would attract U.S. financial aid.

McDonald was put at the head of a new autonomous agency, the High Commission for Refugees (Jewish and Others) Coming from Germany. To establish its independence of the League, and therefore to avoid German obstruction in the League Council, it was sited away from Geneva, in the Palace Hotel, Lausanne. This move was, in fact, unnecessary, since Hitler pulled Germany out of the League shortly after the new high commissioner was appointed. But because the agency did not come under the official League umbrella, it lacked the moral authority that had attached to the Nansen office. It also lacked funding, so that much of McDonald's time was taken up with raising money.

The problem of money dominated much of McDonald's period as commissioner—money to provide food, clothing, shelter, and medical supplies for thousands of Jews living in squalor in makeshift camps in countries bordering Germany. Theoretically, he was not required to act as a fund-raiser, but only "to coordinate and stimulate" the work of international and national charitable agencies. It was the business of his governing body and advisory council to deal with matters like that, but they showed little interest. According to Norman Bentwich, who was McDonald's deputy, the governing body "was composed mainly of non-descript diplomats who knew little, cared little, and wanted to do as little as possible."

International apathy and the refusal of governments to spend money meant that cash was hard to come by. Most governments, as McDonald complained, were "only incidentally or even casually interested in the human problems of the refugees." He had hoped that members of the League would contribute at least a "symbolic" sum toward the cost of the commission: He suggested an annual contribution of $10,000 from each. The U.S. State Department pointed out that the United States was not a member of the League and would wait to see what the other powers contributed; the other powers also chose to wait. John D. Rockefeller, Jr., offered to give $5,000 if McDonald could find $20,000 from other non-Jewish sources. He couldn't. The American Red Cross refused to help, as did the American Friends Service Committee, though later, in 1936, it did become an important refugee organization. The Quaker response varied: American Quakers did not rush to help, unlike their European—and particularly British—counterparts, though in money terms the British only donated £125 in 1935. Other organizations were no more generous: The National Christian Appeal for German Refugees weighed in with only £189 and the International Christian Appeal with £100. McDonald gave his entire salary of $15,000 to the cause—but that, as well as most of the money to finance the commission's work, tens of thousands of dollars, came from Jewish sources, from such organizations as the Jewish Agency for Palestine, the Jewish Colonization Agency, and the Jewish Joint Distribution Committee.

Inevitably, McDonald had his share of criticism. There were charges of "inaction" and "lack of initiative," and "absence of achievements," and even, from some British Jewish leaders, the accusation that he was "somewhat too sympathetic to Germany." For his part, McDonald complained of the difficulty of getting the Jewish refugee organizations to work together, and also that too many people in those organizations seemed to expect him to be able to work miracles. As Norman Bentwich put it, "I worked with a High Commissioner who was expected to be a Messiah."

After just two years of frustration and despair, McDonald decided he had had enough. Worn out by the constant traveling entailed by the job, as well as the emotional wear and tear of dealing with refugees, he resigned on January 1, 1936. In a twenty-seven-page letter of resignation, he pointed out that the position of German refugees had changed drastically since his appointment. "The developments since 1933, and in particular those following the Nuremberg legislation, call for fresh collective action," he wrote. He said he wanted "friendly but firm intercession with the German government, by all pacific means," and that "considerations of diplomatic correctness must yield to those of common humanity."

McDonald's letter of resignation attracted worldwide attention and dominated the editorial columns of the international press for several weeks. In fact, as *The Nation* observed somewhat unkindly, his departure from the job was probably the most effective act of his two years' service— in resigning, he had made more impact than he ever had as high commissioner. And yet his message went unheeded. Inevitably, the furor died down, the press found other scandals to pursue, and as usual no political action was taken. Personal vindication for James Grover McDonald came some twelve years later, when he was appointed as the first U.S. ambassador to the state of Israel.

On Valentine's Day, February 14, 1936, he was succeeded by a League official, Sir Neill Malcolm, a retired British brigadier who had commanded a regiment in Malaya. Malcolm made it clear from the start that in the future the High Commission for Refugees (Jewish and Others) Coming from Germany would not rock the political boat. It would not attempt to make policy, but would merely follow it. "The policy of the League," he declared, "is to deal with the political and legal status of the refugees. It has nothing to do with the domestic policy of Germany. That is not the affair of the League. We deal with persons when they become refugees and not before."

It may have been unintentional, but Hitler was being given a clear signal by the international community that it washed its hands of the so-called "Jewish problem." The member states of the League, it seemed, were prepared neither to condemn him for his anti-Semitic policies nor to concern themselves overmuch with the fate of German Jews.

A similar signal was given two and a half years later, which almost certainly played a significant part in triggering the November pogrom. After the *Anschluss* in March 1938, Jews fled from Austria in thousands— ten thousand in the first month alone. They included some of the great names who had made Vienna a center of European, and indeed world, intellectual life. Sigmund Freud was rescued by his British disciple Dr. Ernest Jones, and settled in England; Nobel Prize winner Professor Otto Loewi went first to Britain and then moved on to the United States, as did Dr. Paneth, a nuclear physicist who was to work on the Manhattan Project, Dr. Gombrich, the art historian, Dr. Wellesz, the musicologist, and many more.

Hundreds of Viennese Jews, however, unable to face the hazards of flight and uncertain of their reception in foreign countries, chose suicide. *The New York Times* carried a report that up to 170 were taking their own lives each day. Later, some reports put the figure as high as two hundred. Goebbels had his own inimitable way of dealing with the subject: In a speech to a rapturous mass meeting of Austrian Nazi party members, he insisted that the number of suicides in Austria had remained unchanged. "The only difference," he declared, "is that whereas it was Germans committing suicide before, now it is Jews."

On March 23, after eleven days of Nazi rule in Austria, President Roosevelt instructed his secretary of state, Cordell Hull, to send an invitation to the governments of interested countries—"France, Belgium, Netherlands, Denmark, Sweden, Norway, Switzerland and Italy, and the governments of all the other American republics"—not to mention Britain—asking "if they would be willing to cooperate with the government of the United States in setting up a special committee . . . for the purpose of facilitating the emigration from Austria and presumably Germany of political refugees." Two days later, at a press conference in the resort of Warm Springs, Georgia, he announced that he was calling an international conference on the world refugee crisis.

At last a world statesman was showing signs of actually wanting to do something. Roosevelt is to be commended for demonstrating such leadership—particularly in view of the fact that it was not a politically opportune moment. Allowing more refugees into the United States was not a gesture likely to be appreciated by a population that had so recently suffered the traumas of the Depression. Although unemployment was falling, the fear of it still haunted the minds of ordinary working people, and Congress was in no mood to permit a further flow of immigrants into the country, particularly if they were Jews.

Roosevelt knew he ran a considerable political risk in espousing such a cause, and no doubt he hoped that an international conference on the question would at least air the subject and perhaps even sanitize it as far as the American public was concerned. "It is my hope," he told Judge Irving Lehmann, a Jew and brother of Herbert H. Lehmann, a distinguished Democratic politician who became lieutenant governor of New York, "that the narrow isolationists will not use this move of ours for purely partisan objectives."

It was, of course, a forlorn hope—the forces of isolationism were everywhere like hungry lions roaring for their prey. As Representative Thomas A. Jenkins, a Republican from Ohio, complained, the president had gone "on a visionary excursion into the warm fields of altruism. He forgets the cold winds of poverty and penury that are sweeping over the one third of our people who are ill-clothed, ill-housed, ill-fed."

One of the principal sources of opposition to Roosevelt's sympathetic attitude toward refugees was the State Department. Cordell Hull, the secretary of state, had been given his job as a reward for his role as an outstanding supporter of Roosevelt for president among southern Democrats. He was a dignified figure with considerable Congressional experience, but was entirely lacking in vision or energy, and was notorious for finding excuses for inaction. In 1934, Hull had publicly disowned General Hugh S. Johnson, head of the National Recovery Association, when the general had said that the anti-Jewish actions of the Nazis in Germany made him sick, "not figuratively, but physically and very actively sick." During his entire tenure at State, Hull rejected or obstructed every opportunity to rescue German Jews.

Many career diplomats, such as Breckinridge Long, later to become assistant secretary of state, firmly believed that bolshevism, not Naziism, was the real threat to Europe and the world, and that if Hitler's persecution of the Jews was the price that had to be paid for not having the red flag flying over Capitol Hill, then so be it. In his book, a bolshevik Germany was much more to be feared than a Nazi Germany.

John Cudahy, a Catholic, onetime ambassador to Poland and in 1938 minister to Eire, was not alone in his view that, although the Nazi treatment of the Jews "may be shocking and revolting . . . [it is] a purely domestic matter and none of our concern." He drew an analogy between Jews in Germany and Negroes in the United States, pointing out that "Germany would have just as much warrant to criticize our handling of the Negro minority if a race war occurred between blacks and whites in the United States."

William C. Bullitt, Roosevelt's foreign-policy adviser during the 1932 presidential election campaign, his first ambassador to the Soviet Union, and now ambassador to France, was equally against Jewish refugees. Bullitt was unusual even in the State Department in being not only anticommunist but also anti-British, anti-Russian, and anti-Semitic, too.

The only country, apart from his own, that he genuinely loved was France. During 1938, he wrote Roosevelt a series of what have been described as "poisonous" letters. In one of these, he reported Daladier as saying that French counterespionage had "recently arrested nearly 200 military spies. Of these spies, more than one half proved to be genuine Jewish refugees from Germany—men and women who had been persecuted and expelled by Hitler—who for gain had entered his employ while enjoying French hospitality."

Even many American Jews were unenthusiastic about the prospect of permitting entry to thousands of their coreligionists from Europe. In April, the *Jewish Examiner,* a paper published in Brooklyn, conducted its own private survey of Jewish opinion. Among those who replied were six Jewish Congressmen, only two of whom turned out to be in favor of easing quota restrictions. In the same survey, three rabbis expressed fears that any such campaign might prove counterproductive and indeed arouse public anger.

If the reaction of the Veterans of Foreign Wars organization was anything to go by, they were right. In New York State, the local chapter of the VFW passed a resolution calling upon the U.S. government to suspend all further immigration into the United States for a period of ten years. This was immediately followed by the next item on the agenda—deciding the winner of the local drum and bugle corps competition.

On the other side of the coin, there was a vociferous pro-refugee lobby in what might be described as liberal circles in the United States, and the president reacted positively to the pressure. Indeed, it has been suggested that the reason for his calling the international conference in the first place was pressure from Rabbi Stephen S. Wise, a personal friend who was leader of the American Jewish Congress, a passionately Zionist organization. Prophetically, Wise feared that Nazi anti-Semitism threatened not only German Jews, but also Jews all over Europe. Another, perhaps more potent force—if only because of her influential weekly radio broadcasts and regular syndicated newspaper column—was the journalist Dorothy Thompson, who campaigned passionately on behalf of refugees.

The president was also said to have been attracted by an economic theory advanced by Hull House's Jane Addams, a Chicago social worker and leading expert on social settlement of immigrants who was brought to his attention by his old friend Professor Felix Frankfurter of the Harvard Law School. Jane Addams argued that, contrary to popular belief, increased immigration was just what the U.S. economy needed. Immigrants brought valuable skills and talents into the country, and their presence in the long run stimulated consumption. But such views carried little weight with any influential Americans.

With so much vociferous opposition in the United States, Roosevelt was forced to trim his sails and minimize the political damage to himself by promising to maintain the existing quota system regulating the entry of immigrants. In announcing his plans for the conference, he stated that "no country would be expected to receive greater numbers than is permitted by its existing legislation"—an admonition that Cordell Hull was no doubt pleased to repeat in his letters to the thirty-two governments who were invited. Hull went further, in fact, by adding the proviso that "any financing of the emergency emigration . . . would be undertaken by private organizations within the respective countries." Since most of the proposed refugees were Jewish, Jewish organizations were expected to finance the exodus.

Hull advised Roosevelt not to invite Germany to the conference, on the grounds that it would be like inviting the lion to lie down with the lamb—though this automatically ruled out any possibility of reaching an agreement with Germany for reducing the miseries of forced emigration. Invitations were limited to those states that might take in refugees, though there were some striking exceptions to this rule. Portugal was not invited, although the Portuguese African colonies of Angola and Mozambique were considered prime sites for resettling Jews, nor was South Africa, though it, too, possessed wide open spaces suitable for resettlement. The South Africans, however, did send an observer to the conference. Italy, although invited, decided to side with Germany and declined to attend.

The British government accepted the invitation readily—but only after it had made a secret deal with the United States over the question of Jewish immigration into Palestine. The British would attend the conference and play a full part, if the U.S. government would guarantee that they would not be pressed to accept more Jewish immigrants into the British Mandated Territory. The State Department agreed and sent a confidential memorandum to each member of the U.S. delegation, advising that "the [conference] committee should reject any attempts to inject into the considerations such political issues as are involved in the Palestine, the Zionist and anti-Zionist questions." These, it was felt, might "stir up bitter passions and might even lead to a disruption of the committee's labor."

*　　*　　*

Washington originally hoped to hold the conference in Switzerland, the home of so many international conferences, but the Swiss politely but firmly declined the honor. With Nazi Germany on their border, they had no wish to offend their powerful neighbor, who, although not invited, would certainly wind up in the dock. There was also the potentially embarrassing question of their own immigration policy, which was becoming increasingly restrictive. Fortunately, the French stepped in and offered the charming spa town of Evian-les-Bains in Haute Savoie, close enough to Switzerland to feel Swiss. Washington gratefully accepted.

Evian-les-Bains is a small town of about six thousand inhabitants that lies on the southern—that is to say, French—shore of Lake Geneva, opposite Ouchy and Lausanne, where the lake is at its widest. From there, on a clear day, one can see the town against the impressive backdrop of Mont Blanc and the French Alps. Famous for its mineral water, which is sold all over Europe, Evian has a small harbor that is the terminus for the excursion boats that crisscross the lake.

The Hotel Royal was the best and certainly the biggest hotel in Evian, one of those Edwardian follies that could be described as Deauville rococo. Looking as if it had been designed with a frivolous summer trade in mind, it had its own tennis courts, and there was a golf course, a beach, and a casino close by. Standing amid several acres of parkland graced with trees, the Hotel Royal was to be the location for what must go down as one of the most ineffectual conferences in history. It has been called, with some justification, the Jewish Munich.

On June 14, the U.S. government sent the agenda to the governments who had agreed to attend and also to the numerous refugee organizations that wished to be present as observers. It read as follows:

1. To consider what steps can be taken to facilitate the settlement in other countries of political refugees from Germany (including Austria). The term "political refugee," for the purpose of the present meeting, is intended to include persons who desire to leave Germany as well as those who have already done so. The conference would, of course, take due account of the work now being done by other agencies in this field and would seek means of supplementing the work done by them.
2. To consider what immediate steps can be taken within the existing immigration laws and regulations of the receiving countries, to assist the most urgent cases. It is anticipated that this would involve each participating government furnishing, in so far as may be practicable, for the strictly confidential information of the committee, a statement of its immigration laws and practices and its present policy regarding the reception of immigrants. It would be helpful for the committee to have a general statement from each participating government of the number and type of

199

immigrants it is now prepared to receive or that it might consider receiving.

3. To consider a system of documentation, acceptable to the participating states, for those refugees who are unable to obtain requisite documents from other sources.

4. To consider the establishment of a continuing body of governmental representatives, to be set up in some European capital, to formulate and to carry out, in cooperation with existing agencies, a long-range program looking forward to the solution or alleviation of the problem in a larger sense.

5. To prepare a Resolution making recommendations to the participating governments with regard to the subjects enumerated above and with regard to such other subjects as may be brought for consideration before the intergovernmental meeting.

It was a document skillfully designed to allay any nervousness on the part of those delegations attending the conference, and clearly limited the possibility of any positive action. At no point did it mention Jews or persecution or even Naziism. The agenda guaranteed there would be no nasty surprises for anyone. The only problem was that it was not clear from it what, if anything, the president hoped the conference would achieve.

Sumner Welles had originally proposed to the president that the U.S. delegation to Evian should be led by the secretary of state with Frances Perkins, secretary of labor, George Messersmith, head of the Foreign Service Personnel Board, and himself as the other delegates. But Roosevelt ignored this advice, shrewdly opting instead for a much less high-profile delegation. To lead it, he chose a man who was not even a member of the government, Myron C. Taylor, a Quaker businessman who had recently retired as chairman of the U.S. Steel Corporation. At one time, in 1930, Taylor had been considered possible presidential timber by certain sections of the Democratic party, but his political career—if he had ever seriously contemplated one—had gone nowhere. Now, the president awarded him the diplomatic rank of ambassador extraordinary and plenipotentiary. The other members of the delegation included James G. McDonald, who was now presidential adviser on refugee affairs, George L. Warren, executive secretary of the Committee on Political Refugees, plus a number of technical assistants. Though worthy enough, heaven knows, none of them carried much political weight.

By and large, the international press welcomed the forthcoming conference. In Paris, L'Oeuvre strongly supported the U.S. initiative: "President Roosevelt sees that the persecution of people on account of their religious beliefs and their race represents a danger for all those nations infected by the Nazi germ. He rightly affirms that this is an international problem that can only be solved by international means." The *Tribune de Genève* declared that "the very fact that the conference is taking place indicates that the American initiative is a clear political warning to the leaders of the German Reich." From Toulouse, *La Dépêche* was positively bullish about the whole thing: "We must hope that if no agreement is reached with the authoritarian countries, it will at least be possible to reach complete agreement between those countries that have remained faithful to the principles of liberty and equality of peoples embodied in the Declaration of the Rights of Man. If these countries, which are many and include the richest countries in the world, succeed in outlining a uniform policy and a suitable sharing out of costs, it can be taken that the political refugee problem will be solved."

The *Journal de Genève* took an altogether more cautious line, however, warning that the conference would achieve nothing if it "appeared to be directed against Germany." The delegates, it said, ought to concern themselves "solely with how to ease the problems of the unhappy refugees and the difficulties they cause Germany's neighbors"—and allow the major powers to negotiate secretly, behind the scenes, with the Nazis. Germany was the greatest power in Europe and would not stand to be humiliated.

But *De Volksgazet*, a Flemish paper published in Brussels, had no illusions about the German plans for the Jews. "What is going on now in 'Greater Germany' is the systematic extinction of a given race, a sort of biological war of extermination waged against one section of humanity." As for the Jews, *De Volksgazet* concluded, the trouble was, if truth were told, that "no one cares about their future fate."

Two days before the start of the conference, on July 4, Anne O'Hare McCormick, in *The New York Times*, wrote movingly "of the queues of desperate human beings around our consulates in Vienna and other cities waiting for what happens at Evian. But the question they underline is not simply humanitarian. It is not a question of how many unemployed this country can safely add to its own unemployed millions. It is a test of civilization . . ."

On July 6, 1938, the Evian Conference opened with a speech of welcome by Senator Henri Bérenger, the leader of the French delegation. A small, balding, bespectacled man with ears like jug handles and the air of a worried notary, Bérenger represented the Caribbean Island of Guadeloupe in the French Senate and had a reputation for espousing humanitarian causes. In his speech, he formally welcomed delegates, journalists, and observers to France, and even assured representatives of the various refugee organizations that, although they had not been officially invited, they were nevertheless welcome. True, they were not allowed to take part in the conference, but that was because its purpose was to create a permanent intergovernmental committee through which the United States and others could collaborate in a direct attempt to solve the international refugee crisis. He expressed the pious hope that something of value for refugees all over the world would emerge from their discussions. He, too, was careful not to use the word "Jew."

Myron C. Taylor began his opening speech in direct and forthright terms. Millions of people, he declared, had become stateless. The number was increasing daily and at a time of serious unemployment in many countries. Everywhere people's standards of living were declining, while the world population was at an all-time high. "Men and women of every race, creed and economic condition, of every profession and of every trade, are being uprooted from the homes where they have long been established and turned adrift without thought or care as to what will become of them or where they will go. A major forced migration is taking place, and the time has come when governments—I refer specifically to those governments which have had the problem of political refugees thrust upon them by the policies of some other governments—must act, and act promptly and effectively in a long-range program of comprehensive scale . . ." It was the closest he came to direct reference to the chaos that had been created by the actions of the German, Polish, and Romanian governments.

The refugee problem he said, was of course "vast and complex"— nevertheless, he hoped that the conference would be able to create the appropriate international administrative machinery to "contribute to a practicable amelioration of the condition of the unfortunate human beings with whom we are concerned." However, although the problem was worldwide, he warned delegates that "we may find that we shall be obliged on this occasion to focus our immediate attention upon the most pressing problem of political refugees from Germany (including Austria)." Accordingly, the U.S. government proposed that, for the purpose of this particular conference—"and without wishing to set a precedent for future meetings"—they should concentrate on "persons . . . who desire to emigrate from Germany (including Austria) . . . by reason of the treatment to which they are subjected on account of their political opinions, religious beliefs or racial origin," as well as those who had already left and were "in the process of migration."

There it was: Taylor had at last discreetly let the cat out of the bag— and yet he had still not mentioned Jews by name.

The United States prided itself, he continued, on its liberal immigration policies and the way in which immigrants were treated in his country. Recently, his government had decided to combine both the German and Austrian immigration quotas, which until then had been separate items, "so that now a total of 27,370 immigrants [per year] may enter the United States on the German quota." This was not as generous a gesture as it might at first have seemed—because for years, in fact ever since 1915, the full annual quota of immigrants into the United States had not been fulfilled. He concluded, "The problem is no longer one of purely private concern. It is a problem for intergovernmental action. If the present currents of migration are permitted to continue to push anarchically upon the receiving states and if some governments are to continue to toss large sections of their populations lightly upon a distressed and unprepared world, then there is catastrophic human suffering ahead. . . ."

After Taylor, the head of the British delegation, Lord Winterton, rose to speak. Winterton was a tall, lean, elegant figure, who looked every inch the British diplomat sent abroad to lie for his country. At a meeting before the start of the conference, Myron Taylor had warned Winterton's deputy, Sir Michael Palairet, that he was under pressure from U.S. Jewish leaders to invite Dr. Chaim Weizmann, head of the Jewish Agency for Palestine, to address the delegates on the subject of a Jewish homeland in Palestine. Sir Michael replied that His Majesty's government would naturally prefer that such a performance not take place. It did not. Dr. Weizmann was successfully muzzled and left on the sidelines as a mere observer, though active behind the scenes, and Lord Winterton was able to make his opening address secure in the confidence that the British government had done everything in its power to keep the subject of Palestine off the conference agenda.

He began by saying that he was in general agreement with the U.S. delegate's speech. But the British government viewed the whole refugee question as a purely humanitarian problem. The British government, he said, had always had a traditional policy of offering asylum "to persons who, for political, racial or religious reasons, have had to leave their countries . . . But the United Kingdom is not a country of immigration. It is highly industrialised, fully populated and is still faced with the problem of unemployment. For economic and social reasons, the traditional policy of granting asylum can only be applied within narrow limits."

His major contribution to the proceedings was the announcement that HMG was "carefully surveying the prospects of the admission of refugees to their colonies and overseas territories." But he warned that there were no simple answers. "Many overseas territories are already overcrowded, others are wholly or partly unsuitable for European settlement, while in others again local political conditions hinder or prevent any considerable immigration." This last was a clear, if unstated reference to Palestine—a subject he was forced to return to on the last day of the conference.

The importance of Palestine as a country of refuge had come up again and again in private meetings and in the appropriate subcommittee, no doubt partly thanks to the efforts of Dr. Weizmann. Some people, Winterton complained, seemed to think that the refugee problem would be solved "if only the gates of Palestine were thrown open to Jewish immigrants without restriction of any kind." But this, he insisted, was simply not possible. The British government had "a direct obligation under the terms of the mandate to facilitate Jewish immigration into Palestine under suitable conditions." But present conditions were far from suitable: "acute problems had arisen"—by which he meant the growing anger of the local Arab population at the continuing immigration of European Jews. It had therefore become necessary to restrict immigration in order to "maintain within reasonable limits the existing balance of population, pending a final decision . . . on the political future of the country." The conference must not continue to regard Palestine as the logical place of Jewish immigration. Instead, he dangled the possibility of settlement in the British East African territory of Kenya. "A scheme," he announced, " . . . is now under active consideration for the acquisition of private land in the colony . . ."

Winterton closed his opening speech by pointing out that no heavily populated, highly industrialized country could be required to take in refugees who were without financial resources. Nor could any of the charitable organizations "be expected to make good the losses which the emigrants have suffered." If the countries of immigration were to help, "then they were entitled to expect the country of origin . . . will equally assist in creating conditions in which emigrants were able to start life in other countries with some prospect of success." It was his most direct criticism of Germany and the Nazi policy of plundering their Jewish population, reducing them to penury before casting them out. Poland and Romania were also guilty of similar behavior, of course, but not to the same extent as Germany.

The *Scotsman* later put the matter with Calvinistic directness: "Finance is . . . one of the crucial issues, for immigrants who would be welcomed if they were provided with sufficient capital, are barred if they lack financial means. . . ."

Senator Henri Bérenger's opening address was briefer than the others, rather more to the point, and, like the others, not without a note of self-congratulation. France, he said, had taken in more refugees than anyone else. His country had "a long-standing tradition of universal hospitality," and would continue to maintain that tradition as far as "her geographical position, her population and her resources permit. Though she has herself reached, if not already passed, the extreme point of saturation as regards admission of refugees, France understands the new effort proposed by President Roosevelt. . . . Like America, France considers the refugee problem to be an international political problem, which can only be solved by the joint and collective action of the governments of the world." But, of course, before anything could be done, there were "various territorial, shipping, financial, monetary and social measures which will first have to be closely and carefully considered in executive subcommittees . . ."

It was clear to many observers from the first day that none of the three principals trusted each other. Indeed, as Clarence K. Streit, writing in *The New York Times*, put it, the atmosphere of Evian reminded him of nothing so much as "a none too trustful poker game, particularly as between the three great democracies, the United States, the United Kingdom and France."

Nearly twenty-five delegates in all spoke at the conference, each reading from a carefully prepared speech written by their various foreign departments, each explaining why their country was unable to accept any refugees. Their logic was impeccable, the arguments unanswerable. They then went out and enjoyed the facilities available in Evian: The golf course and the casino appear to have been the most popular attractions, though many took advantage of the skiing at Chamonix.

The delegate from the Dominican Republic did, however, have a positive contribution to make. He said that his government had for many years been promoting the development of agriculture in his country and "would be prepared to make . . . especially advantageous concessions to Austrian and German exiles, agriculturalists with an unimpeachable record . . ." The Dominican government, it seemed, had large areas of fertile, well-irrigated land at its disposal, and was prepared to give suitable colonists not only land but also seed and technical advice. They were also prepared to recruit technical men—scientists—to help train native Dominicans.

It was left to Sir Neill Malcolm, the League of Nations high commissioner for refugees from Germany, to be thoroughly practical and depressing about the possibilities of resettlement. "There was," he said, "very little chance of our being able to carry through any large-scale settlement in any of the countries overseas . . . In the present conditions of the labour markets in the countries of the world, any large-scale scheme of migration would only arouse hostility." At present, of course, "there was in no one of those countries any anti-Jewish feeling, but . . . such hostility might easily be aroused if the Government were to introduce solid blocks of foreign immigrants who would, almost necessarily, build up an alien element inside the state concerned."

The Australian delegate said that was how his government felt about the issue. His country had no racial problems at the moment—he conveniently ignored the Aborigine question—and had no intention of importing one from Germany. His government therefore rejected any idea of relaxing their immigration restrictions. The New Zealand delegate expressed a similar point of view, though rather less abrasively. Canada, however, was prepared to accept refugees—provided they were farmers—as were Colombia, Uruguay, and Venezuela. Peru turned its face against accepting any Jewish doctors, scientists, or intellectuals. So did Costa Rica, Honduras, Nicaragua, and Panama—though they added Jewish traders to their list of unwanted immigrants. The Argentinian delegate remarked that his country had a population only one tenth that of the United States, and yet they had taken in almost as many immigrants as the United States itself. Surely, in fairness, they could not be expected to take in many more?

When it came the turn of the European countries, Spain and Italy were clearly not in the running. Spain was in the midst of a bloody civil war, while Italy had refused to attend the conference in the first place. As for France, she had already had to accommodate some two hundred thousand refugees, forty thousand of them Jews, many of them her own nationals who had fled from the German remilitarization of the Rhineland in 1936. She was moreover in the throes of attempting to absorb, like some huge boa constrictor, an estimated 3 million aliens at present living within her borders. The French delegate insisted that his country had reached saturation point: She could do no more.

The Dutch and the Danes were similarly placed. Their immigration laws were liberal, but they were small countries and densely populated. Holland, with traditional generosity, had accepted twenty-five thousand Jewish refugees, and Denmark had recently been forced to take in more German refugees than she could conveniently handle.

The Swiss delegate, Dr. H. Rothmund, who was chief of the Police Division in the Swiss Justice and Police Department, spoke at length about his country's liberal tradition regarding political refugees. What he did not tell the conference was that he had already been in negotiation with the Nazi authorities to prevent the immigration of Austrian Jews into Switzerland. He told his listeners bluntly, "Switzerland, which has as little use for these Jews as has Germany, will herself take measures to protect Switzerland from being swamped by Jews with the connivance of the Viennese police." His greatest achievement was later to persuade the Germans—who were delighted with the idea—to stamp the letter "J" on the passports of all German and Austrian Jews, so that the race of the holder of the passport would be immediately obvious to border officials everywhere. This, of course, had the effect of making the passport holder persona non grata in many countries.

One of the unsung heroes of the conference was a delegate from Latin America, Señor M.J.M. Yepes, representing Colombia. He seems to have put into words what everyone felt and no one had the courage, or license, to say. Political refugees, he said, posed two problems to every country. The first was a question of principle, the second of fact—"which each country must settle by its own means and in the light of its special circumstances." Of the two, the question of principle was the most important, because it could determine everyone's approach to the problem for the future. The principle was quite simply, "Can a state, without upsetting the basis of our civilization, and, indeed, of all civilization, arbitrarily withdraw nationality from a whole class of its citizens, thereby making them stateless persons whom no country is compelled to receive on its territory? Can a state, acting in this way, flood other countries with the citizens of whom it wishes to get rid, and can it thrust upon others the consequences of an evil internal policy? The whole tragedy of these thousands of unfortunates who are bandied about from country to country, at the caprice of the alien police and exposed to the boorishness of frontier officials, the whole tragedy lies in the fact that this preliminary question was not settled. . . ." They would be wasting their time finding homes for the present flood of refugees, or listening to the grievances of "those who have come to voice their complaints before this modern Wailing Wall which the Evian Conference has now become." So long as this central problem remained unsolved, everything they did would be useless. He feared that "the bad example of the Old World may be copied in other continents, and the world will then become uninhabitable."

Originally, the conference had been planned to consist of only two full public meetings: an opening and a closing session. The interim would be devoted to the work of subcommittees. However, this was changed at the last minute to six public meetings, so that the various delegates could compete with each other in the eloquence of their speech-making. There was also to be one private session of the full conference. It was decided that the actual work of the conference would be done by two subcommittees. The first would take evidence from the numerous unofficial organizations. The second was a technical subcommittee, chaired by Judge Michel Hansson of Norway, which would study the legal aspects of the international refugee problem. This involved an examination of the laws governing the treatment of refugees in each of the participating states, the number of refugees each country was prepared to accept, and finally the old, old question of documentation. A stateless person, by definition, does not have a valid passport: Therefore, should they revive the Nansen passport? France, Great Britain, and the United States were all represented on this subcommittee as were—among others—Canada, the Netherlands, and Switzerland.

Other delegates obviously found the workings of this committee so tedious in comparison to the activities and delights available to them in the town of Evian that they tended to give it a miss. Faced with serious attendance problems, Judge Hansson—in spite of the embarrassment it was calculated to cause—was forced publicly to ask the delegations from about twenty governments to make a point of attending the meetings of his committee.

It was the first committee that attracted most attention. There were, after all, thirty-nine refugee organizations present at the conference, twenty of them Jewish, and all of them eager to make their own particular voices heard. The committee, under the chairmanship of Lieutenant Colonel White, the Australian minister of commerce, also included representatives of the Big Three—France, Great Britain, and the United States. With all these various groups knocking on its door, so to speak, Colonel White's committee decided it would take evidence only from those "organizations concerned with the relief of political refugees from Germany (including Austria)." In other words, it chose to limit its investigations to the immediate and pressing problem of the continuing Nazi expulsion of Jews from "Greater Germany." Under the circumstances, this was no doubt sensible. Unfortunately, however, it also decreed that each organization should present its views through one representative who would be permitted to speak for a limited time. What no one anticipated was that the time limit would be only ten minutes. None of the public figures chosen to represent these organizations—and they included many distinguished scientists, authors, politicians, and so on—were used to this kind of interrogation. They found that no sooner had they made their plea and perhaps answered a question or two than they were forced to give way to the next spokesman for the next organization. Many found the whole business both disheartening and humiliating, particularly when the committee, grown weary of listening to so many speeches, reduced the time allowed from ten minutes to five.

In the end, in spite of all the rhetoric and fine words, the Evian Conference achieved nothing, apart from setting up an "Intergovernmental Committee to continue and develop the work of the Evian meeting." As it broke up and the delegates departed, reactions in the world's press varied from cautiously optimistic to depressingly gloomy. The views of most of those working in the refugee relief organizations, however, were typified by the comments of Wilfrid Israel, principal director of the Jewish *Hilfsverein* in Berlin.

Israel, whose department store was wrecked by the Nazis on November 10, was a remarkable man, the original for the Bernhard Landauer character in Christopher Isherwood's novel *Goodbye to Berlin*. He was, incidentally, one of those who lost his life, along with film star Leslie Howard, aboard flight 777, the passenger plane from Lisbon that was shot down by the Luftwaffe on June 1, 1943. Writing to a British Quaker friend, Israel told how he had hoped that "the Evian Conference might . . . achieve by direct negotiations with the Reich government some agreement for controlling and humanizing the application of the policy aimed at driving ultimately the whole Jewish population from Germany. There was never any real prospect of modifying the policy itself." But this had not happened—the conference was a disaster, described by Israel as "a catastrophic setback."

Of all the many press reports, *Newsweek* provided perhaps the most telling, summing up the conference in a sentence. Recalling conference chairman Myron Taylor's appeal in his opening address for governments to act and act promptly, *Newsweek* sardonically observed that that is precisely what they had done: "Most governments represented acted promptly by slamming their doors against Jewish refugees."

If Roosevelt had hoped that Evian would bring pressure to bear on the German government—enough at least to force the Nazi authorities to slow down the process of Aryanization—then he was to be disappointed. If anything, Evian had the opposite effect, confirming the Nazis in their belief that, in the final analysis, fine words were all that the international community was prepared to launch in defense of the Jews, or anyone else. Evian simply proved to Hitler that he had nothing to fear from world opinion.

For German Jews, the failure of the free world to rally to their defense at Evian was to have disastrous consequences. Hitler, Goebbels, and the rest of the Nazi leaders were already frustrated at what they saw as the unacceptably slow pace of Jewish emigration, one of the main reasons why they had intensified their persecution during 1938. But obviously the Jews could not leave, however much they may have wanted to, if they had nowhere to go. The violent actions in Austria, together with the other measures taken in the Reich, had been enough to provoke the democracies into holding the conference—bringing hope to the Nazis that at last they were about to take the Jews off their hands. Clearly, however, those actions had not been strong enough to produce the desired solution. The logic was inescapable that what was needed was a more violent action. From that moment, Kristallnacht, or something equally terrible, became inevitable.

"The World Chose Not to Look"

"**N**ovember 10 opened the eyes of even the most devotedly home-loving Jews," Ruth Andreas-Friedrich wrote in her diary. "Everyone who can possibly manage it is trying to get out of the country. It's not easy to get an emigration visa; it almost seems as if all the countries had conspired to make emigration difficult for the German Jews. In one, they restrict immigration; in another, they forbid it altogether. Urgent applications are delayed, important letters lie unanswered. Affidavits are mislaid; sponsorships have to be begged for. A person with no connections abroad, no influential sponsors, must resign himself to staying here as an unwelcome alien. *Sauve qui peut!*"

Andreas-Friedrich's diary entry was made on February 24, 1939—fifteen weeks after Kristallnacht, and seven and a half months after the Evian Conference. The Jews of Germany and Austria were clearly reacting to the pogrom—foreign consulates, especially those of the United States and Britain, but also the French, Dutch, Belgian, and the Scandinavian nations were besieged daily by seemingly endless lines of desperate men and women seeking visas and entry permits. But how were the governments of those countries reacting? How accurate was the impression that they were all conspiring to make emigration difficult?

In some cases, of course, the charge was justified. Mussolini, who naturally sided with Hitler and the Nazis and refused to accept any refugees even had they wanted to go to Fascist Italy, launched a violent attack on the democracies through his mouthpiece, the *Giornale d'Italia*. On November 22, the editor, Dr. Virginio Gayda, put his name to an article entitled "Why Don't They Want Them?," which asked why the democracies, who professed to be so interested in the fate of the Jews, were showing such a remarkable disinclination to accept Jewish immigrants into their own countries. For six months, he said, they had been clamoring against the repressive policies of Germany. Chamberlain, Roosevelt, and Dutch prime minister Colijn had all made pronouncements.

Ever since Evian, people had been studying the problem and promising to help—but there had been no practical results.

According to Dr. Gayda, the reason for this was that the great democracies were themselves beginning to be afraid of the Jews. They saw, he said, that intermixing the races was impossible, that Jewish political influence was dangerous and often subversive, and that Jewish economic power led to capitalistic money-grubbing and speculation.

The next day, another influential Italian paper, *Il Messaggero*, joined in the taunts, proclaiming that it was "owing to Anglo-Saxon prohibitionism, which has closed its doors to European immigration, that the Jewish problem in East-Central Europe has assumed the proportions that we know." Britain, it said, had been able to offer no solution. Nor had the United States. Why was it that those countries where Jews were practically all-powerful, "controlling finance, press, culture, politics and administration," should be most strongly against Jewish immigration? Was it a case of "Israel against Israel"?

Much of what Gayda and *Il Messaggero* had to say in their long and often hysterical articles was deliberately mendacious—like Goebbels, Mussolini was never above using a good lie to score points. But there could be no denying the fact that in their approach to the problem of the Jewish refugees, even after Kristallnacht and all the subsequent outcry, the democracies continued to follow the "not in my backyard" principle.

The Intergovernmental Committee for Refugees, set up to continue the work of the Evian Conference, such as it had been, was established in London in the summer of 1938, with a British chairman, Lord Winterton, and two Americans, Myron Taylor and George S. Rublee, as vice-chairman and director respectively. The involvement, and predominance, of the Anglo-Saxon nations was therefore very clearly established, though the French, Dutch, and various South American countries also played active roles. They spent most of their time trying to find homes for the Jews in countries other than their own.

They also, it must be said in all fairness, tried to find ways of dealing with Germany to alleviate the problem at its source. The man chiefly responsible for this was the director, George Rublee, an old friend of Roosevelt and a fellow Groton alumnus, who had come out of retirement at the age of seventy at the personal request of the president to take on the running of the ICR. He was well qualified for the task, having been a distinguished corporation lawyer as a partner in the Wall Street law firm of Covington, Burling and Rublee, with wide experience in international affairs. He had acted as legal adviser to the U.S. embassy in

Mexico in 1928, and was said to have been instrumental in finding a formula to resolve the tricky Mexican Church-State dispute.

According to Dean Acheson, one of his law associates who later became secretary of state under Harry S. Truman, Rublee was a man given to wildly fluctuating moods—one moment alight with almost demoniacal energy, the next overcome by a "melancholy languor." But in London he appears to have remained in his active mode, setting to work immediately with great fervor. His plan was to negotiate some kind of deal with the German government that would enable large numbers of Jewish refugees to emigrate from Germany in an orderly manner over a period of, say, five years, taking a percentage of their worldly wealth with them.

Rublee made contact first with Dr. Hjalmar Schacht, the "old wizard" of German finance, president of the Reichsbank and Hitler's economic adviser, and later with Dr. Helmut Wohlthat, an expert from the economic department of the German Foreign Office who worked for Göring as a commissioner for the Four-Year Plan. But the ICR director found negotiating with the Nazis much harder than with the Mexicans. They procrastinated, they dragged their feet, they even went so far as to hint that they were hesitant about entering into negotiations with a man like Rublee because they suspected he was not of Aryan descent.

Rublee's problems were made still more difficult by the fact that he had to deal not only with Germany, but also with the countries of potential settlement. Before he could present his plan to the Germans, he had to be able to tell them that there were definite prospects of finding somewhere for the Jews to go—and it seemed none of the other countries were prepared to make any firm commitment.

Everyone, it seemed, had ideas about where the Jews could be settled—and most of these involved what would nowadays be known as Third World countries. One of the earliest and most persistent was Madagascar, the huge island off the east coast of Africa, which was then a French colony. The Madagascar option was suggested by many individuals, notably two Englishmen, Captain Henry Hamilton Beamish, who spoke at Nazi rallies in Germany in the twenties and thirties, and Arnold Spencer Leese, a retired army veterinary surgeon who had spent years in the Middle East and described himself as a camel doctor.

Their idea involved taking over Madagascar from the French and turning it into a kind of racial Elba, to which Europe would banish its entire Jewish population. The costs of this exile, including the building of accommodation, would of course be borne by the Jews themselves, as would the cost of the navy patrol that would provide a *cordon sanitaire* around the island to prevent any Jews from escaping. After the scheme had been in operation for an appropriate time, any Jews found in countries that had become *Judenfrei* would be shot. It was never very clear what was to happen to the native population of Madagascar, except that there would be some form of compensation paid to them—by the Jews, of course.

Over the years, the Madagascar idea surfaced at various times and in various places. In 1937, in Poland, the Lepecki Commission set up by the government to discuss the Jewish question, and which included both Polish and Jewish members, considered—and predictably failed to reach agreement on—the suitability of Madagascar as a site for Jewish resettlement. While the Poles were all in favor of banishing the Jews to the southern Indian Ocean, the representatives of the Jewish community naturally were not.

The French, too, had considerable reservations about sending German Jews to Madagascar or any of their colonies—especially those that had once been German. Astonishingly, their main objection was that as Germans the Jews might turn into a fifth column in the event of war! The French were prepared to settle up to ten thousand refugees in the whole of their empire, including Madagascar, though not more than two thousand in any single territory—but these would not be German refugees. What they proposed was to ship out ten thousand other refugees and allow German Jews to take their places in France. It was never made clear whether the ten thousand German Jews were those who had fled into France immediately after Kristallnacht, and who were to be allowed to stay, but the implication was that they were. The French also added the proviso that their offer depended on other nations playing their full part. If no one else took refugees, then neither would they.

As an alternative to Madagascar, U.S. undersecretary of state Sumner Welles hit on the idea of Angola in West Africa, then a Portuguese colony. Unfortunately, the Portuguese dictator, Dr. Salazar, did not share the U.S. administration's concern for settling the Jews and refused to permit any to enter Portuguese Africa, or indeed Portugal itself, imposing strict visa regulations on German Jews, though other Germans needed no visas.

President Roosevelt himself weighed in with the thought that Ethiopia would be ideal for Jews, and even had his ambassador in Rome, William Phillips, make a formal approach to Mussolini, raising the matter. Mussolini, equally formally, passed the buck, suggesting that Brazil or even the Soviet Union would be more appropriate. When a similar suggestion about the Soviet Union was put to the British government, the Foreign

Office pointed out that although the Soviets had an autonomous Jewish province, the Oblast of Birobijan in eastern Siberia, this had been the scene of particularly brutal purges, and Jews of German origin were believed to have supplied most of the victims. In any case, the Foreign Office rightly noted, the Jews would almost certainly refuse to go there!

William Randolph Hearst, the American newspaper tycoon, suggested buying the Belgian Congo and settling the Jews there. Unfortunately, the Congo proved not to be for sale. Sir Neill Malcolm, the League of Nations high commissioner for refugees, advocated setting up a small state for them in North Borneo—which happened to be an area where he had business interests. James G. McDonald, Malcolm's predecessor, inspired by a suggestion from a former British consul in Costa Rica, proposed Baja California. Many others suggested Mexico, too. Roosevelt himself, with Ethiopia a nonstarter, was intrigued by the possibilities of the Orinoco River valley in Venezuela, and also by the Bukedon Plateau on Mindanao in the Philippines. It was felt that establishing some four thousand Jewish families there—perhaps rising to as many as eleven thousand families—would do much to counter the influence of the Japanese, thirty thousand of whom had settled in the islands. But there was too much opposition from native Filippinos, and the scheme was dropped.

Costa Rica sounded like a good bet, until it was discovered that the proposed area for the settlement was close to the Panamanian border and the canal, which made it strategically sensitive. For all those in the U.S. State Department who equated Central European Jews with bolshevism, it would be seen as placing a large number of Reds next to a vital U.S. waterway, something that could never be contemplated.

Democratic congressman Charles A. Buckley, whose Bronx constituency housed a large Jewish population, wrote to the president on November 18 pressing the claims of Alaska. The northern territory was underpopulated, said Buckley, and had a wealth of resources—immigration was just what it needed. The White House replied that Alaska was not an appropriate place to settle refugees.

The countries of South and Central America and the Caribbean responded to the call after Kristallnacht in various ways. The Brazilians said they would like to help, but immigrants already made up 10 percent of the population and accepting Jews would create "serious difficulties" with the German settlers. Others, however, were quite happy to accept refugees, provided they could control the numbers and pick and choose those with particular skills. Bolivia, for example, would freely take all agricultural workers, families of refugees already in the country, and anyone with capital in excess of five thousand dollars. The Bolivian government also agreed to accept fifty technical experts and the same number of professional men, preferably doctors. This was straightforward enough, but only amounted to two to three hundred people in all. Nevertheless, Bolivia was a popular destination for many, since it was easy to slip across the border into Argentina, an altogether more Europeanized and developed country.

Argentina itself imposed an immediate ban on all Jewish immigrants, even those who already had visas. So, too, did Paraguay. This resulted in trapping sixty-four immigrants who were already on their way, some on board ship, others waiting for transport from Montevideo, capital of Uruguay. Eventually, pressure from the United States and Britain succeeded in settling their case and getting them into Paraguay and Argentina. Anglo-American pressure also persuaded the Argentines, through their minister with the strange portfolio of Foreign Affairs and Public Worship, to agree to take some trained agricultural workers, as long as they had sufficient means "to ensure their settlement and progress on Argentine soil."

The Paraguayans, still recovering from the effects of the Chaco War with Bolivia, also agreed under pressure to take some trained agricultural workers, as long as they had at least ten years' experience. They did not want Jews entering the country as farmers, they said, and immediately engaging in commerce. The Paraguayan ambassador in London was even doubtful if Jews "were capable of becoming steady agricultural colonists who could stay on the land." It seemed as though his government was equally dubious. They certainly did not go out of their way to welcome refugees—when representatives of the Jewish Economic Corporation visited Asunción, the Paraguayan capital, the government attempted to blackmail them. First, they offered them some unsuitable land at a grossly inflated price, and when the offer was refused, threatened to pass a decree closing the country to all Jews in future. In short, it was either pay up or stay out. The JEC decided to stay out.

Many individual Jews, however, did not heed the warning of the JEC, and attempted to obtain visas to Paraguay by bribing officials. Honorary Paraguayan consuls, particularly in France, did a brisk trade selling visas to them, many of which were forged. It is perhaps just as well that few Jews ended up in Paraguay, for the country was about to enter the long night of military dictatorship, first under General Marinigo and then under General Alfredo Stroessner.

In February 1939, Argentina, Paraguay, and Uruguay signed an agreement to reduce trade barriers between the three countries. One of its provisions called for a mutual restriction on immigration, in order to keep out undesirables.

Elsewhere in the region, the Chileans proved in their own way to be as devious as the Paraguayans. They agreed to take two hundred Jewish families, preferably agriculturalists, qualified artisans, and technical experts, but there were problems about where they were intended to settle. Chilean ambassador Edwards, in London, tried to interest a Jewish refugee organization in land in south Chile that he and some friends happened to own. He described the place as ideal for colonization, a land flowing with milk and honey—but it turned out to be near Puerto Aisen, latitude 45° south and therefore in the middle of the "roaring forties," some nine hundred miles south of Santiago and only four hundred miles north of the Straits of Magellan. It was a cold, miserable, inhospitable place. Much to Señor Edwards's indignation, the refugee organization politely turned him down.

In Peru, American ambassador Laurence Steinhardt did his best to persuade the foreign minister, Dr. Concha, to open the doors. Concha promised to study the matter at once, but explained that although Peru had begun to allow refugees to enter with considerable freedom, there had recently been such an influx—he did not specify numbers—that they had had to impose severe restrictions. He did say, however, that they were prepared to accept "a fair number of agriculturalists and a few specialists of a nature to be set forth in writing, and a few businessmen with capital."

Fortunately, there were brighter spots, too. Honduras, for example, Central America's poorest nation, offered to take one thousand refugees, which the British Foreign Office described as "a very respectable number" for a country of its size. But perhaps the most promising scheme of all— on paper, at least—involved the Dominican Republic. At the time of the Evian Conference, the dictator of the island republic, General Rafael Trujillo y Molina, had offered twenty-six thousand acres of his private estate at Sosua, about seventy miles from the border with Haiti, which occupies the other half of the island of Hispaniola. Unlike other leaders, he did not change his mind after Kristallnacht, but pressed on even more eagerly.

Trujillo's motives for making his generous offer were not purely altruistic. He was desperately keen to win American support—and to expunge the memory of the savage massacre of some ten thousand Haitian immigrants by Dominican troops in October 1937, when many Haitians had been burned alive. Nevertheless, it seemed as though his scheme could provide a lifeline for many Jews—the first estimates suggested that the area would be able to absorb between fifty thousand and one hundred thousand people at a cost per head of sixteen hundred dollars for each adult male. The number of settlers was later scaled down to twenty-eight thousand and then to an even more realistic three thousand to five thousand, while the cost almost doubled to three thousand dollars per head. The first contingent of "refugee colonists," as they were to be called, did not arrive in the Dominican Republic until March 1940, to be followed by a further 400–450 men. In the end, the whole Sosua project cost $1 million, and resettled just 474 souls.

The Dominican Republic's effort was, at least, more successful than that of neighboring Cuba, which also started out by offering to take one hundred thousand refugees. Somehow, the offer never got beyond the talking stage, and when, in May 1939, the liner *St. Louis* anchored off the coast of Cuba with 1,128 refugees on board, only 22 were allowed to land, and those after long negotiations. The Cubans refused to provide even a temporary refuge for the others, despite the fact that more than seven hundred of them held quota numbers permitting them entry to the United States in three years' time. The United States also refused to bend its regulations, and the ship was forced to return across the Atlantic with the remaining 1,106 refugees still on board. Britain found homes for 288 of these, while the rest were taken into Holland, Belgium, and France.

For all the charges of anti-Semitism, France continued to set an example to many countries in Europe. Certainly, French ministers had vigorously opposed any government help in financing the settlement of refugees, and at one stage had been seriously considering setting up concentration camps of their own to hold what Bonnet described as "the large numbers of undesirable foreigners." But the French had taken in over forty thousand Jewish refugees in recent years, and Bonnet could with some justification tell the Chamber Foreign Affairs Committee on December 14 that in proportion to her population, France had done as much as Britain and the United States.

But perhaps the best record of all in Europe was that of Holland, which by the same yardstick claimed to have done no less than eight times as much as Britain by December 1938. Since 1933, nearly twenty-five thousand aliens had been admitted to Holland, of whom thirteen thousand were described as pure Jews, four thousand half-Jews, and between seven thousand and eight thousand others. Nearly seventeen thousand of these immigrants had remained in the country, and since Kristallnacht new refugees were arriving at the rate of about one thousand a week.

On December 1, Prime Minister Colijn broadcast an appeal on behalf of the various committees—Jewish, Protestant, Roman Catholic, and a special committee concerned with Jewish children—who were organizing a national collection to raise funds for refugees. Although many refugees were being looked after by friends and relatives, many more had neither, and Colijn stressed that large sums were needed "in order to fulfill our duty of mercy." Since no one knew whether or when the refugees could be sent on to other countries, he said, the Dutch "had to reckon with the necessity of assisting a large number of people for a considerable time, not merely temporarily." This, he told his listeners, was an opportunity for a small nation to show its greatness. In fulfilling their duty to their neighbors, the Dutch people must place the needs of the refugees above those of their own poor.

Belgium, next door to Holland, agreed to accept two thousand Jewish children, had stopped expelling refugees already in the country, and would take "a few hundred more." Although Belgium and Holland both had overseas empires, and the Dutch were investigating the possibility of settling Jews in places like Surinam, they were small countries with limited resources. The Scandinavian countries, with virtually no history of Jewish settlement, put up the barriers and admitted only a few hundred refugees, fearful of arousing latent anti-Semitism. The Swiss allowed in only a trickle, mostly as transients heading elsewhere.

With France already near the saturation point, not prepared to send German Jews into her colonies and about to be swamped by some three hundred thousand Republican Spanish fleeing from Franco at the end of the civil war, the onus of dealing with the refugee problem was therefore almost entirely on America and Britain. America, after all, had been built on immigration, and was traditionally the refuge of those "huddled masses yearning to breathe free." Britain, although a small, crowded nation herself, had the world's greatest empire, with territory in every corner of the globe. The British also held the keys to Palestine, where they were committed to the creation of a Jewish national home. Surely, between them, these two great nations could find some way of looking after those Jews trapped in Nazi Germany?

The shock of Kristallnacht had brought about a modest change of attitude in many parts of the British Empire. Urged on by the secretary of state for the dominions, the Australians, who had earlier declared that they had no intention of importing a racial problem, now announced that they would take fifteen thousand Jewish refugees, over a three-year period. New Zealand also agreed to "do something effective for this unfortunate body of people," though these two promises were offset to some extent by the Canadians, who remained noncommittal, saying they would take a limited number of agricultural workers but that there was "no likelihood of Jews being admitted to enter Canada on a scale and for purposes which would result in displacing persons already in employment in the Dominion." South Africa was even less willing to help, refusing to make special provision for Jewish immigrants, since they were regarded as "not being genuinely assimilable as South Africans."

The colonies responded to the government's request with various plans. The governor of British Guiana said he would make ten thousand square miles of land available at a low rent to voluntary organizations for Jewish settlement, a figure that was rapidly increased to forty thousand square miles. Tanganyika offered about fifty thousand acres and an experimental private scheme to train up to two hundred young Jewish settlers. Kenya, Northern Rhodesia, and Nyasaland suggested similar schemes, each for about 150 young men.

The colonial schemes were so small they could offer little hope to the beleaguered Jews—but even so, there were objections from several quarters after Chamberlain had announced them in the House of Commons on November 21. One of the principal objectors was Marcus Garvey, Jamaican-born president general of the Universal Negro Improvement Association, arguably the most charismatic Negro leader in the United States and the Caribbean in the interwar years. Described by John Bruce, the American radical black columnist, as "a little sawed-off hammered-down black man, with determination written all over his face," Garvey's impact when he first visited the United States was such that J. Edgar Hoover immediately advocated his deportation, an ambition that he achieved in 1927.

The day after Chamberlain's speech, Garvey, who was then based in London, took up the cudgels on behalf of the native populations of Tanganyika, Kenya, and British Guiana. "Without any prejudice toward the Jew," he wrote to Foreign Secretary Lord Halifax, "nor any desire to in any way do anything that would now or henceforth obstruct him, I desire to bring to your notice the following facts: Kenya is native territory, the inherent rights to the same are possessed by natives, even with changes that have been brought about by political accidents. So is Kenya [sic— he presumably meant Tanganyika]. So is British Guiana." Would it not be wiser, he suggested, to think of the future when planning to settle Jews? "I am seriously protesting," he continued, "on behalf of the natives, to whom these countries belong, against the attempt to complicate their national and future existence . . . May I not state that it would be much wiser for the Jews en masse to organise, agitate and do everything for the establishment of a country to which they have moral and legal rights, rather than be shifted from place to place, all over the world, to create problems in other ages."

If Garvey had not upset Halifax by saying Britain's colonies actually belonged to the natives, his final point would certainly have done so—for it was an unmistakable reference to Palestine, which Britain then ruled under a League of Nations mandate, and which was one of the government's biggest headaches.

On the face of it, Palestine offered the perfect, indeed the ultimate, solution to the problem of the Jewish refugees. On November 2, 1917, Arthur Balfour, then British foreign secretary, had sent a letter to Lord Rothschild, one of the Zionist leaders, informing him of "the following declaration of sympathy with Jewish Zionist aspirations which has been submitted to, and approved of, by the Cabinet":

> His Majesty's Government view with favour the establishment in Palestine of a national home for the Jewish people, and will use their best endeavours to facilitate the achievement of this object, it being clearly understood that nothing shall be done which may prejudice the civil and religious rights of the existing non-Jewish communities in Palestine, or the right and political status enjoyed by Jews in any country.

That single paragraph came to be known as the Balfour Declaration. Over the years there was to be a considerable amount of blood spilled because of it, British and Arab as well as Jewish.

After four hundred years of Turkish rule, Palestine became a British mandated territory with the breaking up of the old Ottoman Empire at the end of the First World War. Under the terms of the Treaty of San Remo, signed in 1920, Britain assumed responsibility for governing its people and preserving the balance between the Arabs and the growing Jewish community. It was never easy. By 1929, when the Arabs rose in revolt at increasing Jewish immigration, unrest turned into outright warfare, with 243 deaths that August in fighting in and around Jerusalem. As Jewish immigration continued to rise—from 4,075 in 1931 to a peak of 61,854 in 1935, tensions increased, exploding in a fresh outburst of Arab violence in 1936.

For the British, the situation had become impossible. Caught between two implacably opposed forces, there was no easy solution. On the one hand, they were committed to helping the Jews establish a national home—though not necessarily a Jewish state—and any failure to honor that commitment was bound to provoke the displeasure of the international Jewish community. On the other hand, they were also bound to protect the interests of the Palestinian Arabs—and any failure in this area could cause immense problems with the Arab princes of the Middle East, on whom Britain depended for her oil supplies.

In an attempt to reconcile the irreconcilable, the British government proposed to fall back on the solution that has always seemed the only way out of such dilemmas, but that always causes as many problems as it solves: partition. Palestine would be split into two states, one Arab, one Jewish. For the Jews, this would have the immense benefit that they would be able to control their own rates of immigration. Had the plan succeeded, the Jews of Germany would have had somewhere to run to in 1938 and 1939.

But of course the plan did not succeed—Arab opposition was so vehement that there was never any chance of its doing so. The Arabs were joined by all their allies—there were fears of serious problems with the Muslims in India, for example, and even the Afghans protested strongly. Malcolm Macdonald, secretary of state for the colonies, concluded sadly that if Britain went ahead with partition, "We would forfeit the friendship of the Arab world."

Sir Thomas Inskip, minister for the coordination of Defense, reported to the Cabinet: "The importance to Great Britain of Palestine is that in it are to be found the strategic end of the Iraq pipeline, the end of our eastern air communications, and of various railway communications. In the view of the chiefs of staff, we must safeguard our position in Palestine because of all these interlocking vital strategic interests."

By a terrible accident of timing, the final abandonment of the policy of partition was announced to the world on November 9, 1938. A month later, the British government rejected an appeal from the Jewish Agency for Palestine for an extra twenty-one thousand entry certificates. In May 1939, after a conference in London attended by five Arab countries—Egypt, Saudi Arabia, Iraq, Yemen, and Transjordan—as well as a Palestinian delegation and the Zionist executive in addition, of course, to Britain, the British government issued a white paper that set out its new plans for Palestine. The main points were: no partition, no Jewish state, an independent Palestine state within ten years, and Jewish immigration to be stopped altogether after five years, "unless the Arabs of Palestine were prepared to acquiesce in it." During those five years, a further seventy-five thousand Jews would be allowed in. The door to Palestine, already closing fast, would finally be locked and barred against the Jews forever.

In Britain itself, there was much soul-searching in the government and the higher reaches of the Foreign and Home Offices as to the best way of handling the refugee crisis. Some officials argued there were only two courses they could follow: They could made a direct approach to the German government saying that any further measures against the Jews would make Anglo-German friendship impossible, or they could simply get on with doing everything possible to help the remaining Jews to leave Germany, and provide the money to build reception camps and support them.

One rising star in the Foreign office, Roger Makins, did go so far as to suggest that Britain could bring pressure to bear on Germany by retaliatory measures such as expelling German citizens from Britain, denouncing economic agreements, and "by a clear indication that until the persecution and spoliation of the Jews ceases the policy of appeasement is at an end." But even Makins acknowledged that such steps might well provoke the Nazis into the massacre that many Jews feared was about to happen. And in any case, Chamberlain was far from ready to give up appeasement. Unlike his Dutch counterpart, he chose to leave the broadcasting of an appeal on behalf of the Jews to his predecessor as prime minister, Lord Baldwin. When Baldwin approached the Foreign Office for advice, he was told there would be no objection to his speaking strongly "so long as his words cannot be misrepresented as an attack by a British statesman on the Nazi regime as such."

The dilemma that faced all those trying to help the Jews was that the more they did, the more they encouraged the Germans, and possibly others such as the Poles and Romanians, to believe that persecution worked, and so to increase it. But there seemed to be little alternative, since doing nothing could also provoke more persecution, as the Nazis played ruthlessly on their "soft" consciences.

In the spring and early summer of 1939, there was one other possibility, which could have made an enormous contribution to the problem. In the strict secrecy of a Cabinet committee, senior ministers seriously considered a radical proposition by the home secretary, Sir Samuel Hoare, that Britain should hand over an entire colony to the Jews, rather than trying to find homes for them in five or six different places. With the enthusiastic support of the colonial secretary, Malcolm Macdonald, it was agreed that such a colony could even be allowed to become a sovereign Jewish state. The two most likely colonies were British Honduras and British Guiana. Hoare dismissed British Honduras, saying that he had some personal knowledge of it: It consisted mainly of forest country and was regarded as unhealthy. British Guiana, on the other hand, was a better and a bigger country, and had some mineral wealth, too.

Admirable as this scheme was, however, it was fraught with complex problems that could not be solved quickly—and speed was essential in trying to save the Jews of Germany. Eventually, it was overtaken by the start of the war, and had to be abandoned. Britain's largest contribution, therefore, lay in providing a haven within her own shores for as many refugees as possible, and acting as a transit camp for those heading for shelter elsewhere.

During the eight-year period from 1932 until the end of 1938, Britain accepted 33,675 refugees of all types—the Home Office did not differentiate between Jews and others—from Germany and Austria. During the first nine months of 1939, it took in 49,500, including some 10,000 unaccompanied children, plus another 6,000 refugees from Czechoslovakia.

The British government also did what it could to help George Rublee and the Intergovernmental Committee to deal with the Germans. Sir Montague Norman, governor of the Bank of England, interceded on Rublee's behalf with his friend and fellow banker Hjalmar Schacht, and five weeks after Kristallnacht, on December 14, Schacht arrived in London for a meeting with Rublee, Lord Winterton, and Sir Frederick Leith-Ross, chief economic adviser to the Foreign Office.

Schacht was not a committed Nazi, and even had a certain amount of sympathy for the Jews. At a Christmas party given by the Reichsbank for its office boys, at which many of the boys' parents were also present, he spoke sternly to them about Kristallnacht. "I do hope," he said, "that none of you had any part in that business. If anyone did, I would advise him to leave the Reichsbank at once. There is no room here for people who have no respect for the lives and property of their fellow men."

In London, however, Schacht made it clear that he had not come as a penitent to apologize for the morality of Nazi policy against the Jews, but merely as a financial technician with a plan to cure an unfortunate economic bottleneck. In the past, most emigration schemes had foundered on the problem of money: The fact that Jews were stripped of all they possessed when they left Germany meant they arrived in the country of their choice penniless. Many governments who were otherwise sympathetic to their plight felt constrained to limit the number of refugees they were prepared to take because of the potential cost of supporting them.

Schacht's idea was an ingenious scheme that would both finance Jewish emigration from the Reich and solve Germany's chronic foreign-exchange crisis at one and the same time. It bore a resemblance to the Ha'avara transfer agreement between the Anglo-Palestine Bank and Nazi Germany signed in 1933, which had so far proved to be the only really successful refugee emigration scheme, financing the passage of Jews into Palestine through export credits that helped Germany to avoid the worst effects of the international Jewish boycott on German goods.

In essence, Schacht's plan was nothing more than a subtle form of extortion on a huge scale. What he proposed was that in the future, emigration would be financed by means of an international refugee loan. This would be raised from Jewish sources—"international Jewry" as he put it—and would be sufficient to give every emigrant the equivalent of ten thousand Reichsmarks in whatever was the appropriate foreign currency—the equivalent of about two hundred pounds or one thousand dollars.

In order to secure the loan, Schacht proposed to set up a trust fund with a capital on paper of one and a half billion Reichsmarks, which he estimated to be 25 percent of the value of the property remaining in Jewish hands in Germany. It was a remarkable piece of financial hocus-pocus. The trust fund capital was an estimate of immovable assets that could not be taken out of the country. The only way these assets could be transferred to those countries playing host to the refugees, Schacht suggested, was if the countries concerned purchased German goods. The value of these purchases would be offset against the value of the assets. This meant that Germany would not lose any foreign currency, industrial production would receive a major boost, and valuable Jewish assets would be legally transferred to German ownership.

Under this scheme, Schacht claimed, 400,000 out of the 600,000 Jews he believed were still in the Reich would be enabled to emigrate, 150,000 of them—the Jewish wage earners—in from three to five years. Those who were left, roughly two hundred thousand, would be the old and infirm, who would be permitted to live out their lives in peace. They would, of course, remain as hostages in Germany, thus guaranteeing everyone's good behavior.

President Roosevelt, for one, saw the scheme for what it was—a means of bartering Jewish lives for exports. The Jewish banks, financial institutions, and fund-raising organizations were bitter. As they saw it, Schacht was creating the very monster that Hitler and the Nazis had always inveighed against—a collection of Jewish financial institutions operating together, "international Jewry" no less. He was also proposing to set up a mechanism whereby the Nazis could extort money from overseas Jews whenever they wished. Nevertheless, whatever its effect, no one wanted to risk dismissing the Schacht proposals out of hand; too many lives depended on keeping the Nazis negotiating.

Unfortunately, in Berlin, there was something approaching a palace revolution. After winning Hitler's praise for his refugee loan scheme, on January 20, 1939, Schacht was dismissed by Hitler for refusing to have recourse to the printing press to produce more money. The extremists took over, and they had long since lost patience with the Jewish problem. Their ideas for a solution were far removed from Schacht's subtle schemes.

On January 24, Göring charged Reinhard Heydrich with the task of getting rid of Germany's Jews, an order that was reinforced two years later as the demand for a "final solution." On February 7, Alfred Rosenberg, the so-called "philosopher of Naziism," son of an Estonian mother and a Lithuanian father, held a news conference in Munich. There, looking like an overgrown schoolboy, he announced plans to settle an incredible 15 million Jews—presumably the entire world Jewish population—in Guiana or Madagascar. It is clear from a speech he gave in the summer of that year that what he envisaged was a giant concentration camp with endemic yellow fever. Jews, he said, should be sent to "a wild island with a deadly climate . . . cut off from the outside world like lepers . . . the obnoxious Jewish race will find itself isolated in a reservation from where there is no return, from where there is but one exit—death."

According to George Rublee, there were between fifty thousand and seventy-five thousand Jewish children who needed to be brought out of Germany as quickly as possible. The ten thousand taken by Britain and several hundred by Holland represented a start, but other countries, including the United States, failed to follow their lead. Senator Robert F. Wagner of New York proposed in Congress that quotas should be stretched to allow ten thousand children to find safety in America, but his proposal met with stiff opposition. It was battered to death in congressional committee hearings, largely as a result of testimony from the American Legion and similar patriotic groups, and the children were kept out. A mere five hundred eventually found their way into the Land of the Free.

Far from causing an outcry, this rejection was actually welcomed by

66 percent of people questioned by a Gallup poll in January 1939, which showed only 26 percent in favor of admitting the children. This was, however, an improvement on figures of a month previously, when a CBS poll conducted by Elmo Roper showed that only 8.7 percent were prepared to relax U.S. immigration quota restriction to admit more Jews, despite the coverage given in the press and on the radio to the events in Germany.

The quota system was the biggest stumbling block for any American action. Introduced under the Johnson Immigration Act of 1924, it was intended to bring to an end the open-door approach of the frontier years, when America had needed immigrants to populate the westward expansion across the continent. The system divided immigrants into their countries of origin, regulating the numbers allowed to come from each and thus discreetly choking off the flow from the Old World. If any country failed to fill its quota in one year, the shortfall could not be made up by other countries, nor could it be carried over to another year.

The effect was a dramatic drop in immigration, particularly after 1930, when President Hoover, facing economic collapse at home, ordered U.S. consular officials to apply the terms of the Johnson Act with full rigor. In 1930, the United States accepted 241,700 immigrants; in 1932, this had fallen to 35,576, of which only 2,755 were Jewish.

Roosevelt, when he beat Hoover in the 1932 presidential election, had inherited this situation, and indeed had even endorsed Hoover's order of 1930. In 1938, despite everything that had happened in Europe, he was powerless to do a great deal to alter anything. Faced by a Republican Congress disenchanted with New Deal economics and determined to clip the wings of an overliberal administration, his room to maneuver was severely limited.

There was nothing he could do about the ten thousand children. Nor could he help when the British government begged for its own unused immigration quota to be given to German Jews, to help ease the situation. The old Austrian quota could be lumped in with the German, but even so, this only gave an annual total of 27,350—which was already fully allocated for the next eighteen months—while U.S. consulates in Germany reported more than 150,000 others desperately seeking asylum. The only ray of light fell on some fifteen thousand German Jews who were already in America on temporary, six-month permits. Roosevelt was able to extend their stay indefinitely. At the same time, the government was able to issue many more temporary permits, and extend the quota in this way. Even so, as a response to a terrible disaster it was woefully inadequate.

It was, however, an accurate reflection of popular sentiment in America. It is easy to accuse Roosevelt and the Congress of cynicism and inaction, but it must be remembered that they represented a country that was determined to look the other way, a country that felt it had troubles enough without worrying about a bunch of foreigners. Natural xenophobia was combined with fear of economic hardship to create an atmosphere of paranoia. Americans had vivid memories of the trauma of mass unemployment and the Great Depression of 1929–1934. Thousands of them had been forced to live in cardboard boxes and shantytowns outside cities—even outside the White House itself. Roosevelt and the New Deal had briefly generated a degree of euphoria, but from 1936 onward it was clear that the economic situation had begun to deteriorate again. Everyone was worried.

At the same time, there was in the air, like wood smoke, a whiff of genuine, home-grown anti-Semitism. U.S. Congressmen breathed it in like everyone else, and worried about their political futures when asked to help German Jews. As for the American Jewish community, without doubt the wealthiest and most powerful community of Jews in the world, they were all ex-immigrants themselves, or only a single generation away from it. In spite of their wealth, in spite of their potential political muscle, they remained insecure in the land they had chosen. Consequently, they were afraid to raise their voices, afraid to embarrass the one U.S. president whom they saw as a friend and ally, Franklin Delano Roosevelt.

American Jews for the most part approved of the Johnson Act, seeing it as a protection of their own hard-won status. Many of them had personal experience of anti-Semitism in the United States, and feared it might grow worse if there were a sudden influx of poverty-stricken Jews from Germany. And like many of their fellow Americans, they were concerned lest America become involved once again in the chaos that was Europe.

Throughout 1939, the Nazi persecution of the Jews continued unchecked, while the protests from the democracies faded. The moment had been lost, the opportunity squandered, not simply for protecting the Jews but also for coming together in a massive joint effort of will to stop Hitler from pursuing his other objectives. Hans Bernd Gisevius, the anti-Nazi Abwehr officer, summed up the situation with admirable clarity in his memoirs:

> The significance of the "glassbreakers' week" as it was popularly called cannot be overestimated. . . . After the week of pogroms the world could no longer harbor any doubts as to the ultimate aims of the Nazi movement. Death and

destruction were now being visited on the Jews, but it was clear that very soon indeed all the other accounts would be settled which Hitler had drawn up with such care in *Mein Kampf.* For fifteen years his plan had been written down in black and white for the world to see, but the world chose not to look.

On March 15, emboldened by the impotence and lack of will of his potential enemies, Hitler marched unopposed into Czechoslovakia. Chamberlain and Daladier were finally stung into proclaiming—eventually—that appeasement was finished, but they continued to offer trade and credit agreements, and secretly still tried to find ways of buying him off. On September 1, he invaded Poland, and the Second World War had begun, closing the doors into Britain and France for the remaining German Jews. Around four hundred thousand had escaped from Germany and Austria since 1933, but there were still over half a million left. By the middle of September, with the Allies looking on helplessly, Poland was crushed, and Hitler found himself with another 3.25 million Jews on his hands. The escalation of the Holocaust had become inevitable.

There was little anyone could do for the Polish Jews, as they were rounded up by Heydrich's SS *Einsatzgruppen* squads and either shot or herded into ghettos, but in Germany U.S. consulates continued to issue quota certificates for later years. In June 1940, however, at the time of the fall of France, the State Department refused, for security reasons, to accept any more refugees directly from German or German-occupied territories, with or without certificates. This effectively halved the flow of refugees into the United States. It was stopped altogether a year later, in July 1941, when Hitler ordered the closure of all U.S. consulates in Germany and German-occupied territories, in retaliation for the closing of German consulates in the United States because of their subversive activities in backing the isolationist America First Committee. Between them, Hitler and Roosevelt had finally plugged the dyke—there was nowhere for the Jews to go but Auschwitz, Treblinka, and the other death camps.

Epilogue

What Became of Herschel Grynszpan

At 9:00 P.M. Eastern Standard Time on Monday, November 14, 1938, some 5 million radio sets throughout the United States were tuned to *The General Electric Hour* for the weekly broadcast by a woman who had become an American institution, Dorothy Thompson. After a little sweet music from Phil Spitaly and his All-Girl Orchestra—included by the sponsors to soften the belligerent tone of her often controversial messages—Thompson launched into an emotional resumé of the events in Europe during the preceding week. The focus of her attention was the young assassin in Paris.

"I feel as though I know that boy," she told her listeners, "for in the past five years I have met so many whose story is the same—the same except for this unique, desperate act. Herschel Grynszpan was one of the hundreds of thousands of refugees whom the terror east of the Rhine has turned loose in the world. He could not leave France, for no country would take him in. . . .

"Herschel read the newspapers, and all that he could read filled him with dark anxiety and wild despair. . . . Thousands of men and women of his race had killed themselves in the last years, rather than live like animals . . . he got a letter from his father . . . he had been summoned from his bed and herded with thousands of others into a train of boxcars, and shipped over the border, into Poland . . . Herschel walked into the German embassy and shot Herr vom Rath. Herschel made no attempt to escape. . . .

"Every Jew in Germany was held responsible for this boy's deed. In every city an organized and methodical mob was turned loose on the Jewish population. . . . But in Paris, a boy who had hoped to make some gesture of protest which would call attention to the wrongs done his race burst into hysterical sobs . . . he realized that half a million of his fellows had been sentenced to extinction on the excuse of his deed. . . . They

231

say he will go to the guillotine, without a trial by jury, without the rights any common murderer has. . . .

"Who is on trial in this case? I say we are all on trial. I say the Christian world is on trial. . . . If any Jews, anywhere in the world, protest at what is happening, further oppressive measures will be taken. . . . Therefore, we who are not Jews must speak, speak our sorrow and indignation and disgust in so many voices that they will be heard. . . ."

It was fine, dramatic stuff, if slightly inaccurate in some of its details. Backed up by two equally potent articles in Thompson's widely syndicated newspaper column, it evoked a remarkable response from the American public: Over three thousand letters poured in over the next few days, many of them enclosing money. Thompson found herself willy-nilly directing a fund for the defense of Herschel Grynszpan, which she established as the Journalists' Defense Fund, with offices at 730 Fifth Avenue, New York, co-opting a number of other well-known figures as a committee. These included the editor of *Foreign Affairs*, Hamilton Fish Armstrong, columnists Heywood Broun, General Hugh Johnson, Frank R. Kent, and Westbrook Pegler, journalist John Gunther, Teddy Roosevelt's daughter, Alice Roosevelt Longworth, Leland Stowe, Raymond Gram Swing, onetime correspondent in Berlin for the *Chicago Daily News* and the New York *Herald* and now another well-known radio personality, William Allen White, editor of the *Emporia Gazette*, and the Broadway wit, critic, and columnist Alexander Woollcott.

Westbrook Pegler sounded a note of warning in a letter to Thompson on November 17, writing that he had "one great doubt of the wisdom of raising a great fund. It will suggest an attempt to corrupt the issues of the trial." In addition, he pointed out that it would be sensible to agree in advance as to what should be done with any excess cash left over from Herschel's defense, since questions would almost certainly be asked later. He suggested that any remaining money should be given to "a relief or emigration fund," an eminently sound proposal.

Bearing Pegler's points in mind, Thompson published an open letter to fellow journalists and anyone as yet uninvolved in the Grynszpan case. She began by stating the position clearly and forcefully:

Firstly, despite the fact that hundreds of thousands of their people have been driven into exile and thousands have perished, this is only the second act of counter-violence committed by a Jew.

Second, the boy who did this deed is only seventeen years old.

Third, he is penniless.

Fourth, none of his people had any possible recourse to redress of their grievance by law.

Fifth, the international political pressure is such that the case will be tried in an atmosphere of extreme fear.

She declared that the purpose of the fund was "to provide for a first-rate and adequate defense. . . . We do not want to make a hero out of Grynszpan. We only want to give him a chance to have his case presented and the facts aired openly." Later in the letter, she shrewdly made the point that "[w]e want every cent of this money to come from Americans who are not Jewish. The reason is a simple one. All the Jews in Germany are being held hostages for whatever the members of their race do abroad, and we want to be able to say that not a Jew has contributed to this defense fund." She concluded the letter by saying that any money left over would be given to organizations aiding refugees, on the advice of Myron C. Taylor, American representative on the Intergovernmental Committee for Political Refugees, the man who had been President Roosevelt's delegate to the Evian Conference that July.

Dorothy Thompson, known as "the First Lady of American Journalism," was a passionate anti-Nazi. Born in Lancaster, an industrial town near Buffalo, New York, she was the daughter of an English Methodist minister, and began her writing career as publicist for a Bible society, following a period as an organizer for the women's suffrage movement. Graduating from there by way of free-lance articles for various publications, she established her credentials as a foreign correspondent by covering the "Troubles" in Ireland and then going on as an unsalaried Austrian correspondent for the *Philadelphia Public Ledger* in Vienna, where her forceful personality soon made itself felt. "Two things happened in central Europe during the decade of the twenties, people in Vienna still say," wrote John Gunther, "the economic crisis and Dorothy Thompson."

As a correspondent in Austria and later in Germany during the twenties and early thirties, Thompson witnessed the rise of the Nazis firsthand. Initially, she was not impressed by the party, or by Hitler himself, whom she interviewed in 1932 for *Cosmopolitan* magazine. "When finally I walked into Adolf Hitler's salon in the Kaiserhof Hotel," she wrote, "I was convinced that I was meeting the future dictator of Germany. In something less than fifty seconds I was quite sure I was not. It took just that time to measure the startling insignificance of this man who has set the whole world agog."

Hitler never forgave her for those words. In 1934, following a series of articles she had written criticizing Nazi measures against the Jews, he ordered her out of the country. Thompson, by then already well on her way to becoming a household name, returned home to complete the process by using the new medium of radio as well as the printed word to impress the strength of her character on America.

Although her regular broadcasts and columns covered a wide range of topics, her campaign against the Nazis remained a constant feature. A *New Yorker* cartoon by Gardner Rea as Europe teetered on the brink of war in 1939 aptly covers both her obsession and her forcefulness: A Scarsdale matron trimming flowers for a vase questions her newspaper-reading husband, "Has Germany answered Dorothy Thompson yet?"

It would be a mistake to dismiss Dorothy Thompson's efforts on behalf of Herschel Grynszpan as a cynical exercise in self-publicity, making use of a pitiful youth's misfortunes. Certainly, by choosing to focus on the highly emotional image of a hapless young man forced into a desperate act to draw attention to the plight of his people, she was personalizing and no doubt sensationalizing the greater issues involved. But there can be no doubt that the subjective treatment of the story was remarkably effective in bringing home to the ordinary reader and listener the truth of what was going on in Germany. And unlike those who made a great deal of noise but achieved little more than the emptiness of righteous indignation, she did do something positive in arranging Herschel's defense in a trial that would inevitably become a political jamboree.

Because her work kept her in New York, Thompson relied on her old friend Edgar Ansel Mowrer, head of the Paris bureau of the *Chicago Daily News*, to organize things on the spot. Mowrer, who like Thompson had been forced out of Berlin where he had been a correspondent for many years, was an excellent and capable choice. On the morning of Thursday, November 19, 1938, he went to see the most celebrated advocate in France, a Corsican lawyer called Maître Vincent de Moro-Giafferi.

"I am not altogether pleased with the choice," Mowrer wrote Thompson, "because Moro is considered here as being extreme left. But he is one of the big shots and will do a good job and manage to put Hitler in the prisoners' dock."

Mowrer went on to say that Moro "had already been asked to defend young G., whom he calls 'the child.' He therefore gladly accepts to represent your Committee at the same time." At this stage, the two men did not discuss money, but Mowrer made an appointment to see the lawyer at the beginning of the following week, when, as he promised Thompson, he would "impress upon him that a newspaper committee is nothing that ought to be milked." The problem was, he said, that the Corsican was used to drawing "prodigious fees."

Despite his pricey label, Moro-Giafferi was in great demand. Not only had he already been asked by the Grynszpan family to defend Herschel, but he had also been approached by the vom Rath family, who had, he said, "offered him a fortune to represent their civil interest in the case." (In a French murder trial, there is often an extra counsel to be found in court, acting neither for the defense nor for the prosecution, but representing those who have in some way been injured by the crime—usually the victim's family—who are known as the *partie civile* and who wish to seek damages from the accused.) Needless to say, Moro had refused the vom Raths: Quite apart from any moral or financial considerations, there was clearly much more kudos in the star role of defense counsel.

Herschel, meanwhile, was being held in the young offenders section of Paris's Fresnes Prison, a section of the jail that was regarded as a model penitentiary for minors. Dr. Alain Cuenot, a French physician who spent years collecting every piece of available material concerning Herschel, may have stretched the truth slightly in comparing it to "a seaside town, clean light and airy," but it was certainly no grim Bastille. It was seen as a "rehabilitation center," and the youngsters, including Herschel, enjoyed a certain degree of freedom. They were encouraged to keep a journal of their stay in Fresnes, and to write their life stories, which were later studied by the examining magistrate in charge of each case and, if necessary, by psychiatric experts, too.

Herschel filled two notebooks during his time in Fresnes. In some ways, he enjoyed his stay in prison: For the first time in his life, he felt important, having become a celebrity, the central figure in what would inevitably be a big political trial. He began to develop inflated ideas of his own importance, seeing himself as a freedom fighter, a Maccabee battling for the Jewish cause, and as a result he turned into something of a prima donna. For a start, he announced that he intended to handle his own defense and appoint his own lawyers.

In the absence of Uncle Abraham and Aunt Chawa, who had been arrested on a charge of aiding and abetting the illegal entry and residence of Herschel Grynszpan in France, a trio of uncles, Abraham Berenbaum, Salomon Grynszpan, and Jacques Wykhodz, formed a family council to look after his case. They were all out of their depth from the beginning. When Herschel made his announcement, they hurried over to the prison on November 14 to talk to him.

"They greeted me in the name of my family and in the name of world Jewry, for whom I had risked my life," he recorded rather grandly in his journal. They then explained to him that as his trial would be an important one, "I ought to have the best lawyer in France, de Moro-Giafferi." Herschel allowed himself to be persuaded—on condition that the uncles arranged to have "my dear parents and my sister and my brother come to Paris." According to the journal, they swore on the heads of their children that as soon as Moro-Giafferi was appointed, he would see to it that Herschel's family traveled from Poland to see him. They then gave him money to buy special foods—he had suffered from stomach trouble ever since arriving in Paris—and left, telling him not to worry and assuring him that "the whole world" was behind him. Their assurance was only a slight exaggeration, for it was that same evening that Dorothy Thompson made her first radio broadcast on the subject.

Before his own arrest, Uncle Abraham had appointed three Jewish lawyers, Maîtres Swarc, Fränkel, and Vessiné-Larue, to handle Herschel's case. The appointment of Moro-Giafferi over their heads, and by an outside agency in America of all places, did not sit well with them, and they were soon complaining that they were being excluded from the legal decision-making process. This was, of course, perfectly true, but since virtually all the money was coming from Dorothy Thompson and her fund, there was little they could do about it if they wanted to go on getting their share.

Conscious of her responsibilities to the American public who had contributed to the fund, Thompson was determined to see that she got value for its money. She disbursed the cash to Paris in installments, a little at a time, sending it to the office of another lawyer, Maître Gillet, at 150 Rue de Rivoli, who passed it on to Moro-Giafferi and the Grynszpan committee's appointed agent, one Elie Sofer, proprietor of a manicure salon and treasurer of the Union Contre La Persécution Hitlerienne, who together kept a tight rein on expenditure. Moro insisted that no money could be paid out without his cosignature on the check.

Expenses continued to mount, however. In all, over several months, some 300,000 francs—around $30,000 or £6,000—was sent from New York to Paris. Some of this was used to pay the lawyers: twenty-two thousand francs in November 1938, a further two thousand francs in December, twenty thousand more in January 1939, and so on. Money was also spent in trying to get Herschel's parents out of Poland, as the uncles had promised. A British journalist, A. R. Pirie, volunteered to go to Zbaszyn and escort them personally to Paris, in return for exclusive rights to Herschel's prison journal for his paper. The plan backfired, however, when Herschel refused to go along with the deal and even wrote to his parents at Zbaszyn telling them not to sign anything with the journalist. In the event, Pirie was unsuccessful. He went to Poland, but failed to bring out the Grynszpans. The venture cost the fund some fifty thousand francs.

Moro, meanwhile, was getting into his stride in typically flamboyant style. Since promising to represent Herschel, he told Thompson in a message through Dr. Goldman (chairman of the administrative committee of the World Jewish Congress, who had called on him in Paris on his way to New York), he had received "innumerable threatening letters," presumably from Nazi sympathizers and anti-Semites. He had, however, found an original method of countering these threats: He had, he said, officially informed the German embassy that he was a Corsican, and that Corsicans were not civilized people like the Jews, but believed in the blood feud. If, therefore, anything untoward should happen to him while he was defending Herschel Grynszpan, there would not be just one death in the embassy—they would be lucky if anyone at all was left alive at 78 Rue de Lille!

On a more serious note, Moro indicated that he was optimistic about the outcome of the trial. Herschel, he said, was "very beautiful . . . an extremely fine type, straightforward, earnest, with no complications of communism or any political tie-ups." This would be a greater benefit when the case came to trial, since in many people's minds—and not just in France—the Jew was perceived to adopt the shape of the latest painted devil of popular political demonology. What Moro did not tell Thompson was that he and Herschel had heartily disliked each other on sight. Herschel felt Moro had been forced on him against his will, but he could not fire him since he was not paying his fees. The strong personal antipathy was strengthened by the very real language barrier between them: Moro spoke no Yiddish, and Herschel's French was not up to grasping subtle legal argument. And on top of that, there was the question of religion—the fact that Moro was not Jewish might be a positive advantage in court, but initially it must have made the lawyer seem alien and vaguely threatening to a young man who had never had any friends outside the Jewish community.

Herschel clearly felt more at ease with his original three lawyers, who were Jewish and spoke Yiddish, though as advocates they were not in the same class as Moro. Unlike the Corsican, however, it seems that Maître Swarc in particular was especially adept at, or interested in, stroking his young client's tender and easily bruised ego, even helping him draft letters to many of the world's leaders, including—incredible as it may seem—

Adolf Hitler. Unfortunately, the text of his letter to Hitler has not survived, and there is no record of the führer ever receiving it. But Herschel was obviously proud of his efforts, and described its contents at some length in his journal: He advised Hitler to turn back the clock, saying it was still not too late. He must "rebuild that which had been destroyed . . . [and] return to us [the Jews] those things that had been . . . taken. If he did this, we would be ready to pardon him immediately."

In spite of his dislike of his client, and his concern for controlling expenditure, Moro proceeded to recruit more heavyweight lawyers to make up a remarkably impressive defense team. As his own assistant, he hired Maître Weill-Goudchaux, a bouncy, hard-working, energetic little man, who referred to Moro as "le Grand Patron." Weill-Goudchaux's main job was to concentrate on the political and public-relations aspects of the case. He was an ideal choice in this respect, for he and Moro complemented each other perfectly, taking in between them the whole range of anti-Nazi opinion in France. Moro was highly acceptable to those on the French left, having represented his native Corsica as a radical in the Chamber of Deputies and served as undersecretary for education in Edouard Herriot's government. Weill-Goudchaux, on the other hand, had many friends among politicians and journalists of the right, especially those who were anti-Nazi and opposed to French and British policy over the betrayal of Czechoslovakia at Munich. These included figures such as Georges Mandel, the Jewish ex–Radical party politician who had been Clemenceau's chief assistant in 1917 and who held several ministries between 1934 and 1940; the mercurial journalist Henri de Kérillis, who wrote for *L'Epoque* and *Echo de Paris*, two right-wing papers; Mme. Geneviève Tabouis, foreign editor of *L'Oeuvre*, and many others.

Weill-Goudchaux also had excellent connections with the Franco-Jewish establishment and with international Jewish organizations, notably the World Jewish Congress. Together with various other Jewish groups all over the world, they helped him assemble a formidable dossier on German atrocities against the Jews, which Moro planned to make full use of at the trial.

To complete his team, Moro called on an old friend—described by *The New York Times* as "yet another high-priced advocate"—Maître Henri Torrès, a great Jewish lawyer who had successfully defended an earlier Jewish assassin, Samuel Schwartzbard, in 1926. Schwartzbard, Ukrainian by birth, had shot and mortally wounded Simon Petlioura, who had been responsible for a series of massacres of Jews in the Ukraine during the Russian civil war of 1918–20. During his celebrated defense, Torrès had called no fewer than eighty witnesses ranging from the former president of Hungary to the famous French actor Grèmier, who was then playing Shylock in the *Merchant of Venice* in Paris. Torrès had had Grèmier deliver Shylock's speech from Act 3, scene 1—"I am a Jew. Hath not a Jew eyes? Hath not a Jew hands, organs, dimensions, senses, affections, passions?"—from the witness stand, a performance that had helped persuade the court to find Schwartzbard not guilty. Although there were considerable differences between the two cases, no doubt Moro was hoping to make use of Torrès's flair to repeat the earlier triumph. Whatever happened, Herschel was to be given a show trial with a political impact that would resound across the entire civilized world.

On Friday, November 25, 1938, a phalanx of seven of Herschel's lawyers, led by Moro-Giafferi, assembled to represent him at the preliminary hearing. They made an impressive sight, dressed in the traditional garb of the French *avocat*—pleated linen jabot at the throat and full-sleeved black silk robes, some trimmed with a double border of rabbit fur in lieu of ermine. The international press was there in force—Herschel was news, and editors the world over were panting for stories about the teenage assassin.

With a grand flourish of his flowing sleeves, Moro rose to announce what everyone in France must by then have known—that he had been appointed to defend the accused. He had accepted the task, he explained, "on international and humanitarian grounds," encouraged by the interest shown in the case in the United States. He was of course serving notice on the French government that the defense did not propose to ignore the political implications of the trial. The United States, for one, he ominously implied, would be closely watching the French court proceedings.

Judge Tesnière then formally charged the prisoner with premeditated murder, and cautioned him that he was free to make a statement if he so wished, but that anything he said could be used in evidence against him at any subsequent trial. Herschel, never one to pass up any opportunity of holding center stage, chose to make a statement.

"I did it all," he declared, "as if I had been asleep. I might have appeared calm because I was making great efforts to conceal my emotions, but I was acting like an automaton, as though I had been hypnotized." He went on to describe his purchase of the gun, and his subsequent actions in the light of his intention to commit suicide in the German embassy.

This was the latest version of Herschel's story, which he had developed and modified since his arrest. On the way from the embassy to the police station in the Rue de Bourgogne, he had told Officer Autret that he had shot a man in order to avenge his parents, who were suffering at the hands of the Germans, and that he did not regret it. Three days later, when questioned by Judge Tesnière, he had said that he had not acted out of personal hatred for vom Rath, or from a desire for vengeance against any particular person. "I did not wish to kill," he had told the examining magistrate. "When I committed that act, I was obeying an overwhelming and inexplicable force." Then he had added a fresh detail: Vom Rath, he declared, "called me a dirty Jew."

"Was that before or after the shooting?" Judge Tesnière had asked.

"I couldn't tell you exactly," Herschel had replied. "I was overcome by emotion."

Later, it occurred to Herschel that vom Rath had struck him when he called him a dirty Jew, and that that was why he had shot him. It had been an instinctive act, an act almost of self-defense. He had intended, he explained, to shoot himself in front of a portrait of Adolf Hitler. It seemed he was sticking to this version in court.

Judge Tesnière proposed to retain the photograph found in Herschel's pocket at the time of his arrest as an exhibit for the forthcoming trial, believing that the words written on the back—"I have to protest in such a way that the whole world hears my protest, and this I intend to do"— indicated premeditation of murder. Moro, however, contended that the words indicated that Herschel had intended taking his own life. In the event, the three distinguished psychiatric experts appointed by the magistrate to examine Herschel concluded in an eighty-four-page report delivered at the end of February 1939 that Herschel had not been in a hypnotic state, nor had he intended to commit suicide, but that he "should be considered entirely responsible mentally" for his actions.

Judge Tesnière concluded the preliminary hearing on November 25 by notifying Herschel that he would be required to appear in court again the following Wednesday, when Uncle Abraham and Aunt Chawa were tried for aiding and abetting his illegal entry and residence in France.

When the two older Grynszpans stood in the dock of the Seventeenth Division of the Civil Court of the Seine on November 30, the court was packed—but this time with lawyers rather than journalists. Moro-Giafferi was defending Abraham and Chawa in person, and some twenty lawyers crowded into the small courtroom to hear him plead his case. He did not disappoint them.

After the public prosecutor had rather ineptly presented his case and demanded the heaviest penalty for the accused—under Article 4 of the

Penal Code this was one year in prison—Moro rose and spoke eloquently for over an hour. He based his defense on Article 11 of the same decree under which the two Grynszpans were charged, which stated that "a foreigner who is proven to be unable to leave the country shall not be subject to the provisions of Articles 8 and 9 of this decree." It was obvious, Moro told the court, that Herschel was unable to return to Germany or Poland, and therefore it followed that he was covered by Article 11.

It may have been obvious to Moro, but it was not to the court. Uncle Abraham and Aunt Chawa were found guilty and sentenced to four months in prison plus a fine of one hundred francs. On January 10, 1939, the Court of Appeal increased Uncle Abraham's sentence to six months, but reduced Aunt Chawa's to three. However, after less than a month in prison, both were discreetly released.

As the appalling aftereffects of Kristallnacht became clear, with the suffering of the thirty thousand Jewish men who had been dragged off to concentration camps, the growing numbers of deaths, and the futility of international protests in the face of increased persecution of Germany's remaining Jews, Moro and the Grynszpan committee began to have second thoughts about Herschel's defense strategy. Where once they had all been eager to politicize the trial by placing Nazi Germany in the dock, now Moro began to fear the consequences of such an approach. How would the Nazi government react to being pilloried in a French court? What more frightful excesses might they commit against innocent Jews in reprisal?

It was one thing to present Herschel to the world as a boy avenger attacking a brutal regime that had evicted his parents from their home in Germany and driven them, with appalling hardships, into Poland. But was the defense morally justified in making political propaganda out of the trial knowing that more of the four hundred thousand Jews still trapped in Greater Germany would suffer as a result? Moro and those members of the committee who were not members of the Grynszpan family did not think so.

Moro's new strategy was ingenious and, to say the least, unconventional. It involved nothing less than a deliberate defamation of the characters not only of Ernst vom Rath but also of Herschel himself. Moro proposed that Herschel should now declare to the examining magistrate that he and vom Rath had been lovers and that he had shot him in a jealous rage because the diplomat had found another lover, or—in an alternative scenario—because vom Rath had refused to pay Herschel for his services as a male prostitute. Either way, a political assassination

would be instantly transformed into a murderous tiff between two homosexuals, no longer an act of political vengeance but a sordid *crime pas-
sionelle*, the kind of story on which the gutter press has always thrived.

There would be two immediate and highly desirable consequences of
the new approach. In the first place, the Nazis could hardly seek to vent
their rage upon German Jews because a Jewish boy prostitute and his
Nazi client had fallen out. And in the second place, it would make the
Reich a laughingstock: Even though the lawyers acting for the *partie civile*
might be able to do something to defend the late vom Rath's name in
court, the world's press would have a field day at Germany's expense.

It was a typically Corsican strategy in its deviousness, and it might even
have worked. Because of his age and impoverished circumstances, Herschel would have been seen by the court more as victim than as culprit,
thus greatly increasing the chances of an acquittal. At worst, he could
have expected a minimum, or even a suspended sentence. Even supposing he were sentenced to a period of imprisonment, it was unlikely
it would have been for longer than three or four years, and under French
law remission of sentence was always possible where the term was less
than five years. The likelihood of Herschel's spending much time in
prison, therefore, would have been virtually nil.

But it was not to be. In spite of the fact that Moro made it clear to
him that this unhallowing of his crime would be to his own advantage,
Herschel indignantly refused to cooperate. Moro was furious. "That
young man is a fool and infatuated with himself," he told a friend whom
he met in the Boulevard St. Michel as he was returning from visiting his
client in the Fresnes prison. "He refuses to give his actions a nonpolitical
character . . . yet it is necessary to do so in order to save the Jews of the
Third Reich."

For all his sophistication, Moro seems to have had a strangely naïve
view of Nazi motives and intentions. His belief that they still needed
some excuse for attacking the Jews demonstrated all too clearly the difficulties experienced by civilized people outside Germany in grasping
what was really going on, even after Kristallnacht. From this stance, he
found Herschel's attitude incomprehensible. "If only he would deny the
political motives of his crime," he declared to his friend in the Boulevard
St. Michel, "the Nazis would lose their best pretext for inflicting reprisals
on the German Jews!" In his opinion, he said, those Jews had become
"the victims of his [Herschel's] fit of madness, and now, of his obstinacy."

Asked whether there was any truth in the story of a homosexual liaison,
Moro shook his head. "Absolutely not!" he replied. And when it was

suggested that surely it was his duty not only to defend his client's interests but also his honor as well, he became almost apoplectic with rage.

"Honor! Honor!" he shouted. "What is the honor of that absurd little Jew in the face of the criminal actions of Hitler? What does the honor of Herschel Grynszpan weigh in the face of the survival of hundreds of thousands of Jews?"

When the friend asked if vom Rath was known to be homosexual or not, Moro shrugged his shoulders. "I don't know," he said. "And besides, it doesn't interest me."

In the event, neither Moro's devious plans nor Herschel's obstinate refusal to go along with them were of any significance as the months dragged by with no date set for the trial. There is no doubt that the case could have been ready by July 1939, but the French government, worried by the increasing international tension, was in no hurry to rush such a politically sensitive matter. According to Maître Weill-Goudchaux, French foreign minister Georges Bonnet was afraid that a sympathetic French court might well acquit the boy or, what might be even worse, find him guilty but, after taking into consideration the German treatment of the Jews, and in particular his parents, impose some purely nominal sentence. Either way was certain to antagonize Hitler, not against the Jews but against France.

On the other hand, if the court did sentence Herschel to death or impose a heavy prison sentence, then Jewish opinion in the United States and in France itself would be affronted. None of the options looked particularly attractive. All in all, the simplest and safest thing was to keep him locked up, certainly for the time being.

Herschel himself did not take kindly to such treatment. Having, with the aid of Maîtres Szwarc and Fränkel, developed a taste for writing to the famous, he had been spraying letters in all directions like a scatter gun. On August 28, 1939, he wrote to the minister of justice demanding the right to enlist in the French Army. He wished, he said, to make amends for all the trouble he had caused "the country that accorded me its hospitality." The minister's reply, if any, must have been negative, because Herschel remained locked up in Fresnes as war was declared on September 3.

After the end of the fighting in Poland, through the autumn and winter of 1939 and the spring of 1940, the Second World War remained in that curious state of suspended animation known as *"la drôle de guerre,"* "the phony war." The two sides faced each other warily but made no aggressive moves. The French and British rearmed frantically, building tanks, guns, aircraft, as fast as their factories could turn them out, while the smaller nations, Belgium, Holland, the Scandinavians, Switzerland, clung to their neutrality, wrapping it around themselves like a cloak in the vain hope that it would protect them when the bullets started flying. Across the Atlantic, America stood aloof, still firmly in the grip of the isolationist majority who were determined not to get drawn into what they saw as another family squabble among the decadent Europeans. To the east, the Soviet Union was busy assimilating the territory Stalin had gained by the deal he had struck with Hitler in the Nazi-Soviet pact, and greedily eyeing further juicy morsels in the Baltic.

Hitler was content for the moment to concentrate on reequipping his army after the Polish campaign, building up his strength for the eventual confrontation with the Western powers and the Soviet Union, and digesting the territory and the people he had conquered. In addition to some 27 million Poles, ethnic Germans, and other minorities, he had acquired an extra 3.25 million Jews, who would now have to be dealt with. He started immediately. His SS *Einsatzgruppen*—"cleansing squads," as they were known—had moved in right behind the fighting troops of the army and started their task with gusto, removing or shooting all potential troublemakers: Polish intellectuals, socialists, local leaders, and Jews, who were herded into ghettos. Central Poland was designated as a "sink" area, into which could be poured the "waste" from the Reich and from the other conquered lands. On October 7, Hitler signed a decree entitled "Strengthening of German Manhood," which provided for "the elimination of the harmful influence of nationally alien populations, which constitute a danger to the Reich and the German community." On October 12, the first Czech and Austrian Jews were transported to Poland. The Holocaust had begun.

While everyone waited for the war to explode in the West, Herschel Grynszpan remained in the Fresnes prison, waiting for his trial. Judge Tesnière, his examining magistrate, had been called up for military service in early September 1939, and was replaced by Judge Glorian, who naturally needed time to familiarize himself with the facts of the case, thus delaying any possible trial still further. Maître de Moro-Giafferi and Herschel both appealed to the minister of justice for action, but he now refused to authorize the start of legal proceedings on the grounds that the *partie civile*—that is, the vom Rath family and the German government—were unable to be represented in court because of the war. Herschel was furious. On January 11, 1940, he wrote to the public prosecutor in tones of high indignation, demanding to know when his trial would take place, and complaining that he had written about this several times before. He had by then been in custody for fourteen months. "If I do not have an answer by March 1," he wrote, "I shall be obliged to go on hunger strike for twenty-four hours as a warning. And if the trial is not held by March 31, I shall find it necessary to go on hunger strike until my strength fails." From then on, he was constantly threatening to go on hunger strike, but as far as is known, he never did so.

On April 9, Europe's uneasy calm was shattered when Hitler marched into Denmark, which did not resist, and Norway, which did, fighting valiantly for several weeks with British and French support. A month later, on May 10, the war in the west began in earnest as the German armies invaded Holland and Belgium in order to outflank the fortifications of the Maginot Line, which ran along the Franco-German border. As the French and British armies rushed north to intercept them, Hitler's panzers struck through the hills and forests of the Ardennes, which until then had been thought impassable for tanks and were only lightly defended. They crossed the river Meuse into France on May 13. The Allied armies were caught in a vast trap as the German armor scythed its way across their rear, drove swiftly to the Channel coast, and then began sweeping inexorably south toward Paris.

The speed of the German advance took everyone, including the Germans themselves, by surprise. By May 29, they had already taken Ypres, Ostend, and Lille. Clearly, it would not be long before they reached Paris itself. On June 1, the French government decided to transfer the Court of Paris to Angers, a town on the river Loire some 275 kilometers from the capital, and to evacuate the Paris prison population to other parts of the country, away from the war zone. The prisoners to be moved included a number of "politicals," among them Herschel Grynszpan.

By then, Herschel had been in custody for twenty months, longer than any juvenile in French legal history, in spite of continuous efforts by Moro and others to get him freed. The last attempt had been in April 1940, when Victor Basch, president of the League of Human Rights, had pleaded for "liberty or judgment"—but this, like all the others, was ignored. Now, Herschel and a group of other prisoners were taken from Fresnes and delivered by road to the prison at Orléans, 115 kilometers south of Paris. They did not stay there long: As the German advance continued, the authorities decided to evacuate the Orléans prison, too. On roads jammed with refugees, Herschel and ninety-six other prisoners were driven south again, their destination this time being Bourges, 115 kilometers from Orléans. On the way, they were attacked by German aircraft. Guards and prisoners alike piled out of their buses and trucks and took cover as best they could by the roadside. The demoralized guards fled as the German planes dive-bombed and strafed the convoy with machine-gun fire. Most of the prisoners took the opportunity of disappearing permanently, but a small group of men, including Herschel, stayed behind.

Herschel, not unnaturally, was terrified of being captured by the Germans, who he thought would shoot him on the spot. He calculated that he stood a better chance of surviving under French jurisdiction, so when the guards eventually returned to what was left of the convoy, he begged to be taken to the Bourges prison. A single subofficer obliged, and escorted Herschel and the small party of remaining prisoners there, arriving on Sunday, June 17, the day France surrendered.

The situation at the Bourges prison was chaotic. With the extraordinary influx of refugees from the north, the authorities had been forced to turn it into a reception center where families who had become separated on the long march from the war could meet up once more. In the midst of this heartrending confusion, the arrival of a prison officer with a handful of prisoners, one of them a political hot potato who would certainly be sought by the Germans, merely served to make things worse. It seemed to be Herschel's destiny to complicate life for his host country.

The following day, the prison governor went to see the local public prosecutor, Paul Ribeyre, to ask his advice on what should be done with Herschel. After consulting his friend M. Taviani, the local prefect of police, Ribeyre advised the governor simply to lose him. He should fail to register Herschel's arrival on the prison roll and get him out of the city as soon as possible, ideally under his own steam—the road to Châteauroux, some sixty-five kilometers to the southwest, was still open.

Thus began what must be one of the most remarkable odysseys in penal history, as Herschel journeyed across France from prison to prison, from police station to police station, desperately seeking some jail that would take him in, some cell where he could be safely locked up. Although he had no money, knew nobody, and spoke French with a strong German accent, one would have thought that after his upbringing in Hanover and his experiences in Paris and the Fresnes prison he would have developed some survival skills and would try to help himself. But he did not. He made no attempt to escape to Spain or Switzerland, no attempt to contact his lawyers or any of his many well-wishers in France or abroad, no attempt even to seek the help of other Jews. In the end, half-starved, bewildered, lost, he knocked on the door of the Toulouse prison and begged to be let in.

There is another version of the story—indeed, there are usually several versions of any story concerning Herschel, many of them the products of his own overheated imagination. In 1957, Herschel's older brother, Marcus, published a statement in which he repeated a story supposedly told to him by Maître Fränkel. According to this, Fränkel had been told by a lawyer friend in Toulouse how one day in 1940 Herschel had come to his office begging his help in obtaining the necessary papers to cross the border into Spain. The Toulouse lawyer had apparently agreed to do what he could, and had contacted someone he thought could fix things. But the man he contacted must have gone to the Vichy French authorities, because Herschel was arrested when he returned to the lawyer's office.

There is some indirect evidence to support this version of events: By an odd coincidence, Uncle Abraham, Aunt Chawa, Chawa's brother Barenbaum, and Maître Fränkel were all in Toulouse at the same time as Herschel, having fled from the advancing Germans. At it happened, Moro-Giafferi was also in the region, some 130 kilometers away along the road to Bordeaux in the small town of Aiguillon, but they were not in contact with him. The Grynszpans and Fränkel met by chance in Toulouse, but none of them knew of Herschel's presence in the city until it was too late. When Fränkel did learn that his client was in the local prison, he applied immediately for permission to visit him, but missed him by twenty-four hours. By the time the permit came through, Herschel was on his way back to Paris.

In the evening of the day the Germans marched into Paris, a thirty-year-old SS *Standartenführer* (colonel) with a doctorate in English literature, Helmut Knochen, moved into the Hôtel du Louvre by the Palais Royal with a team of twenty men. Under direct orders from SD chief Reinhard Heydrich, his job was to round up enemies of the Nazis in France: Jews, communists, Freemasons, antifascists of whatever political persuasion, and refugees from Germany who were by definition against the regime. Herschel Grynszpan figured prominently on the list, and Knochen assigned his case to SS Sturmbannführer (Major) Karl Bömelburg, who was already familiar with the details since he had worked in Paris before the war as Interpol liaison between the German embassy and the French police.

Bömelburg immediately applied to the French attorney general, M.

Cavarroc, for Herschel's dossier, only to be told that it had been sent out of Paris two weeks earlier, at the same time as Herschel himself. The documents had been entrusted to the secretary general of the court, M. Menegaud, who had personally taken them in his own car to Angers, where the court had been transferred. What the attorney general did not know, however, was that Menegaud had stopped off at Orléans on the way, and there his car had been destroyed in an air raid. He had therefore left his suitcase, which contained not only numerous legal dossiers, including Herschel's, but also the state seals, with the concierge of the court. Neither the dossiers nor the seals had been seen again. Without Herschel and his dossier, the Germans could not proceed with the show trial they had planned.

The search for Herschel continued, however. On June 19, only hours after Herschel had been sent on his way to Châteauroux, men from Dr. Knochen's office arrived in Bourges to arrest him. The prison governor, following the public prosecutor's instructions, denied any knowledge of anyone called Herschel Grynszpan. But Knochen's men were not so easily satisfied: They soon located the subofficer who had been responsible for escorting the small group of prisoners to Bourges after the air attack on the road from Orléans. They questioned him fiercely, and it was only a matter of time before he confessed his part in the events, implicating Public Prosecutor Ribeyre and Prefect of Police Taviani in the process. Both men denied all knowledge of Herschel. Even when Ribeyre was arrested and dragged off for further questioning, to the Cherche-Midi prison in Paris, where he was terrorized for two nerve-racking weeks by a slightly mad German officer who went around threatening the prisoners with his revolver, he maintained his silence. After two weeks, he was released unharmed and shortly afterward was offered a safe post with the court in Algiers, away from the reach of the Germans.

By that time, Herschel had been found. Under the terms of the Franco-German Armistice Convention, the French were obliged to hand over on request any German subjects found in the Unoccupied Zone of Vichy France. For the past two weeks, while Ribeyre was keeping silent, the Vichy authorities had been conducting a trawl through their prison population, searching for—among others—Herschel Grynszpan. They located him in Toulouse, and on July 5 transferred him to Vichy. On July 18, having waived the need for proper extradition papers, they meekly handed him over to Sturmbannführer Bömelburg's men at the demarcation line with German-occupied France. Two days later, he found himself in the Berlin headquarters of the Central Office for Reich Security, the RSHA, facing interrogation once again.

In the face of the German questioning, which does not seem to have been too intense, Herschel began to repeat one of his earlier versions of the events of November 7—he had by now fallen into the old con's habit of rearranging the facts to suit each particular interrogator. He had originally gone to the Rue de Lille, he said, with the intention of shooting himself as a protest against the inhuman treatment of his parents, but Ernst vom Rath had insulted him, calling him a "filthy Jew," and in his rage and despair he had shot him. When he was interrogated yet again on Sunday, July 23, he stuck to the same story, even writing out a statement to that effect in his own hand, and there the matter rested for several months.

On January 18, 1941, he was taken to the Sachsenhausen concentration camp outside Berlin. There, he was housed in an area known as the Bunker, along with other special prisoners, the *"Prominente,"* such as Pastor Niemöller, who had incurred Hitler's wrath because of his anti-Nazi sermons, various generals, politicians, and foreign dignitaries. Like the other *Prominente*, Herschel was relatively well fed, eating the same food as his guards, and was not required to do any heavy work—in fact, his most arduous task appears to have been acting as an orderly for his SS guards, who nicknamed him "Bubi" ("Baby"), though whether affectionately or contemptuously is not known.

Like Hansel being fattened up in the witch's gingerbread house, Herschel was being kept alive and well by the German authorities for a purpose: They needed him as a sacrifice to the pride of Dr. Goebbels. The Nazi propaganda minister had been robbed of his chance to justify Kristallnacht by French procrastination and delay in bringing Herschel to trial before the war. He had been unable to demonstrate to the world the existence of a bolshevik-Jewish plot to foment trouble between Germany and France by murdering a German diplomat. Now, however, with the assassin safely tucked away in Sachsenhausen, the old scenario could be dusted off, brought out again, and put into effect. All the French files on the case had been recovered and sent to Berlin. An indictment was drawn up, and submitted on October 30, 1941.

Amazingly, considering the times and the nature of the Nazi regime, the jurists of the Reich Ministry of Justice declared themselves uneasy about the whole matter, which in their view posed serious legal problems. These can be summed up in two words—nationality and extraterritoriality: Herschel was a Polish national who had committed murder in France, a foreigner who had committed a crime in a foreign country. The fact that the victim was German was, in the eyes of the law, irrelevant. Under those circumstances, hazarded the jurists, did the German People's Court

249

have legal jurisdiction? The normal course would be for the case to be tried in France by a French court—but that would hardly suit Hitler and Goebbels, who wanted a show trial and did not trust the French to stage it. Rather like Pontius Pilate turning to Caiaphas, the Ministry of Justice passed the whole question over to Hitler himself, who soon came up with a solution. When Herschel shot vom Rath, he ruled, the gun was aimed not just at the man but at the very government of the Reich itself. Therefore it was not an act of murder, but of high treason. Article 1 of the Penal Law, April 24, 1934, stated that such an offense was punishable by death—and Article 3 of the same law stated that if it was treason, as defined under Article 1, then it came within the jurisdiction of the People's Court, which was therefore competent to try the case.

At the beginning of January 1942, the representatives of the various ministries involved—Justice, Foreign Affairs and Propaganda—met to coordinate logistics and legal strategy under the chairmanship of Dr. Engert, president of the Second Chamber of the People's Court, who had been chosen to preside at the trial. The meeting, in fact, was held in Engert's apartment, where it was decided that the trial should be provisionally scheduled for February 18 and should last for one week. A number of the original witnesses who had given evidence to the French examining magistrate—Officer Autret, Dr. Paul, M. and Mme. Carpe, and so on—plus Judge Tesnière himself, were to be brought to Berlin to give evidence.

Dr. Engert was determined to avoid any danger of this trial developing into a judicial farce, as had been the case with an earlier Nazi show trial, after the Reichstag fire in 1933. That case had been seriously mishandled: The proceedings had been unconvincing, no one had believed that the communists had been responsible for the fire, and the whole thing had done great damage to Germany's image abroad. The Grynszpan trial, by contrast, was to be a model of its type—professional, brief, with the minimum of ideological verbosity, and above all with an unassailable verdict at the end.

Almost immediately, however, things started to go wrong. For a start, when the witnesses were approached, their reactions were hardly encouraging. In the main, as far as it was in their power, they declined the honor of appearing in a German court. There was a sudden outbreak of convenient illnesses that prevented many of them from traveling; others, such as Officer Autret, could not be released from duty at that time, or were unable to give evidence for reasons of professional secrecy. Even the former ambassador, Count von Welczek, had retired to his family castle in Upper Silesia and showed little inclination to be involved in the proceedings.

But it was—inevitably—Herschel who really fouled up the Nazi plans. When a Ministry of Justice interrogator, a Herr Jagusch, went to Sachsenhausen to question him in order to prepare the ground for the trial, he found Herschel, as usual, only too willing to talk. What he said, however, sent Herr Jagusch scurrying back to Berlin to consult his superiors.

Herschel had at last started to learn the art of survival. He was now twenty years old, and had spent over a sixth of his life in prisons or concentration camp, rubbing shoulders with criminals of all kinds. The naïveté and lack of sophistication of his Paris days had long since worn off, and he was finally becoming streetwise. This time, he did not simply change the details of his story, he offered a totally different version of the events of November 7, 1938. Remembering the advice given to him by Maître de Moro-Giafferi three years before, Herschel now gave Herr Jagusch a remarkably detailed account of his seduction by Ernst vom Rath.

He said that the diplomat, who had been wearing a light-colored overcoat, had picked him up one Saturday afternoon in the Place de la République, only a few streets away from the Grynszpans' home. Vom Rath had hailed a taxi and taken him to one of those hotels in Montmartre that rent rooms by the hour, where he had paid him to have sex. Afterward, he had persuaded the boy to meet him again a few days later. Herschel had decided that the whole business was distasteful and that he would never see vom Rath again, but the man had somehow discovered his address and had turned up outside the house on the Rue des Petites Ecuries where his uncle and aunt lived. Vom Rath had tried to arrange another rendezvous, but Herschel had refused, determined to end the affair. He explained that he had been worried in case vom Rath should call at the house and tell Uncle Abraham or Aunt Chawa what had happened between them, so had decided that the only thing to do was to go and see vom Rath in his office. That, he said, was why he had gone to the German embassy on November 7. The two lovers had met. They had exchanged insults—whereupon Herschel had taken out his revolver and shot his seducer.

The whole story was, of course, a total fabrication. Investigation revealed that Ernst vom Rath was not a homosexual, had never owned a light-colored overcoat, and could not have picked Herschel up in the Place de la République when Herschel claimed he had, because he was known to have been out of Paris at that time. Herschel had also got other dates wrong: The Grynszpans were still living at 8 Rue Martel when he claimed he had found vom Rath waiting for him outside their home in the Rue des Petites Ecuries. And there was another serious flaw in his argument: Even if one accepted his story, with all its errors and inconsistencies, as more or less true, was it likely that anyone in vom Rath's position would give a boy prostitute his correct name and place of work while making love to him in a sleazy hotel? Surely, for a diplomat, with all he had to lose, the possibility of blackmail would loom too large. In any case, the evidence given by Officer Autret to the French examining magistrate stated that when arrested at 78 Rue de Lille, Herschel had said he did not know the name of the man he had shot—that as far as he was concerned, he had shot a complete stranger.

Herschel, however, stuck to his story, with occasional slight variations. When he was interviewed by two German psychiatrists, Professor Muller-Hess and Dr. Rommeney, who had been assigned to write a report on his mental state, he insisted that he and vom Rath had been lovers. According to Dr. Rommeney, he told them vom Rath had deceived and tricked him, and that he had allowed himself to be seduced on a promise from the diplomat that his parents would not be deported to Poland.

Although Herschel's story could easily be demolished by the prosecution, its potential as an anti-Nazi smear was enormous. Vom Rath had been sold to the world as an official martyr, shot down in the service of the führer. He had even been given a state funeral at which Hitler himself had been a mourner. Was he now to be portrayed in the world's press as a queer with a taste for seventeen-year-old boys?

It now seems quite obscene that at a time when they were committing incredible atrocities on a mass scale, and were about to step up the organized genocide of an entire race in specially built death factories, the Nazis should care about their image in such matters. And yet they did. Goebbels angrily confided to his diary on January 24, 1942: "Grynszpan has found an insolent argument. He pretends to have had homosexual relations with the counselor of the embassy, vom Rath, whom he assassinated. It is, of course, a shameless lie. But . . . it was a skillful move on his part, for if he reveals this to the public, it will certainly be used by our adversaries as a propaganda weapon." The only solution Goebbels could see was to have part of the trial held in camera—but that would defeat the whole purpose of a show trial. Inevitably, the trial was postponed.

Herschel was still important enough to be kept alive, and continued to live in the Bunker at Sachsenhausen in at least a minimum of comfort. Dr. Engert at the Ministry of Justice was replaced by Dr. Otto Thierack, who held the rank of *Gruppenführer* (major general) in the SS and could be relied upon to push things through with the greatest dispatch. The trial was now set to start at 10:00 A.M. on Monday, May 10, 1942, in the large courtroom of the People's Court at 15 Bellevuestrasse, Berlin.

The delay gave Goebbels the time to create a new myth about the late Ernst vom Rath, and he set about it in a highly ingenious manner. He arranged for the letters of French prisoners of war to be specially vetted by one of his men, who seized the more passionate and erotic messages. The letters were then doctored to make it appear that they had all been written to vom Rath by various mistresses, with the aim of producing them in court as written evidence of his heterosexuality. At one stroke, Goebbels would have created a new Don Juan, a German womanizer irresistible to Frenchwomen.

Ribbentrop, who was having serious second thoughts about the wisdom of proceeding with the trial, came up with an equally elaborate and even more farfetched scheme to counter Herschel's story. An official named Günther from the Foreign Ministry's legal department claimed to have discovered a secret message that had been hidden in Herschel's clothing. Not only was the message in Hebrew, it was also in a secret code. It had supposedly been dictated to a fellow prisoner in his Gestapo cell by Herschel, who had been unable to write it himself, since his hands were manacled. Swearing everyone to absolute secrecy, Günther gave the message to the Foreign Ministry's cipher department for decoding. The department failed, handing the message back with the excuse that they did not have the manpower or facilities to cope with it. Günther then took it to the military experts of the OKW, again with many exhortations to secrecy—but then announced that the Foreign Ministry's own crypt-analysts had, in fact, succeeded in cracking the code. The message, he said, was a statement by Herschel saying that his homosexual story was untrue.

In the end, neither Goebbels's letters nor Ribbentrop's secret document was used, for the third branch of government involved in the case, the Justice Ministry, had come up with two pieces of information of its own. The first was that since 1941 a story had been circulating in public that Herschel had in fact been vom Rath's male whore and procurer for some time in 1938, and that vom Rath had been known in Parisian homosexual circles as "the ambassadress" and "Notre Dame de Paris." This was only a rumor, of course, but the second story was fact: On June 6, 1941, vom Rath's brother, a cavalry *Oberleutnant* and troop commander, had been court-martialed and dismissed from the service for homosexual offenses.

This was all too much for Hitler, who abhorred even the slightest suggestion of homosexuality in the party ranks. He ordered another post-ponement of the trial, until at least the autumn of 1942, when he would reconsider the possibility.

By then, however, the war situation had changed. German forces were no longer all-conquering: They had been routed by the British at El Alamein, thrown back from Moscow and trapped in Stalingrad by the Russians, and were now facing American troops for the first time in North Africa. Clearly, it was no time to be holding a show trial. The question must have been asked in high places in the Third Reich—did they need Herschel Grynszpan any longer? It was at that point that his name ceased appearing on German documents. At the end of 1942, he simply vanished.

Various people have subsequently claimed to have met him or seen him in various prisons and concentration camps after that date. One story places him in the Brandenburg prison as late as January 1945, registered under the name of Otto Schneider—though why he should have been held under a false name is not clear. It has been suggested that he was either executed in Brandenburg or taken to the Magdeburg police station and there murdered by the Gestapo. Another story places him in the Sonnenburg prison to the east of Berlin, where some 685 political pris-oners were shot in the courtyard on January 30, 1945, the day before Soviet troops arrived. Was he one of them? No one knows for sure.

Other stories claim that, like Butch Cassidy or King Arthur, he did not die, but in the confusion of the end of the war escaped from Germany and returned to France, where he still lives today, approaching seventy years of age, married, the father of a family and the proprietor of a garage outside Paris. Another version says he lives in the United States, where he owns a record store.

The trouble with such legends is that they ignore the nature of the man. Herschel was no blushing violet, content to bloom unseen: He saw himself as a heroic figure, a Jewish warrior fighting against Naziism, revenging himself against Germany. He had lived in obscurity in Hanover and Paris, and had not liked it. He had longed for a starring role, and by murdering Ernst vom Rath he had found one. If Herschel had survived the war, the world would have known about it, and if not the world then certainly those members of the Grynszpan family who did survive, for Herschel, as we have seen, was deeply attached to his family and would surely have contacted them for a joyful reunion.

Herschel's parents and brother and sister all survived the war. When the Germans invaded Poland, the Grynszpans fled to the Soviet Union and settled safely in Astrakhan, on the Volga. Marcus joined the Red

Army and fought the Germans. Eventually, they found a home in Israel, where Sendel gave evidence in the trial of Adolf Eichmann. Uncle Abraham and Aunt Chawa, who had fled south in 1940, lived peacefully for a time in Toulouse, but were then arrested and sent to a Vichy French concentration camp at Gurs in the town of Navarrenx about fifty kilometers from Pau, near the Pyrenean border with Spain. Aunt Chawa was put to work on a farm and remained there, unharmed, until the liberation. But Uncle Abraham, with his usual wretched luck, was sent to Auschwitz, where he died, just another victim among the millions. After the war, Aunt Chawa returned to Paris, to the apartment in the Rue des Petites Ecuries. She was still only in her early forties, and soon remarried. Her new husband was another tailor, and they set up shop at the old address, but, whether from respect, or sentiment, or superstition, they did not trade under the name Maison Albert—it had not, after all, brought Abraham Grynszpan much good fortune.

For some time, Sendel Grynszpan did his best to find some trace of Herschel—the last time he had heard from him was a Red Cross letter in 1940. Both he and Marcus went to Paris, but neither they nor any of their relatives could discover anything. In September 1958, Sendel applied through the office of the United Restitution Organization, which represented Jews seeking reparations from the West German government, for compensation for the death of his younger son at the hands of the Nazis. His application was finally rejected, but not before the legal machinery had been set in motion. On June 1, 1960, after extensive archival research, the Hanover Tribunal concluded that, under Article 12, Chapter 2, of the Missing Persons Law of January 15, 1951, Herschel Feibel Grynszpan was presumed to be dead. They even announced a nominal date for his death: May 8, 1945—VE Day, the day the war ended in Europe. It is somehow fitting that, although he almost certainly perished in the Sachsenhausen concentration camp at the end of 1942 or the beginning of 1943, Herschel should have officially died the day after Germany surrendered.

Source Notes

Detailed information concerning the books referred to in shortened form
in these notes will be found in the Bibliography. The following abbre-
viations are used to identify documents and records consulted:

AA   German Foreign Office files, Bonn
AA, PA   German Foreign Office Political Archives
BA   Federal German Archives, Koblenz
BDC   Berlin Documents Center
CAB   British Cabinet Papers, Public Record Office, Kew
CDJ   Centre de Documentation Juive Contemporaine, Paris
DBFP   Documents on British Foreign Policy
DGFP   Documents on German Foreign Policy
FFMA   French Foreign Ministry Archives
FO   British Foreign Office papers, Public Record Office, Kew
FRUS   Foreign Relations of the United States
IMT   International Military Tribunal, Nuremberg: Transcripts and
            Documents in Evidence, Trials of the Major War Criminals
MK   *Mein Kampf*
NA   National Archives, Washington
RGB   *Reichsgesetzblatt*
VB   *Völkischer Beobachter*
ZStA   Central State Archives, German Democratic Republic,
            Potsdam

Prologue: The Spark

page
3–8   Details of Herschel Grynszpan's preparations, and of the assas-
            sination attempt, are taken from the records of the examining
            magistrate's investigation, given in *"Affaire Grynszpan," Mem-
            oire de M. Gustave vom Rath, Partie Civile*, ref. 237, 239, 266;
            CDJ 13:8312. Also in Cuenot.
3–8   Geography and physical details of buildings, etc.: personal ob-
            servations by authors.
6   "As he did so, a casually dressed man . . .": Bonnet, *Le Monde
            Juif*, April/June 1964.

6   "The Germans operated an active espionage . . .": *L'Intransigeant*, November 8, 1938.

7   "Vom Rath half rose from his chair . . .": Cuenot.

7   Vom Rath's injuries: Professor James Cameron, David Pryor, Ballistics Section, Metropolitan Police Laboratories, personally to authors.

Chapter 1: "Down with the November Criminals!"

11   " 'No, not down with France . . .' ": Baynes.

13   " 'It happens sometimes that peace treaties . . .' ": MK.

14   " 'The frontiers of 1914 . . .' ": Ibid.

14   " 'If I had the Ural Mountains . . .' ": Baynes.

16   " 'To catch the electric hare . . .' ": Air Vice-Marshal Sir John Slessor, *The Central Blue.*

18   " 'It is my unshakable resolve . . .' ": DGFP, Series D, Vol. II, 221.

19   " 'At Fouquet's, at Maxim's . . .' ": Shirer, *Berlin Diary*, 150.

19   " 'Already our people is coming to its senses . . .' ": AA, 2536 H/D520527.

Chapter 2: "Jews Not Wanted"

22   "The first mention of a Jewish congregation . . .": Bach.

22–23   "In his pamphlet *That Jesus Christ Was Born* . . .": Haille.

23   " 'First, their synagogues . . .' ": Luther, *Against the Jews and Their Lies.*

24   Party orders for boycott: IMT, 374-PS.

25–26   Nuremberg Laws: RGB, 1935, part 1, pp 1146–7. Jewish emigration figures: League of Nations report, November 18, 1938, FO 371/24079; Simpson, *Refugees: Preliminary Report.*

27   Jewish population in Austria: Fraenkel.

28   " 'Jewellery, furs and even furniture . . .' ": Gedye.

28   "No Jew was safe . . .": Bentwich, in Fraenkel.

29   "Eichmann's methods . . .": Morse.

29   "On April 26, Göring decreed . . .": RGB, 1938.

29–30   Report from Frankfurt: FO 371/21635.

30   Foley's report for June: Ibid.

30   Jewish names decree, etc.: RGB, 1938.

Chapter 3: A Postcard from Poland

32–40	Details of the Grynszpan family history: AA, PA, *Rechtsabteilung, Strafrecht*, No. 21; CDJ 13:8312.
32	"The Ukraine was in ferment . . .": Ascherson.
33	Report of the French doctors: CDJ 13:8312.
33	Hanover and "the Butcher": Bolitho.
33–40	Herschel's education, journey to Paris, etc.: CDJ 13:8312; Cuenot.
39–40	Berta's postcard from Poland: ZStA Potsdam, *Reichspropagandaministerium* File 991, 61–64; CDJ 13:8312.

Chapter 4: The Making of a Martyr

41	Early Jewish settlement in Poland: Gieyszta, in Abramsky.
41	". . . the population census": Davies.
41	"In more recent times . . .": Davies; Ascherson.
42	"Pilsudski's successors . . .": Marcus.
42	"In 1936, with unemployment . . .": Polonsky.
43	Przytyk pogrom: Shtokfish.
43	Emigration figures for Polish Jews: World Federation of Polish Jews Yearbook, 1964.
43	Numbers of Jews and Arabs killed: *Palestine Post.*
44	"The counselor of the Polish embassy in London . . .": FO 371/21636.
45	Polish passports decree, October 6, 1938: DGFP.
45	" 'By this decree . . .' ": Ibid.
46–47	Sendel Grynszpan's description of deportation: Eichmann Trial, session 14, April 25, 1961.
46	"The stationmaster of Hanover . . .": Gilbert, *Final Journey.*
47	"The village was Zbaszyn . . .": *Jewish Chronicle*, September 28, 1979.
48	Berta's postcard from Zbaszyn: ZStA Potsdam, *Reichspropagandaministerium* File 991, 61–64.
48–51	Herschel Grynszpan's movements, family quarrel, etc.: *Affaire Grynszpan*, CDJ 13:8312.
51	"After the shooting . . .": AA, PA, *Rechtsabteilung, Strafrecht* No. 21, Report of Ambassador Welczek.
52	" 'I have just had a narrow escape!' ": Bonnet.
53	"The two doctors . . .": *Le Figaro*, November 9, 1938; Thalmann and Feinermann.
53	"The vom Raths were an old, conservative . . .": Cuenot.

54–55   Ernst vom Rath's career details: Personal File, AA; BA Koblenz, NL Grimm II, 112.

55–56   Interrogation of Herschel Grynszpan: *Affaire Grynszpan*, CDJ 13:8312; Cuenot.

Chapter 5: "The SA Should Be Allowed to Have a Fling"

60   "The ceremonies of 1935 became the model . . .": Fest, *Hitler*.

60   1938 ceremonies: VB, November 10, 1938.

61   " 'The circle of non-Jewish friends . . .' ": J. Littner, *Aufzeich-nungen aus einem Erdloch*, Munich, 1948, p. 20.

62   Goebbels's testimony: IMT 3063-PS.

62   Goebbels's speech and reactions to it: *Der Stürmer*, November 15, 1938; IMT, Vol. X, evidence of Julius Streicher and Joachim von Ribbentrop.

63   SA action report: BDC File 240/I.

63–66   Gestapo teleprint messages: IMT 374-PS, 3063-PS.

64   "They claimed their haul in Berlin along . . .": VB, November 9, 1938.

66   "This dichotomy was not accidental.": IMT 3063-PS.

Chapter 6: The Pogrom

68   ". . . at least 7,500 stores . . .": IMT 1816-PS.

68–69   Heydrich's report to Göring: IMT 3058-PS.

70   "The sacking of Israel's . . .": Shepherd; FO 371/21636.

72   "Franz Rinkel had a fine house . . .": IMT 1759-PS.

72–73   ". . . Ruth Schemel and Selma Ginsberg . . .": Mrs. Ruth Leggett, personally to authors.

73–74   "Inge Fehr was the niece . . .": Mrs. Inge Samson, personally to authors.

74–75   "The Freyhans had an apartment . . .": Mrs. Kate Freyhan, personally to authors.

75–76   "The Sinzheimers were a well-to-do . . .": Mrs. Elizabeth Abrahams, personally to authors.

76–77   "Colonel (later General) Hans Oster . . .": Mrs. C. K. Rosenthal, personally to authors.

77   "Over the years, Bremers . . . ": FO 371/21637.

77   " 'All Jewish stores are to be destroyed . . .' ": IMT 3063-PS.

78–79   Consul T. B. Wildman's report from Bremen: FO 371/21637.

81   Consul General L. K. Robinson's report from Hamburg: FO 371/21637.

82   "Elmshorn is a small town . . .": Lore Boas, personally to authors.

83   "Before the war, Leipzig . . .": Report from U.S. consul David H. Buffum to U.S. consul general in Berlin, November 21, 1938.

83–84 "A twenty-five-year-old Dutch Jew . . .": Wim van Leer, *The Time of My Life*, Jerusalem, 1984.

84   " 'In one of the Jewish sections . . .' ": Buffum, op. cit.

85–86 "The family of Abraham Rose . . .": Frederick Rose, personally to authors.

86   "Another survivor from Leipzig, Alfred Glaser . . .": *Leipziger Blätter* 13, Autumn 1988.

86–87 "At an isolated Jewish educational farm . . .": Lili Durlacher, personally to authors.

88   "Charlotte Singer was the wife . . .": Mrs. Charlotte Singer, personally to authors.

89   " 'In Düsseldorf . . .' ": FO 371/21637.

89   "So did Kerry Weinberg . . .": Weinberg, *Jewish Frontier*.

90–91 "Twenty-four kilometers east of Düsseldorf . . .": Francis H. Schott, *The New York Times*, November 9, 1988.

91   "An anonymous letter . . .": FO 371/21638.

92–93 "Lotte Kramer attended the Jewish school . . .": Lotte Kramer, personally to authors.

93–96 Acting Consul General Dowden's reports from Frankfurt-am-Main: F0371/21638.

96–97 "Baden-Baden was one . . .": Dr. Arthur Flehinger, *Jewish Chronicle*, November 9, 1979.

97   Munich Fire Department reports: *Das Parlament*, November 1963.

97–98 "The first death in Munich . . .": IMT 3063-PS.

98   "The Munich police chief . . .": von Eberstein's evidence, IMT Vol. 20.

98   "At 2:16 A.M., the head office of the Gestapo . . .": IMT 374-PS.

98   " 'There was little looting . . .' ": FO 371/21638.

99   Wagner's speech: VB, Munich edition, November 12, 1938.

99   ". . . Wagner continued to satisfy his greed . . .": Bavarian State Chancellery File MA 1957/178.

100   ". . . Streicher was asleep . . .": IMT Vol. X, Streicher's evidence.

101   "Nine Jews in all were murdered . . .": NA, Captured German documents, T81, R57, RD27.

101   "Old-fashioned, gangster-style extortion . . .": FO 371/21638.

101   "By November 14, the local party . . .": IMT 1757-PS.

102   "The Würzburg pogrom . . .": Rockemaier.

103   "In some places . . . a less tragic outcome.": Peterson.

103   ". . . small acts of kindness . . .": Peterson.

104   ". . . individual acts of betrayal . . .": *AJR Information*, November 1958.

105   "The village of Warmsried . . .": Peterson.

106–7   "Hoengen, a small community near Aachen . . .": Eric Lucas, manuscript, "The Sovereigns," quoted in Gilbert, *The Holocaust*.

107–9   The pogrom in Vienna: FO 371/21636, reports of Consul General D. St. Clair Gainer.

109   Goebbels's statement: FO 371/21637.

Chapter 7: The Camps

110–11 Herbert Finkelstein's experiences: Herbert Finkelstein, personally to authors.

111–12 Gestapo messages: IMT 710-PS.

112   Numbers in concentration camps: Krausnick & Bröszat; Wiener Library, London, File PIId No. 750.

112   "New building programs . . .": Krausnick & Bröszat.

113   "Twenty-year-old Gerd Treuhaft . . .": Treuhaft, *The Times*, November 7, 1988.

113   "One of those on the buses . . .": Dr. Georg Wilde, personally to authors.

114   "Another survivor, Kurt Hirschbert . . .": Andreas-Friedrich.

115–22 History of the camps: Krausnick & Bröszat; Bernt Engelmann; Noakes & Pridham.

119   "Sometimes they knew their victims . . .": Engelmann.

121–22 "Edward Engelberg remembers . . .": *The New York Times*, November 9, 1988.

Chapter 8: "The Stifling Silence"

123   Recollections of Dorothea Illigens and Hugo Krick: *The Home Movie Front*, BBC TV, November 29, 1985.

124   " 'The conclusions that were forced . . .' ": Gisevius.

124   "One of Germany's leading playwrights . . .": *Die Welt*, November 10, 1962.

124–25   Consul L. M. Robinson's report: FO 371/21638.

125   ". . . the woman in Bremen . . .": FO 371/21638, Consul T. B. Wildman.

125   " 'Look, Father, beautiful, isn't it?' ": Charlotte Loose, personally to authors.

125   Pastor Julius von Jan: Leuner.

126   Attacks on cardinals' palaces in Vienna and Munich: FO 371/21637.

126   Consul Wildman's report from Bremen: FO 371/21638.

126–27   A letter writer in the *Daily Telegraph*: Leonard Wilde.

127   "In a Munich street . . .": Report from Wolstan Weld-Forrester, acting consul general, FO 371/21637.

127–28   Consul General R. T. Smallbones's report: FO 371/21638.

129   Albert Adler's experiences: Albert Adler, personally to authors.

129   "Hitler's favorite architect . . .": Speer.

129–30   Melita Maschmann's experiences: Maschmann.

131   Funk's telephone call to Goebbels: Frau Funk affidavit, November 5, 1945.

131–32   Göring's reactions: IMT Vol. IX, Göring's evidence; Körner's evidence.

132   "It is terrible . . .": Frau Gerdy Troost, quoted in Toland.

132   Hitler's speech on November 10, 1938: Kotze.

133   Goebbels's statement: FO 371/21636.

133   Göring's meeting with Hitler: IMT Vol. IX, Göring's evidence.

134   Göring's assistance to Jews: IMT Vol. IX, Bodenschatz's evidence.

136   " 'Very critical situation . . .' ": NA, captured German documents, T120/624; also IMT Vol. IX, Göring's evidence.

Chapter 9: "Atonement"

137–49   The incomplete stenographic record of the meeting on November 12, 1938, is given in IMT Vol. XXVII, 1816-PS.

146–49   Göring's three decrees: RGB.

Chapter 10: "Humanity Stands Aghast"

150–52 Newspaper reports are taken from the named journals.
152–53 Mayor La Guardia's "Nazi Guardian Squad": *New York Herald Tribune*.
153 Cardinal O'Connell's speech: *The New York Times*.
153–54 Ambassador Dieckhoff's report: DGFP.
154 "North of the border . . .": FO 371/21639.
157 Belgian reactions: FO 371/21637.
157–58 Polish reactions: FO 371/21636; 21638.
158–59 Soviet reactions: FO 371/21636; 21638.
160–62 Goebbels's press conference: FO 371/21637.

Chapter 11: "A Wasps' Nest"

163–64 Conversation with von Pfeffer: FO 371/21638.
164–65 Weizmann's telephone call to Halifax, and advice from Ogilvie Forbes: FO 371/21636.
166 Education minister's order: FO 371/21637.
166 "Goebbels was at pains . . .": Ibid.
167 Goebbels's release of Fritz Wisten, etc.: *Philadelphia Inquirer*.
167 "Oh, what tedious people . . .": Sir Kingsley Wood, quoted in Mosley.
167–68 Chamberlain's reply to Private Notice Question: Hansard.
168 Chamberlain's letter to the German Shakespeare Society: *The Times*.
169 Phipps's reports: FO 371/21637.
170 "At noon, Bonnet had another appointment . . .": Bonnet; Zay.
170 Dirksen's meeting with Kennedy: DGFP.
171 Roosevelt's briefing of Dodd: Dodd.
172 "Ironically, Wilson himself was unhappy . . .": Wilson.
172–73 "Lieutenant Colonel Truman Smith . . .": Shafir.
173–76 Ernst vom Rath's funeral: AA, PA, *Rechtsabteilung, Strafrecht*, report of Professor Friedrich Grimm; VB; *Le Temps*; *New York Herald Tribune*.
176–77 Italian reactions: FO 371/21638.

Chapter 12: "We Do Not Wish to Export Anti-Semitism"

178–79 Regulations of December 6, 1938: FO 371/21638; RGB; VB.
179 ". . . abortion ceased to be a crime . . .": FO 371/21638.
180 "While the screws were being tightened . . .": IMT 3063-PS, Report of the Party Supreme Court.

181   Goebbels's speech on November 20: *Daily Telegraph*.
181–82   Kennedy's visit to Foreign Office: FO 371/21637.
182–83   Hoare's speech: *Daily Telegraph*; *New York Herald Tribune*.
184   " 'The Government White Paper . . .' ": Colville.
185   ". . . Bonnet renewed his invitation . . .": FFMA; DGFP.
185–86   "There was a fair amount of grumbling . . .": Zay; Adamthwaite.
186   "But Bonnet was undeterred . . .": DGFP; FFMA.
186   "Anxious to secure American approval . . .": FRUS, 1938, Vol. I; FFMA; Bonnet.
186–87   Coulondre's visit to Ribbentrop: DGFP; FFMA.
187   Ribbentrop's visit to Paris: FFMA; DGFP; Bonnet; Ribbentrop; Schmidt.
189   Anglo-French competition in economic relations with Germany: DGFP; FFMA; DBFP.
189   £1 billion in loans and credits: DGFP.
190   Hitler's speech on January 30, 1939: Baynes; VB.

Chapter 13: "The Jewish Munich"

191   " '. . . six million Jews . . .' ": Peel Commission minutes, 1937.
192   ". . . the new wave of refugees from Nazi Germany . . .": Simpson.
192–93   James Grover McDonald: Genizi, in Wiener Library *Bulletin* 1977, Vol. XXX Nos. 43, 44.
193   Criticism of McDonald: Bentwich.
195   Goebbels's speech on Jewish suicides: VB; *Der Angriff*.
195   Roosevelt's instruction to Cordell Hull: FRUS, 1938, I.
196   Hull disowning Johnson: Alsop.
196   Cudahy's views: FRUS, 1938, Vol. I; Morgan.
197   Bullitt's letters to Roosevelt: Morgan.
197   Reactions of VFW: Morse.
197   ". . . pressure from Rabbi Stephen S. Wise . . .": Feingold.
198–99   Plans and invitations for conference: FRUS, 1938, Vol. I.
200   ". . . not clear what, if anything, the president hoped the conference would achieve.": Simpson; Adler-Rudel in Leo Baeck Institute Year Book XIII, 1968.
201–9   Details of Evian Conference: Proceedings of the Intergovernmental Committee, Verbatim Record, London 1938.
209   Comments of Wilfrid Israel: Shepherd.

Chapter 14: "The World Chose Not to Look"

211   " 'November 10 opened the eyes . . .' ": Andreas-Friedrich.
212   Intergovernmental Committee for Refugees set up in London: FO 371/22439.
212–13 Rublee's character: Acheson.
213   "The Madagascar option was suggested . . .": Thayer; Gorman, in Wiener Library *Bulletin* 1977, Vol. XXX Nos. 43, 44.
214   French reservations on Jews in colonies: FFMA; FRUS, 1938, Vol. I; FRUS, 1939, Vol. II.
215–18 South American countries' response: FO 371/22539.
218   Dominican Republic scheme: Schecktmann; FO 371/22539.
218   ". . . France had done as much as Britain . . .": Minutes of Chamber Foreign Affairs Committee, December 14, 1938.
218–19 Dutch record, and Prime Minister Colijn's broadcast: FO 371/22539.
220   Description of Garvey: Lewis.
220–21 Garvey's letter to Halifax: FO 371/21637.
221   Jewish immigration into Palestine: Palestine Royal Commission (Peel Commission) Report, CMD 5479, 1937; Simpson.
222   Abandonment of policy of partition: CAB 27/651.
223   Roger Makins's suggestion for pressure on Germany: FO 371/22539.
223   Advice to Lord Baldwin for broadcast: Ibid.
223   Hoare's proposal to hand over an entire colony: CAB 27/651.
224   Numbers of refugees admitted to Britain: Home Office, Reports under the Aliens Order, 1920, in House of Commons Papers; Sherman; Simpson.
224–25 Schacht's visit to London: FO 371/22539; Schacht.
226   Rosenberg's speech: Cecil.
226   "According to George Rublee . . .": FO 371/22539.
227   Roosevelt's quota restrictions: Lookstein.
227   ". . . the British government begged for its own unused immigration quota . . .": FO 371/21637.
228–29 " 'The significance of the "glassbreakers' week" . . .' ": Gisevius.

Epilogue: What Became of Herschel Grynszpan

231–32 Dorothy Thompson broadcast: Sanders.
232–35 Details of Journalists' Defense Fund and engaging of Moro-Giafferi: Dorothy Thompson Papers, Syracuse University.

233   "When finally I walked into Adolf Hitler's salon . . .": Thompson.

236   "They greeted me in the name of my family . . .": Herschel Grynszpan's journal, quoted by Cuenot; CDJ 13:8312.

237   Moro's description of Herschel: Dorothy Thompson Papers.

238   "To complete his team, Moro . . .": Torrès.

239   "With a grand flourish . . .": *The New York Times.*

239–40 "This was the latest version . . .": CDJ 13:8312; AA, PA, *Rechtsabteilung, Strafrecht,* No. 21; Cuenot.

241   Sentencing of Abraham and Chawa Grynszpan: Ibid.

241–42 "Moro's new strategy . . .": Cuenot.

243–45 Herschel's letters to minister of justice and Public Prosecutor: Cuenot; CDJ 13:8312.

246–48 Herschel's flight from Germans and Nazi search for him: Cuenot; AA, PA, *Rechtsabteilung, Strafrecht,* No. 21.

249   Herschel's interrogation in Berlin: Ibid.

249   Herschel in Sachsenhausen: Naujocks; Cuenot; BA Koblenz, R 60 II, 79.

250   Indictment against Herschel: BA Koblenz, R 60 II, 79.

250   January 1942 meeting of ministries concerned: AA, PA, *Sonderakten Krümmer* 2/1.

250–51 Problems with witnesses, von Welczek's retirement: Ibid.

251–52 Herschel's homosexual affair story: Ibid.; Cuenot.

253   Goebbels doctoring of letters: Cuenot; ZStA Potsdam, *Reichspropagandaministerium* File 991.

253   Herschel's "secret message": AA, PA, *Sonderakten Krümmer* 2/1.

255   Sendel Grynszpan's search for Herschel: Statement given under oath to Dr. Joel Adiv, lawyer, Haifa, October 6, 1957.

255   Declaration of Herschel's death: *Oberstaatsanwalt Hannover,* File 18, Book G5/60, December 16, 1960.

Bibliography

Unless otherwise stated, publication was in London.

<u>BOOKS</u>

Abel, Theodore.	*Why Hitler Came into Power.* Harvard University Press, Cambridge, Mass., 1986.
Acheson, Dean.	*Morning & Noon.* Houghton Mifflin, Boston, 1965.
Adamthwaite, Anthony.	*France and the Coming of the Second World War, 1936–39.* Frank Cass, 1977.
Alsop, Joseph.	*FDR: The Life and Times of Franklin D. Roosevelt.* Thames & Hudson, 1982.
Andreas-Friedrich, Ruth.	*Berlin Underground.* Latimer House, 1948.
Ascherson, Neal.	*The Struggle for Poland.* Michael Joseph, 1987.
Bach, H. I.	*The German Jew: A Synthesis of Judaism & Western Civilisation 1730–1930.* Littman Library, Oxford University Press, 1984.
Beard, Charles A.	*American Foreign Policy in the Making 1932–1940: A Study in Responsibilities.* Yale University Press, New Haven, CT, 1946.
Bennecke, Heinrich.	*Die Reichswehr und der "Röhm-Putsch."* Gunter Olzog Verlag, Vienna, 1962.

Bentwich, Norman.   *My Seventy-seven Years: An Account of My Life and Times 1883–1960.* Routledge & Kegan Paul, 1962.

Bettelheim, Bruno.   "Individual & Mass Behavior in Extreme Situations (1943)," from *Surviving & Other Essays.* New York, 1980.

Bolitho, William.   *Murder For Profit.* Cape, 1926.

Bonnet, Georges.   *Dans La Tourmente, 1938–1948.* Fayard, Paris, 1971.

Bullock, Alan.   *Hitler: A Study in Tyranny.* Odhams Press, 1954.

Cadogan, Sir Alexander.   *Diaries 1938–1945;* ed.: David Dilks. Cassell, 1971.

Cecil, Robert.   *The Myth of the Master Race: Alfred Rosenberg & Nazi Ideology.* Batsford, 1972.

Céline.   *L'Ecole des Cadavres.* Paris, 1938.

Cohn, Norman.   *Warrant for Genocide.* London, 1967.

Colville, John.   *The Fringes of Power, Downing Street Diaries, 1939–1955.* Hodder & Stoughton, 1985.

Cuenot, Dr. Alain.   *The Herschel Grynszpan Case.* Unpublished manuscript, the Wiener Library.

Dallek, Robert.   *Franklin D. Roosevelt & American Foreign Policy 1932–1945.* Oxford University Press, 1979.

Davies, Norman.   *God's Playground: The Story of Poland, Vol. 2.* Clarendon Press, Oxford, 1987.

Dodd, William.

Ambassador Dodd's Diary 1933–1938; eds.: Dodd, William E., Jr., & Dodd, Martha. Gollancz, 1941.

Döscher, Hans-Jurgen.

"Reichskristallnacht," Die November-Pogrom 1938. Ullstein, Berlin, 1988.

Eban, Abba.

My People, The Story of the Jews. Weidenfeld & Nicolson, 1969.

Engelmann, Bernt.

In Hitler's Germany: Everyday Life In The Third Reich. Methuen, 1988.

Fest, Joachim C.

Hitler. Harcourt Brace Jovanovich, New York, 1974.

———.

The Face of the Third Reich. Weidenfeld & Nicolson, 1970.

Feingold, Henry L.

The Politics of Rescue: The Roosevelt Administration & The Holocaust 1938–1945. Holocaust Library, New York, 1980.

Fischer, Conan.

Stormtroopers, A Social, Economic & Ideological Analysis 1929–1935. George Allen & Unwin, 1983.

Friedmann, Philip.

Their Brothers' Keepers. Crown Publishers, New York, 1957.

Gedye, G.E.R.

Fallen Bastions. 1939.

Gilbert, Martin.

The Holocaust. Collins, 1986.

———.

Final Journey: The Fate of the Jews in Nazi Europe. George Allen & Unwin, 1970.

Giradoux, Jean.

Pleins Pouvoirs. Paris.

Gisevius, Hans Bernd.   *To The Bitter End*. Cape, 1948.

Grunberger, Richard.   A *Social History of the Third Reich*. Weidenfeld & Nicolson, 1971.

Haille, H. G.   *Luther*. Sheldon Press, 1981.

Hauner, Milan.   *Hitler, A Chronology of His Life and Times*. Macmillan, 1983.

Heiden, Konrad.   A *History of National Socialism*. 1936.

Hitler, Adolf.   *Mein Kampf*. Hutchinson, 1969.

Hoess, Rudolf.   *Commandant in Auschwitz*. 1959.

Höhne, Heinz.   *The Order of the Death's Head: The Story of Hitler's SS*. Martin Secker & Warburg, 1969.

Hyman, Paula.   *From Dreyfus to Vichy: The Remaking of French Jewry 1906–1939*. Columbia University Press, New York, 1978.

Ickes, Harold.   *The Secret Diary of Harold Ickes: Vol. 2, The Inside Struggle 1936–1938*. Belknap Press, Harvard University Press, Cambridge, Mass., 1969.

Irving, David.   *The War Path*. Michael Joseph, 1978.

Jones, Nigel H.   *Hitler's Heralds: The Story of the Freikorps 1918–1923*. John Murray, 1987.

Kater, Michael H.   *The Nazi Party: A Social Profile*. Basil Blackwell, Oxford, 1983.

Kochan, Lionel.   *Pogrom 10 November 1938*. André Deutsch, 1957.

Kotze, H., and Krausnick, H., eds. — *Es Spricht Der Führer*. Gütersloh, 1966.

Krausnick, Helmut, and Bröszat, Martin. — *Anatomy of the SS State*. Panther, 1970.

Leuner, H. D. — *When Compassion Was A Crime: Germany's Silent Heroes 1933–1945*. Oswald Wolff, 1966.

Levy, Guenter. — *The Catholic Church & Nazi Germany*. McGraw-Hill Book Company, New York, 1964.

Lewis, Rupert. — *Marcus Garvey: Anti-Colonial Champion*. Karia Press, 1987.

Lookstein, Haskel. — *Were We Our Brothers' Keepers? The Public Response of American Jews to the Holocaust, 1938–1944*. Hartmore House, New York, 1985.

Luther, Martin. — "Against the Jews & Their Lies" and "Introduction to 'Romans,' " A. J. Holman, ed., *Works of Martin Luther*. Col Phil, 1915–1932.

Marcus, Joseph. — *Social & Political History of the Jews in Poland 1919–1939*. Mouton, 1983.

Marrus, Michael R. — *The Unwanted: European Refugees in the Twentieth Century*. Oxford University Press, 1985.

Maschmann, A. — *Account Rendered*. Abelard-Schuman, 1963.

Merkl, Peter H. — *The Making of a Stormtrooper*. Princeton University Press, Princeton, N.J., 1980.

Morgan, Ted.

FDR. Grafton Books, 1986.

Morse, Arthur D.

While Six Million Died: A Chronicle of American Apathy. Random House, New York, 1967.

Mosley, Leonard.

On Borrowed Time. Weidenfeld & Nicolson, 1969.

Naujoks, Harry.

Mein Leben in KZ Sachsenhausen 1936–1942. Erinerungen des ehemaligen Lagerältesten, Cologne, 1987.

O'Brien, Conor Cruise.

The Siege. Weidenfeld & Nicolson, 1986.

Offner, Arnold A.

American Appeasement: United States Foreign Policy & Germany 1933–1938. Belknap Press, Harvard University Press, Cambridge, Mass., 1969.

Orlow, Dietrich.

The History of the Nazi Party, Vol. 2, 1933–1945. David & Charles, Exeter, 1973.

Pauley, Bruce F.

Hitler & the Forgotten Nazis. University of North Carolina Press, Chapel Hill, N.C., 1981.

Petersen, Edward N.

The Limits of Hitler's Power. Princeton University Press, Princeton, N.J., 1969.

Polonsky, Anthony.

Politics in Independent Poland 1921–1934. Clarendon Press, Oxford, 1972.

Rich, Norman.

Hitler's War Aims: Ideology, the Nazi State and the Course of Expansion. Norton, New York, 1973.

Rockemaier, Dieter W.

Das Dritte Reich und Würzburg: Versuch einer Bestandsaufnahme. 1983.

Sanders, Marion.

Dorothy Thompson: A Legend in Her Time. Houghton Mifflin, Boston, 1973.

Schacht, H.

Abrechnung mit Hitler. Hamburg, 1948.

Schoenbaum, David.

Hitler's Social Revolution: Class & Status in Nazi Germany 1933–1939. Thames & Hudson, 1974.

Schuschnigg, Kurt von.

Austrian Requiem. Gollancz, 1947.

Sharf, Andrew.

The British Press & Jews Under Nazi Rule. Oxford University Press, 1964.

Shepherd, Naomi.

Wilfrid Israel: German Jewry's Secret Ambassador. Weidenfeld & Nicolson, 1984.

Sherman, A. J.

Island Refuge: Britain & Refugees from the Third Reich 1933–1938. Elek, 1973.

Shirer, William L.

The Rise and Fall of the Third Reich. Secker & Warburg, 1960.

———.

The Collapse of the Third Republic. William Heinemann, 1969.

———.

The Nightmare Years. Little, Brown & Company, Boston, 1984.

———.

Berlin Diary. Bonanza Books, New York, 1984.

Shtokfish, David, ed.

Pshitik. A Memorial to the Jewish community of Pshitik (Przytyk). Tel Aviv, 1973.

Simpson, Sir John Hope.   *The Refugee Problem.* Oxford University Press, 1939.

———.   *Refugees: Preliminary Report of a Survey.* Royal Institute of International Affairs, July 1935.

Speer, Albert.   *Inside the Third Reich.* Weidenfeld & Nicolson, 1970.

Stevens, Austin.   *The Dispossessed.* Barrie & Jenkins, 1975.

Stone, Norman.   *Hitler.* Hodder & Stoughton, 1980.

Taylor, A. J. P.   *The Origins of the Second World War.* Penguin, 1961.

Thalmann, Rita, and Feinermann, Emmanuel.   *Crystal Night 9–10 November 1939.* Thames & Hudson, 1974.

Thayer, George.   *The British Political Fringe.* Anthony Blond, 1965.

Thompson, Dorothy.   *I Saw Hitler.* Farrar & Rinehart, New York, 1934.

Toland, John.   *Adolf Hitler.* Doubleday, New York, 1976.

Torrès, Henri.   *Accusés Hors Série.* Gallimard, Paris, 1957.

Vansittart, Lord.   *The Mist Procession.* Hutchinson, 1958.

Wagner, Dieter, and Tornkowitz, Gerhard.   *Ein Volk, Ein Reich, Ein Führer.* Longman, 1971.

276

Wilson, Hugh R.

A *Career Diplomat, The Third Chapter: The Third Reich.* Unpublished manuscript.

Wyman, David S.

Paper Walls: America & the Refugee Crisis 1938–1941. University of Massachusetts Press, Amherst, Mass., 1968.

————.

The Abandonment of the Jews: America & the Holocaust 1941–1945. Pantheon Books, New York, 1984.

COLLECTIONS

Abramsky et al, eds.

The Jews in Poland. Blackwell, Oxford, 1986. See especially:
Aleksander Gieyszta: "The Beginning of Jewish Settlement in Polish Lands."
Ezra Mendelsohn: "Interwar Poland: Good for the Jews or Bad for the Jews."

Fraenkel, Josef, ed.

The Jews of Austria: Essays on their Life, History & Destruction. Valentine Mitchell, 1967. See especially:
Bentwich, Norman: "The Destruction of the Jewish Community in Austria."
Rosenkrantz, Herbert: *The Anschluss & the Tragedy of Austrian Jewry 1938–1945.*

Noakes, J., and Pridham, G., eds.

Nazism 1919–1945: A Documentary Reader.
Vol. 1. *The Rise to Power 1919–1934.*
Vol. 2. *State, Economy & Society 1933–1939.*
Vol. 3. *Foreign Policy, War & Racial Extermination.*

Reinharz, Jehuda, and Schatzberg, Walter, eds.

The Jewish Response to German Culture: From the Enlightenment to the Second World War. University Press of New England, Hanover, N.H., 1985.

ARTICLES

Adler-Rudel, S.

"The Evian Conference On The Refugee Question," Leo Baeck Institute Year Book Vol. XIII, 1968.

Bonnet, Georges.

"Le Monde Juif," Paris, April/June 1964.

Brugel, J. W.

"The Bernheim Petition: A Challenge to Nazi Germany in 1938, Patterns of Prejudice," Vol. 17 No. 2, 1983.

Engelberg, Edward.

". . . And In Munich," *The New York Times*, November 1988.

Genizi, Heim.

"James G. McDonald: High Commissioner for Refugees 1933–1935, *The Wiener Library Bulletin*, Vol. XXX Nos. 43, 44, 1977.

Gorman, Robert M.

"Racial Antisemitism in England: The Legacy of Arnold Leese," *Wiener Library Bulletin*, Vol. XXX Nos. 43, 44 1977.

Katz, Shlomo Z.

"Public Opinion in Western Europe & the Evian Conference of July 1938," *Yad Vashem Studies*, Vol. IX, 1973.

Loewenberg, Peter.

"The Kristallnacht as a Public Degradation Ritual," Leo Baeck Institute Year Book, Vol. XXXII, 1987.

O'Brien, Conor Cruise.

"Denounced for the Truth," *The Times*, November 16, 1988.

Schecktmann, J.   "Failure of the Dominican Scheme,"
                                     Congress, January 8, 1943.

Shafir, Shlomo.   "American Diplomats in Berlin (1933–
                                     1939) & their Attitude to the Nazi Per-
                                     secution of the Jews," *Yad Vashem
                                     Studies*, Vol. IX, 1973.

Steinfels, Peter.   "The Road to Extermination," *The
                                     New York Times*, November 9, 1988.

Treuhaft, Gerd.   "The Darkest Night," *The Times*, No-
                                     vember 7, 1988.

Uhlig, Heinrich, and Free-   *"Der Nackten Gewalt und der Feigheit
den, Herbert H.   Begegnet . . ." Das Parlament*, No-
                                     vember 1963.

Weinberg, Kerry.   "The Kristallnacht & After: Memoir,"
                                     Jewish Frontier.

NEWSPAPERS, MAGAZINES, ETC.

Action Française
Der Angriff
Atlanta Journal
Baltimore Sun
Berliner Nachtausgabe
Bornaer Tageblatt
Bremer Nachrichten
Daily Express
Daily Herald
Daily Mail
Daily Telegraph
Danziger Vorposten
La Dépêche
The Economist
Le Figaro
Giornale d'Italia
Hartford Courant

The Independent
L'Intransigeant
Jewish Chronicle
Jewish Examiner
Jewish Frontier
Le Journal
Het Laatste Nieuws
Leipziger Blätter
La Lumière
Le Matin
Manchester Guardian
Messaggero
Nation
Nation Belge
*Nationalisozialistische
    Parteikorrespondenz*
Nation Zeitung

News Chronicle
New Statesman
Newsweek
New Yorker
New York Herald Tribune
The New York Times
The Observer
L'Ordre
Osnabrücker Tageblatt
Le Peuple
Philadelphia Inquirer
Le Populaire
Pravda
Regime Fascista
Richmond Times Dispatch
St. Paul Dispatch
The Scotsman

Spectator
Springfield Republican
Standard
Der Stürmer
Le Temps
Tevere
Time and Tide
Tribune de Genève
Trud
Völkischer Beobachter
Washington Post
The Weekly Review
Yorkshire Post

BBC Television:
    The Home Movie Front

Index

Permissions Acknowledgments

Excerpts from the Dorothy Thompson Collection at the George Arenst Research Library for Special Collections at Syracuse University.

Excerpts from the British Foreign Office papers: Public Records Office, London, and document reference.

Excerpt from *The Fringes of Power: Downing Street Diaries, 1939–1955* by John Colville originally published by W. W. Norton and Company.

Grateful acknowledgment is made to the following for permission to reprint previously published material:

Blackie and Son Limited: Excerpt from *Account Rendered* by A. Maschmann. Reprinted by permission of Blackie and Son Limited.
Collins Publishers: Excerpt from *The Holocaust* by Martin Gilbert. Reprinted by permission of Collins Publishers.
Jonathan Cape Ltd.: Excerpt from *To the Bitter End* by Hans Bernd Gisevius. Reprinted by permission of Jonathan Cape, Ltd.
Don Congdon Associates, Inc.: Excerpt from *Berlin Diary* by William Shirer. Reprinted by permission of Don Congdon Associates, Inc.
The Daily Telegraph: Excerpt from *The Daily Telegraph* of November 11, 1938. © The Daily Telegraph plc. Reprinted by permission of *The Daily Telegraph*.
Houghton Mifflin Company and Century, a division of Century Hutchinson Limited: Excerpts from *Mein Kampf* by Adolf Hitler, translated by Ralph Manheim. Copyright 1943 and copyright renewed 1971 by Houghton Mifflin Company. Rights in the British Commonwealth and Canada are administered by Century, a division of Century Hutchinson, Limited. Reprinted by permission of Houghton Mifflin Company and Century, a division of Century Hutchinson, Limited.
Macmillan Publishing Company and Weidenfeld and Nicolson Limited: Excerpts from *Inside the Third Reich* by Albert Speer. Copyright © 1970 by Macmillan Publishing Company. Rights on the Open Market administered by Weidenfeld and Nicolson Limited. Reprinted by permission of Macmillan Publishing Company and Weidenfeld and Nicolson Limited.
The New York Times: Excerpts from "Kristallnacht, in Solingen . . ." by

Francis H. Schott and from ". . . And in Munich" by Edward Engleberg, both from the November 9, 1988, issue of *The New York Times*. Copyright © 1988 by The New York Times Company. Reprinted by permission of *The New York Times*.

The Philadelphia Inquirer: Excerpts from an editorial on Hitler's Reich from the November 16, 1938, issue of *The Philadelphia Inquirer*. Reprinted by permission of *The Philadelphia Inquirer*.

Times Newspapers Limited: Excerpt from an article by Gerd Treuhaft which appeared in the November 7, 1988, issue of *The Times*. Reprinted by permission of Times Newspapers, Limited.